HOW
RICH ASIANS
THINK

HOW
RICH ASIANS
THINK

A THINK AND GROW RICH
PUBLICATION

JOHN C. SHIN

Published and distributed by:

SOUND WISDOM
P.O. Box 310
Shippensburg, PA 17257-0310
717-530-2122

info@soundwisdom.com

www.soundwisdom.com

Jacket design by Eileen Rockwell

ISBN 13 TP: 978-1-64095-125-9

ISBN 13 HC: 978-1-64095-123-5

ISBN 13 eBook: 978-1-64095-124-2

For Worldwide Distribution, Printed in the U.S.A.

1 2 3 4 5 6 7 8 / 23 22 21 20 19

May you have the courage to DREAM BIG, live life on your own terms, and follow your heart.

Whatever you can conceive and believe, you can achieve.

ACKNOWLEDGMENTS

How *Rich Asians Think* reflects the influence and impact of Napoleon Hill's masterpiece *Think and Grow Rich* on all areas of my life. I am grateful for Hill's timeless guidance and wisdom. Hill's legacy continues through the dedication and commitment of Don Green, Robert Johnson Jr., and the caring family at the Napoleon Hill Foundation. This book would not have been possible without their belief in the project.

Think and Grow Rich collected insights that Napoleon Hill gathered while interviewing the most successful thought leaders of his time. It made sense to follow his approach as I wrote my version of Hill's book for a new audience. Thank you to the men and women who generously talked with me and shared their knowledge and experiences so that others can learn and grow. Thank you, Brad Lea, Hannah and Marissa Brandt, David Fishof, George Chanos, Gregg Godfrey, Ilana Muhlstein, Jaime and Shawn Villalovos, Jessica Cox, John Ashworth, Julian Serrano, Justin Chon, Katsuya Uechi, Kevin Harrington, Lawrence Jackson, Dr. Marissa Pei, Maury

Gallagher, Penney Ooi, Raja Dhaliwal, Ray Parker Jr., Scott Williams, and Steve Aoki. I also wish to thank Dwayne "The Rock" Johnson, Jack Ma, Keanu Reeves, and Lucy Liu, whose valuable insights and examples of leadership help shape the world for the better.

A project of this magnitude requires a team of experts to take raw thoughts and ideas and polish them into gems. I am grateful to David Wildasin and the fine folks at Sound Wisdom Publishing for producing this book and Jonathan Badanguio for his initial creative cover designs. Special thanks to Ken and Michele Budka, the editorial team at Full Sail Publishing, who consistently take my reams of data, raw thoughts, and ideas and turn them into gold. Bravo! And thank you, Lisa Lockwood, for introducing us.

Every success can be traced back to a single, critical step— the first step. Thank you to my dear friends and mentors, Monte and Lisa Holm, who gave me my first copy of *Think and Grow Rich* in 1996. Thank you, Rich and Cindy Thawley, who inspired me to study the book, quoting chapters and paragraphs, solidifying its life-changing messages. Thank you, John Maxwell, for encouraging me to write this book; once I started, there was no turning back. Sharon Lechter and Greg Reid, thank you for coaching me throughout the book-writing process.

Finally, thank you to my loving family, who cheers for me and supports me in everything I do. To my father and mother, Dong and Susan Shin—your work ethic and courage shaped my dedication, commitment, and perseverance in every area of my life. My sister, Dr. Stella Erbes, has always been my greatest supporter, always inspiring us to be all we can be. My children,

Matthew, Kayla, Andrew, and Jenna, inspire me and fill my heart with joy every day. Arlene, my partner in business, love, and life—you make life a joyful adventure and everything I do worthwhile. I love you.

—John C. Shin, J.D.

CONTENTS

Preface   13

Thoughts Are Things   25
Conceive, believe, and achieve your dreams

Desire   51
The starting point of all achievement

Faith   91
Visualization of, and belief in,
the attainment of desire

Autosuggestion   109
The medium for influencing the subconscious mind

Specialized Knowledge   133
Personal experiences or observations

Imagination   159
The workshop of the mind

Organized Planning   183
The crystallization of desire into action

Decision   205
The mastery of procrastination

Persistence   221
The sustained effort necessary to induce faith

Power of the Mastermind   259
The driving force

The Mystery of Sex Transmutation   291
Redirecting your energy toward success

The Subconscious Mind   303
The connecting link

The Brain   321
A broadcasting and receiving station for thought

The Sixth Sense   335
The door to the temple of wisdom

The Six Ghosts of Fear   347
The grand illusion

Notes   373

Special Thanks   375

About the Author   377

PREFACE

Think and Grow Rich by Napoleon Hill is one of the best-selling books of all time, responsible for influencing and improving the lives of countless individuals, including me.

My mentor, Monte Holm, gave me a copy in 1996 and told me to read it. At the time, most of my reading focused on dry college textbooks about biology and chemistry. *Think and Grow Rich* sparked a huge interest in me because I immediately felt it could change my life.

I felt energized rereading it before I sat down to write this book and have found it reminds me of movies like *The Matrix* and *Inception* where each time you watch them, you pick up new details and nuances of the story. Although *Think and Grow Rich* is a short book, each chapter is packed with movie-worthy content.

The 13 principles of success Napoleon Hill outlines in *Think and Grow Rich* work for everyone and are as relevant today as they were when the book was first published in 1937, though the world today is a much different place than it was in 1937.

So, why write a version of *Think and Grow Rich* specifically for Asians? Versions of the original book have been created for Latinos, African Americans, and women. Why not Asians? It makes sense that one of the most significant cultures on the planet should be represented.

As an Asian American, I believe it is my responsibility to help other Asian people succeed. As a human being, I'd like to help as many people as I can, period. The success stories and perspectives shared by people from different backgrounds in this book will inspire you and link you to others who are farther down the path you have chosen to follow.

Asian people have encouraged me to create a reference companion to *Think and Grow Rich* that outlines the keys to my success in words and examples that echo their own stories and heritage.

My work has been influenced by the examples of successful Asian authors, mentors, celebrities, and leaders. I am honored to share their perspectives, beliefs, and experiences, illustrating qualities and approaches to challenges that are unique to the Asian culture.

I use the terms "Asian American" and "Asians" a lot in this book. The term "Asian American" was coined by historian Yuji Ichioka when he referred to a new "inter-ethnic-pan-Asian-American self-defining political group" in the late 1960s. Today, it remains one of the most accepted and respected terms to identify the diversity within Asian cultures in America. On a global scale, I intend to treat all Asian cultures and descendants of them with great respect.

According to the Napoleon Hill Foundation, the original *Think and Grow Rich* sells more copies in Asia than in any other two continents combined! The NOP World Culture Score Index lists the top four reading countries (based on average time spent reading per week) as India, Thailand, China, and the Philippines. Being an Asian American living in the United States, I decided to zero in on a smaller sample, focusing mostly on Asians living in the United States, instead of looking at massive numbers of the Asian community worldwide.

Statistics gathered by the Pew Research Center in 2015 show that the impact of Asian Americans immigrating to the United States can be felt across the board:

DEMOGRAPHICS

- 20 million Asian Americans trace their roots to more than 20 countries in East and Southeast Asia and the Indian subcontinent.[1]

- The US Asian population grew 72 percent between 2000 and 2015 (from 11.9 million to 20.4 million), the fastest growth rate of any racial or ethnic group.[2]

- No single country-of-origin group dominates the US Asian population, but the largest groups are of Chinese, Indian, and Filipino origin, with Chinese being the largest at 4.9 million people.[3]

- Asians are projected to become the largest immigrant group in the country, surpassing Hispanics in 2055.[4]

My parents immigrated to the United States from South Korea in 1969. For them, everything was about education. They believed what you learned and applied helped you become rich. They also believed in service to mankind. When you combine the two, you have two possible career choices—doctor or lawyer. Saving lives, helping people, making lots of money—those were the goals my parents drilled into me. This is a common theme throughout many Asian families.

My parents instilled three guiding principles in me: respect, humility, and patience. I've mastered respect and patience, though I'm still working on humility.

Following my parents' plan, I became a lawyer, though I had no burning desire to do so. Their definition of success was simple—sending your children to college; watching them go out and get a good job; and most importantly, having them be happy at the end of the day.

Many Asian people who immigrate to America come from a background that may include difficult times, war, struggle, and oppression. My parents had to learn Chinese and Japanese during their lifetime.

Difficult times can fuel a burning desire. People become committed to doing whatever it takes to achieve success, like having to leave what is familiar behind in search of greater opportunity.

Even in the Land of Opportunity, Asians still have to deal with racism and stereotypes. People usually expect me to have an accent because I am obviously Asian. Some people squint while talking to me and assume I own a dry cleaning business, a restaurant, or a liquor store, or that I am a math whiz, a programmer, or a computer tech.

Once I met a woman who asked where I was from. When I told her I am from Los Angeles, she said, "I didn't realize there was a Los Angeles in China."

After clarifying I meant Los Angeles, California, and telling her I was originally from South Korea, she went on to say, "Oh, I love Chinese food."

My children get this too. One of my daughters is in the process of rushing college sororities. The feedback she received from her first choice was, "You will never get in here." When she asked why not, she was told, "You don't have blond hair and blue eyes."

Breaking stereotypes is a complicated process. Change will come as we educate and enlighten people about the impact Asian people have on the world today. Clearly, some of the old stereotypes are not relevant anymore.

EDUCATION

- In 2015, about 54 percent of Asians had a college degree.[5]

- 85.7 percent of Asians in America, age 25 and older, are high school graduates.[6]

- 21.2 percent of Asians in America, age 25 and older, have an advanced degree (e.g., Master's, PhD, MD, or JD).[7]

ECONOMICS AND EMPLOYMENT

- 49.1 percent of employed Asians 16 and older hold management and professional positions such as financial managers, engineers, teachers, and registered nurses.[8]

- Of the 87 US startup companies valued at over $1 billion, 19 were founded by Asian-American immigrants.[9]

- The estimated number of Asian-owned employer firms in the United States in 2015 was 530,406.[10]

- Asian American-owned businesses employed a total of 2.8 million people, and their average revenue was $338,400 per company.[11]

- In 2015, Asians had an estimated buying power of $825 billion, which is expected to grow to $1.1 trillion in 2020, according to the Selig Center for Economic Growth.[12]

- The average household income of Asian Americans is $74,105.[13]

According to the Pew Research Center, Asian Americans are highly satisfied with their lives and their finances, and they place a high value on marriage, parenthood, hard work, and career success.[14]

Every day, I meet people and read stories about individuals who refuse to let racism, stereotypes, and old thinking limit them. Many of them have read and applied the principles of the original *Think and Grow Rich* and gone on to achieve success and improve their lives.

Millions of people share a similar experience or can relate to being driven by fear due to negative past experiences. Think back to a moment when you may have been bullied, excluded, or made to feel "less than"—a time when you were told you weren't smart enough or good enough or that you were too heavy, too light, too tall, or too small. Maybe you were the wrong race, color, or creed and were excluded or made the subject of gossip and judgment as a result. These negative seeds can become magnified and amplified during your life until you begin believing them and creating your own self-imposed limitations.

When writing this book, my goal was to discuss Napoleon Hill's principles of success through the eyes of Asians for the benefit of all readers, regardless of their ethnicity, heritage, or background. I quote Hill along with successful, influential people from the Asian community and cultural knowledge bank. I also include many non-Asian sources who have influenced my life. No one can achieve success without embracing teamwork. Working with people from different backgrounds and cultures elevates us faster and better than working with a group of like-minded people who share our experiences. My general focus, however, will remain on the Asian experience.

It is important to note that the Asian and Asian American experiences are unique and were not specifically addressed in *Think and Grow Rich.*

Reviewing the collected wisdom of others presented in this book will help you understand the principles as you hear them from the perspective of others. At the end of each chapter are quotes from the "Asian Mastermind." If you find yourself struggling in any particular area, start your day by reading these.

How Rich Asians Think: A Think and Grow Rich Publication will give you the tools to eliminate excuses and overcome your fears so that you can begin to turn your dreams into reality. As you read, I hope you feel my conviction that you can achieve anything you truly desire.

This book will develop your inner strength so that you can stand up and face your fears and be the person you were meant to be. Stand tall and confront the bullies and the naysayers and the gossips of the world, and let them know you are a force to be reckoned with that will not stop, ever.

How Rich Asians Think follows the chapter outline of the original *Think and Grow Rich*. Each chapter begins with my interpretation of the key points found in the original text written by Napoleon Hill. Then, I share success stories and examples from my interviews with Asian and non-Asian leaders relating to the content found in each chapter. I will connect these stories and examples to Hill's key points in a short summary before leaving you with select inspirational quotes exclusively from notable Asians.

Each chapter concludes with exercises and action steps for you to apply what you have learned. A notepad or a journal is an excellent companion to this book. As you read, write your thoughts and ideas, clarify your goals, and organize your plan.

How Rich Asians Think celebrates the Asian culture and honors trailblazers who have succeeded despite numerous challenges, forging a path for others to follow.

There are Asian people throughout the world who are continually seeking, appreciating, and genuinely valuing every opportunity. The wisdom they have gained and their approaches to obstacles can be found throughout this book.

During the last Winter Olympic Games, I learned a new acronym from Marissa Brandt, one of the members of the 2018 Korean hockey team—TWIG, which stands for "take what is given."

Marissa recollects that when she got the call to be on the Korean team, she just said yes without taking time to think it over, taking what was given and running with it.

You get to choose. You decide what value to assign. When you are grateful for the opportunity—any opportunity—you win!

Regardless of your background, I believe *How Rich Asians Think* has the power to change your life. Your personal success goes beyond the boundaries of race, ethnicity, and culture. If you follow the 13 success principles taught by Napoleon Hill almost a century ago, you will succeed.

Take what is given and make the most of this gift.

You can do it!

—**John Shin**

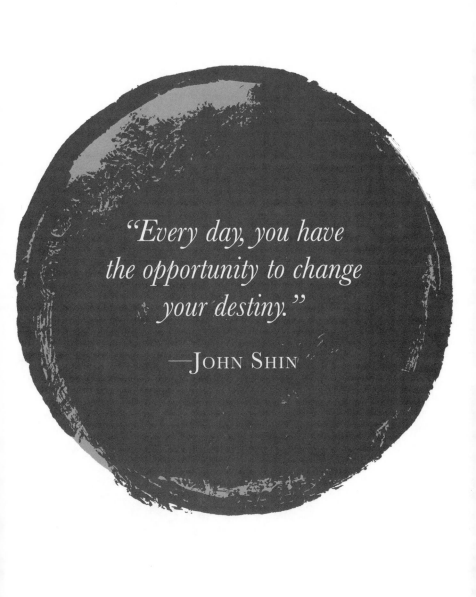

"*Every day, you have the opportunity to change your destiny.*"

—JOHN SHIN

THOUGHTS ARE THINGS

Conceive, believe, and achieve your dreams

What holds you back? If you're like most people, it's fear. Fear of rejection. Fear of failure. Fear of abandonment, ill health, old age, or death. No matter what label you assign it, failure usually boils down to one thing—fear of the unknown.

"All that a man thinks and achieves and all that he fails to achieve is the direct result of his own thoughts...as a man thinks, so he is; as he continues to think, so he remains," said James Allen.

Napoleon Hill also believed thoughts can and do become things. *Think and Grow Rich* opens with "Truly, thoughts are things, and powerful things at that, when they are mixed with definiteness of purpose, persistence, and a burning desire for their translation into riches, or other material objects."

Definite purpose, persistence, and burning desire make all the difference. Without these aspects, thoughts are unlikely to go beyond your head.

If fear keeps you from dreaming big, create a dream that is larger than your fear. Imagine your dream coming true. Visualize it, and make it so vivid and real that it energizes you above and beyond your feelings of uncertainty. Make the good outweigh the bad. Keep in mind that feeling anxious is much the same as feeling excited.

Use this acronym to reframe fear in a positive light: Feeling Excited and Ready (FEAR).

Fear is no laughing matter. Or is it? Have you ever tried laughing at your fear? Have you ever asked yourself what you are afraid of? What's the worst that could happen? Can you live with failure, assuming you survive? Try asking your brain, "Is this all you've got? Is this the best you can do?"

Developing the ability to laugh at yourself will carry you past the small obstacles your brain throws out whenever you try something new.

Fear is not the only thing holding people back. Some wander through life staying busy with mundane and insignificant tasks, taking it easy. It takes energy and effort to conceive, believe, and achieve your dreams. A comfortable routine is a perfect distraction. Unfortunately, this familiar pattern leads nowhere.

It is merely one of many tools we all use to mask our fears. Such tools often work together, at times so elaborately that we cannot unravel the truth from the stories we tell ourselves.

- Excuses
- A sense of entitlement
- A victim mentality
- A lack of purpose

- Poor habits
- Poor choices
- Poor planning
- Quitting early
- A lack of confidence and belief in yourself

The reasons why we don't follow our dreams are endless. Let's take a closer look at them and clear the deck for better things.

EXCUSES, ENTITLEMENT, AND THE VICTIM MENTALITY

The world is filled with people who want more money, a bigger house, a nicer car, and a better life. But most people are unwilling to improve themselves and make the changes necessary to obtain these things. Their expectations and sense of entitlement exceed their willingness to change. Instead of attracting what they want, they continually attract things that reflect who they are at their core. Ironically, many of these people get angry, point their fingers, and blame other people, circumstances beyond their control, politics, or even the weather for their struggles.

Hill explains, "We refuse to believe that which we do not understand. We foolishly believe that our own limitations are the proper measure of limitations."

If you believe you're a victim of circumstance, you will remain stuck. You will be boxed in by your own self-imposed limitations. The minute you begin to realize your own creative power to control your destiny, you will become a master of self, and everything will start to change.

Dr. Marissa Pei, inspirational speaker, TV commentator, consulting psychologist, author, and life coach known as the "Asian Oprah," seems about as far from stuck as one can get, but it wasn't always that way. Growing up, Marissa was not proud of her Chinese roots. "I was Canadian-born Chinese in the predominantly German town of Kitchener, Canada, and the only Chinese girl in my school. I was made fun of a lot for something I could not change and called fat, ugly, and clumsy. In hindsight, I'm grateful I am Chinese. Embracing my roots served as a helping point for those who are not happy with all parts of them. My journey has been a wonderful one because it chiseled me into valuing all aspects of myself, which is a life journey all human beings benefit from."

When Marissa was growing up, her mom tried to protect her and keep her from being a person who stands up and speaks out. "My mother used to say, 'The nail that stands up gets hammered down.' It's an old Chinese expression."

Initially, Marissa thought she knew what path she would take in life. "I thought I would go into medicine because all Asians should either do medicine or law, right? But I dated a guy in high school who died of leukemia. I watched him die and knew I couldn't do medicine as a career, so I picked my favorite elective, psychology."

Instead of taking her childhood experiences and pain to heart and turning others' negative thoughts and ideas into things that defined her, Marissa used them to motivate her into building a life she could be proud of, starting with a career as a model. "I became a model to prove people wrong and discovered I loved business and the behind-the-scenes-activities of the agency more."

Marissa already had a degree in psychology but had realized she didn't have the patience to become a clinical psychologist. "I went into organizational psychology to combine my interest in business with psychology and dynamics of behavior at work." And she was very successful, consulting with Fortune 500 businesses and teaching at UCLA for six years.

"People said I should get into public speaking because they thought my presentations were dynamic and inspiring. So, I got involved in on-camera work and started doing keynotes."

Marissa followed a path to success that meandered (as many do), always remembering where she started, using her painful beginnings to push her to the next rung on the ladder she'd put before herself. But she stalled at times, dealing with many of the same negative thoughts that once had motivated her. "Along the way, I married a man who made me feel less than, not good enough, and who brought me down. An expensive and painful divorce led to the belief in a higher power greater than me. I started examining my life and my inner landscape, trying to find my true purpose. Then, it hit me. I realized I was not alone. We are all a part of life, of energy. We all struggle. But what to do with that knowledge?"

Psychologists have correctly said that when one is truly ready for a thing, it puts in its appearance.

In Marissa's case, this is exactly what happened. "I woke up at 4:30 A.M. one day to a voice in my head that said, 'Radio.' I got up and spent 45 minutes writing a prospectus, a business plan, and a manifesto for a talk radio show on business, health, and happiness called 'Take My Advice, I'm Not Using It: Get Balanced with Dr. Marissa.'"

The rest is history. Five hundred thousand people have downloaded Marissa's show, and she has over 180,000 regular listeners in over 100 countries. She combined her life experience with her newfound purpose in life and turned a middle-of-the-night idea into success on her terms, going on to write best-selling books, appear on television shows and in documentaries, speak in front of large audiences worldwide, and receive award after award, including the Iconic Woman of the Year Award in 2017.

"What a different story men would have to tell if only they would adopt a definite purpose and stand by that purpose until it had time to become an all-consuming obsession!" Hill said.

Hannah and Marissa Brandt, 2018 Olympic hockey players (Hannah with Team USA and Marissa with Team Korea), started playing hockey when they were only five years old. The sisters were always very close. The Brandts adopted Marissa from South Korea when she was an infant, and Hannah was born 11 months later.

"We grew up in Minnesota. Our dad owned a carpet cleaning business, and Mom owned a store. They supported us with every opportunity," Marissa recalled. "My parents even sent us to Korean culture camp. Hannah kept going back because she loved the food and learning about the Korean culture."

Hannah says she never thought of her sister as being adopted. They did everything together, including learning to skate. "I went to preschool with another girl named Hannah. One day, our medications got mixed up, and in the process of sorting it out, we became friends with the family. That family was into hockey, and ours was not. As a result of this friendship, I started skating. The other Hannah went on to figure skating, but I continued with hockey, the sport I love more than any other," Hannah said.

Hannah recalls watching the Olympics in 2002 in Salt Lake City and telling her mom she wanted to play in the Olympics one day. "My mom told me to keep working hard, and they'd find me. I constantly practiced, shooting pucks in the driveway and working on my skills."

While Marissa didn't share her sister's dream of playing in the Olympics and started out wanting to be a figure skater, she loved the sport, the team aspect, and being with her sister more than the girly outfits that initially drew her to figure skating.

Although they came to it in different ways, the sisters adopted definite purposes early in life, never wavering from their goals, and creating lifelong habits that aided them on their road to Olympic glory.

Thought quickly matures into habit, and habit sets into condition. One cannot choose circumstances, but you can choose your thoughts, which indirectly shape your circumstances.

Or, as Hill puts it, "Success comes to those who become success conscious. Failure comes to those who indifferently allow themselves to become failure conscious. Another weakness, found in altogether too many people, is the habit of measuring everything, and everyone, by their own impressions and beliefs."

When it comes to money, we all have a default mode based on complex programming we learned as children. Hill asks, "Are you money conscious or poverty conscious?"

Musician Ray Parker Jr. learned how to manage money from his dad. "He taught me to save my money and live off the interest. Preserve the golden goose and eat the eggs."

Ray grew up in Detroit, about ten blocks from the heart of the Motown music scene. He is a guitarist, singer-songwriter, record producer, and actor best known for writing and performing the theme song to the 1984 movie *Ghostbusters* and playing with his band Raydio and with Barry White. He has written numerous songs for top stars, but the guitar is his focus.

In 1994, he married his wife, Elaine. They have four sons: Ray III (Little Ray), Redmen, Gibson, and Jericho. In 2014, Parker received a star on the Hollywood Walk of Fame for his contributions to music. But he's remained a humble man with a healthy relationship with money.

"I have friends who tried to convince me to buy an $8 million house in Beverly Hills. I decided to buy a $1.1 million house next to Frank Sinatra back in 1980. My friends all thought it was too small. They were the ones who couldn't hang in there down the road. I'm glad I didn't cave to the social pressure and stuck to my core values regarding health and finance. Today, I'm in good shape in both respects."

Riches come in many forms. What's important is to spend time dialing in on what being rich means to you. If money is your prime motivator, that's okay. The important thing is to put money in perspective for yourself.

What do you think about when you think about money? What's the first thing you thought when you read the question? Deeper still, what are your beliefs about money?

Let's look at Mr. Hill's question again.

Are you money conscious or poverty conscious?

Be honest.

When you examine your income history, do you see an increase, a decrease, or a steady number? Most people find that they stay within a narrow margin of earning. If you are accustomed to making $40,000 each year, you've most likely developed a habit of living within this income level. To break free of this earnings rut, something needs to change. You've already started this process by thinking about it.

CHANGE YOUR DEFAULT

Poverty is the default mode, the baseline of having no money or barely enough to survive. No effort is required to live in poverty. Without deliberately creating a plan to attract and earn money, you will live at the default level. If your thoughts surrounding money are mostly fearful or negative, you're also thinking from a position of poverty.

"Poverty is attracted to the one whose mind is favorable to it, as money is attracted to one whose mind has been deliberately prepared to attract it," said Hill.

To move from poverty thinking to money thinking, be conscious and clear about what success looks like to you. Images and pictures are an enormous help because pictures speak the language of our minds.

Spend time immersed in dreams, collecting images that resonate with you, reviewing your plans and goals, and taking the steps necessary to achieve success. When you begin to look at money as something exciting and ditch the thoughts holding you back, the door to change opens. Once it opens, act with a plan and dreams in hand. Because without action, it's all talk, hopes, and wishes. Execute, my friend!

POOR CHOICES

Every day, you have the opportunity to change your destiny.

Everything you've accomplished in your life started off as a single moment. You took your first step, made your first move, and made things happen. Everything you are today, and all you have right now, are the results of every choice and every action you made in the past. Everything you will become hinges upon today, in this very moment.

You may feel like you're stuck. You're too busy. You have other obligations. Life is hard. All of these things are true only if you believe them. Only if you believe the stories you create. We're all storytellers with unlimited imaginations. You could just as easily believe life is great no matter what happens. You could believe nothing that happens is inherently bad; it's your choice.

Perhaps you are struggling financially. You may find (as I have) that money isn't everything. Money won't necessarily make you happy, nor will a lack of money make you unhappy. There are plenty of miserable millionaires who attempt to find internal peace and fulfillment by spending money, putting on masks, and showing off their wealth. And we all know people with very little money or material possessions who radiate a glow of peace and calm that cannot be bought.

You have a priceless piece of computerized technology with the highest precision virtual reality unit working between your ears, twenty-four seven. And nobody has one exactly like you. You are unique.

All change starts in a single moment. Every moment has potential. When I say change, I mean your perspective. Your feelings of frustration, your feelings of pressure and worry, even hopelessness can easily become ease and optimism. You have the power. You are the magician. You have the magic in you, at your fingertips. Only you can decide to use it.

THREE FEET FROM GOLD

In *Think and Grow Rich*, Hill uses a powerful visual. Imagine being a gold miner digging and searching for buried treasure, repeatedly coming up empty. After a few weeks of nothing, you give up. You've had enough and throw in the towel. Now imagine a camera that is capable of showing the network of tunnels you've made panning back to reveal a massive vein of gold a mere three feet from where you quit. Ouch, right?

According to Hill, one of the most common causes of failure is the habit of quitting when one is overtaken by temporary defeat. Everyone has made this mistake. I made it so often that I formed the habit of giving a little extra when I am coming up short on things. I figure I've come this far, what's a little extra?

Have you ever struggled with paying a little more for a better-quality item? If the basic model costs $20 and the better one costs $25, your decision is only about the $5 difference. You're spending at least $20 no matter which option you choose. This change in perspective often makes it easier to give a little more.

OPERATING WITHOUT A PLAN

You've all heard the expression "slow and steady wins the race." In the classic tortoise versus the hare road race, the hare rockets off to an almost insurmountable lead while the tortoise slowly plods along. Everyone expects the hare to win without challenge, but he runs into unexpected obstacles: distraction, overconfidence, and the lure of old habits. He's so far in front that he loses sight of his goal and primary purpose, which is to win the race. Although he made significant strides at first, ultimately, he never crosses the finish line. This is the pattern many people experience as they begin pursuing their New Year's resolutions. They set the bar high without thinking their resolutions through; then they start to lose interest because they lose focus or don't create the habits necessary to sustain their efforts.

The tortoise, on the other hand, was clear about his objective—to become the winner of the race. He was clear about his game plan and focused on what he needed to achieve. He broke it all down into more deliberate, manageable steps.

The key to achieving any goal is to be clear about the big picture and then work backward to the milestones and, finally, the daily steps. The beautiful example the tortoise sets is that because he is clear about who he wants to be, he can pace himself and keep moving forward toward his goal.

Be clear about who you want to be and why. Once you are clear on this goal, break it down into daily resolutions, designed to keep you moving forward each day.

FOCUS BUILDS CONFIDENCE AND ENERGY

When you think with purpose and communicate your desires persistently, people sit up and take notice. This is when the magic happens. Your idea gets picked up by others; then it gets magnified, altered, and augmented. It expands and grows exponentially. It becomes an avalanche of energy. Almost immediately, you receive resources, input, and modifications to your idea, both directly and indirectly. Your concept moves from an "if" to a "when." The only question that remains is whether you stay the steward of your idea or it gets picked up by another to carry it to fruition.

Multimillionaire and business mogul Penney Ooi said, "Once I set a goal to have $2 million in cash by the time I was 40, earning 5 percent so I would have $100,000 in passive income. I wrote it down and reviewed it everywhere in my house and around my office. Can you believe I made it before I turned 40?

"I credit my sureness of thought, the purpose that I communicated persistently, the dream I worked toward. I know my next 50 years will be 10 times bigger than my first 50. My reach and impact on people will be that much bigger," Penney said. "Hard work is fundamental, and saving money plays a major role in success. My parents taught me that."

Our thoughts are direct results of our inputs: books, media, education, and personal influences. If you feel stuck or as if you are drifting aimlessly, without any goals, it may be time to change the station and begin managing your inputs. Doing the same things and thinking the same thoughts but expecting different results is insane. So, how do we change our programming?

STOP IT

Our thoughts impact how we feel. How we feel impacts our actions. Our actions directly affect our results. So, it makes sense that if we want to change our results, we must begin by changing our thoughts, especially when they are not serving us.

When you wake up in the morning and your head is a swirl of negative thoughts, it's not long before you're feeling down, depressed, and even hopeless. We've all been there. And it can feel impossible to break free of this pattern once it starts. But you can.

Begin focusing on being wealthy and successful. If this is not currently your habit, start believing you are already wealthy and successful. Why? Because you are. Remember, it's not all about money. It may take a little time to shift your perspective, and this may be the "not-so-good news" because it requires some effort and change on your part.

You must define what wealth and success mean to you. For some people, being wealthy is all about money, assets, and unlimited options to purchase the latest and greatest trinkets and material goods. For others, wealth and success mean freedom, family, relationships, flexibility, and time to do what they want, when they want—not how much money they have in the bank.

David Fishof, the founder of Rock and Roll Fantasy Camp, believes success is something different for everyone. "Over the years, what I thought was success for other people wasn't success to me." This observation raises an interesting point about the way we all tend to measure our success against that of others. This can create discomfort and uncertainty for some people as they pursue goals that might lead them away from the traditional view of success.

David's early career as a concert and event promoter and sports agent meant that he was surrounded by the rich and famous—people like Ringo Starr, players with the New York Yankees and Giants, and the Monkees. Although he was successful by any measure, his idea of success didn't waver. "Success for me has always been my family, seeing my kids and grandkids, and hoping my children will out-succeed me. With the camp, I am not necessarily getting rich, but I love what I do."

Hill gives us the "secret" formula in *Think and Grow Rich*: "Whatever the mind of man can conceive and believe, it can achieve."

So simple, yet powerful. Unlimited potential for those who believe. Flexible in definition, recognizing success is how you define it for yourself.

Let's break it down.

CONCEIVE

Hill devotes an entire chapter in *Think and Grow Rich* to the imagination and reminds us that humans can create anything they can imagine: machines, music, architecture, food, works of art, and constructions of every conceivable kind. If it doesn't exist in nature or come from the planet, everything we know was created first in the imagination of a human mind.

Although he may not have foreseen the future of cell phones, Gene Roddenberry's concept of the flip-open communicator used in the original *Star Trek* series inspired Motorola to produce one of the earliest commercial cell phone designs in 1996, a flip phone appropriately named StarTAC. What began as a thought became a thing once the crazy-genius idea was released into the world, making it real. Today, others have harnessed the energy of that idea and augmented and expanded it well beyond Roddenberry's wildest imagination. Captain Kirk would be proud.

Imagination is a blank canvas unrestricted, ungoverned, and unlimited in its potential. There is no end to the possibilities of what can be drawn, painted, written, designed, or placed upon the imagination's blank slate. In this area, the only limitations are ones we place upon ourselves.

Hill says, "There are no limitations to the mind except those that we acknowledge."

Self-imposed limitations form the walls we build around ourselves. These figurative walls provide a sense of safety, security, and order. They also confine, define, and undermine our efforts to spread our wings and fly. Venturing out of our comfort zone is difficult, which is why many people limit their thinking to create the illusion of control.

The reality is that our thoughts are the only thing we can control. "Nature has endowed man with absolute control over but one thing, and that is thought," Hill points out in *Think and Grow Rich*.

BELIEF

Belief is perhaps the most essential ingredient in achieving success in any area of life. Our beliefs form our operating system. They run in the background, subconsciously and imperceptibly affecting our results. Whether you believe you can or you believe you can't, the results will be automatic, like a self-fulfilling machine.

Most people tend to place limitations on their thinking and expression in specific areas because they don't believe the results they desire are possible. It is common among people in Asian cultures to be more reserved when expressing their thoughts and ideas, to value silence, and to avoid speaking out of turn or rocking the boat.

Although times are changing, heritage and multigenerational family values are still a potent force among many Asian cultures today.

Sometimes the disparity holding us back is the difference between what we think we deserve and what we honestly believe is possible. It's one thing to have a great idea and get all fired up about it, but it's another to think the idea is possible and to act and follow through on it. Your results are directly related to your belief in your ideas and yourself.

Believing in yourself takes courage. Following your heart is painful at times. If what you want is something you genuinely think you can accomplish, you will find a way. Period.

Napoleon Hill and other notable authorities on success and achievement have taught me to express my thoughts and ideas and expand my thinking about what I deserve and believe is possible. The more I share with others, the more they advance and grow too, perfectly illustrating Hill's concept that thoughts are things.

ACHIEVEMENT

Whatever you can conceive and believe, you can achieve. Your position in life and what you have accomplished so far are the result of your actions.

I've had some fantastic dreams I've acted upon, producing tangible results. I also have my share of dreams that are still sitting on the shelf in my library of unfulfilled dreams. And that's okay. There is nothing wrong with having an active imagination or unfulfilled dreams. There are only so many hours in a day and so many dreams we can pursue at once.

How does this idea make you feel? Where do you set the bar for settling? How much is good enough? Only you can answer these questions. There is no judgment and no right or wrong answer. If you are living your life by your own design and getting the results you desire, then congratulations! Bravo! Good for you! If not, review what's holding you back. My bet is the answer lies somewhere in your belief system, specifically in your beliefs about yourself and what you can or should achieve.

On the surface, the big issue may appear to be a lack of time and being too busy to do more. But too busy is a symptom of a deeper issue. Life is complicated and demanding. We all tend to pack our schedules with false priorities. These are distractions—excuses, really. Sometimes they are necessary distractions, but they are distractions from your goals and dreams nonetheless.

YOUR FUTURE STARTS NOW

Your future starts today, right now, at this very moment. Every breath you take represents the present moment. Your previous breath is already in the past. Life, energy, and unlimited potential course through your veins, waiting to be unleashed in the pursuit of your goals and dreams. You are a miracle. What's holding you back?

THE BIG TAKEAWAY

What you think repeatedly you will believe. The more you think you can, the more you believe you can. Be careful because the opposite is also true.

WISDOM FROM THE ASIAN MASTERMIND

"What you habitually think largely determines what you will ultimately become."

—Bruce Lee,
actor and martial arts master

"The mind is everything. What you think you become."

    —Buddha, prince, warrior, meditator, and teacher

"I try to believe like I believed when I was five, when your heart tells you everything you need to know."

    —Lucy Liu, actor

"The key to growth is the introduction of higher dimensions of consciousness into our awareness."

    —Lao Tzu, Chinese philosopher, author of the *Tao Te Ching,* and founder of Taoism

"Rule your mind, or it will rule you."

    —Buddha

"We're never in lack of money. We lack people with dreams, [people] who can die for those dreams."

—Jack Ma, Chinese businessman, philanthropist, and the founder and executive chairman of Alibaba Group. He is the wealthiest person in Asia.

"Life's battles don't always go to the stronger or faster man. But sooner or later the man who wins is the man who thinks he can."

—Bruce Lee

"Money is really just an idea."

—Robert Kiyosaki, bestselling author and founder of the Rich Dad Company

"Happiness does not depend on what you have or who you are. It solely relies on what you think."

—Buddha

"Kindness in words creates confidence. Kindness in thinking creates profoundness. Kindness in giving creates love."

—Lao Tzu

"The men I idolized built their bodies and became somebody like Sylvester Stallone and Arnold Schwarzenegger. I thought, 'That can be me.' So I started working out. The funny thing is, I didn't realize back then that I was having a defining moment."

—Dwayne Johnson (The Rock), actor

"None of us are getting out of here alive, so please stop treating yourself like an afterthought. Eat the delicious food. Walk in the sunshine. Jump in the ocean. Say the truth that you're carrying in your heart like hidden treasure. Be silly. Be kind. Be weird. There's no time for anything else."

—Keanu Reeves, actor

GROWTH EXERCISES

Perfect your elevator speech.

Explain your beliefs about wealth and success by communicating them to someone else in 30 seconds or less. You should be able to convey, with authority and crystal clarity, why you want to be wealthy and successful and what you intend to do in exchange for that wealth.

1. Craft one sentence that clearly states your objective.

2. Write a paragraph that clearly explains your objective.

3. Print them out.

4. Review and practice your speech twice a day for the next month.

Feed your thoughts.

1. Practice gratitude. Start a gratitude journal or whatever works for you. Pinterest is fun. The important thing is to record at least three things you are grateful for each day. This can be something fun to share with your partner or children. Try journal drawing.

2. Say "no" more often to drudgeries and "yes" more often to fun.

3. Find and start working with three autosuggestions designed to improve the quality of your self-talk (see the chapter on Autosuggestion for guidance).

4. Clearly define what success means to you.

5. Do little things today to achieve bigger things tomorrow.

6. Don't blame others or make up excuses.

7. Learn from others. Ask one person for advice this week on something related to your ultimate dream.

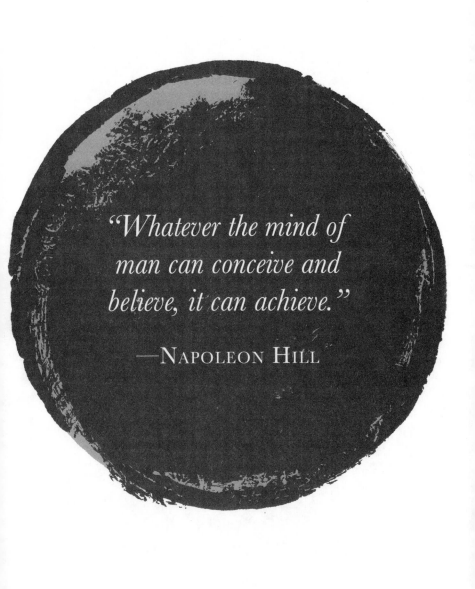

"Whatever the mind of man can conceive and believe, it can achieve."

—NAPOLEON HILL

DESIRE

The starting point of all achievement

Actor Lucy Liu explains, "I didn't really have an idea of what I wanted to do until I really went to college. When I was younger, I wanted to be an actress, but it just wasn't something that was going to be feasible. My parents didn't understand that. I didn't even mention it to them. I didn't actually bring it up until I started pursuing it because it would just be, you know, this kind of blob that they couldn't really connect to. You have to give them something tangible. Like I have a stethoscope on, I'm going to be a doctor. Or I'm going to be a lawyer. But I think the arts is not something they really understood or focused on. My parents were very focused on education and business, things like that."

My parents said something similar to me when I was young: "You need to be a doctor or a lawyer," the two most common professions Asian parents want for their children.

Lucy attributes her success and ability to break through in her pursuit of the arts to her burning desire and determination. "I think it was just about this passion that I had for the arts. I really knew that this was what I wanted to do, and I was going to pursue it with everything that I had. I also wanted to show my parents and prove to them that I could do something. I mean, I had no evidence. I had no proof of it."

Putting a label on Lucy Liu is hard. Actress, director, artist, UNICEF ambassador, and single mother, Lucy is the youngest of three children born to Cecilia, a biochemist, and Tom Liu, a trained engineer who sold digital clock pens to make a living.

She said, "They are definitely people that worked very hard and had that whole idea of the American dream, and they pursued it."

She did not learn English until the age of five when she entered public school. "We didn't have many traditions in our family. My parents were immigrants coming from China, and they spoke English haltingly. They both held down full-time jobs. There wasn't time for niceties. It was about survival. It wasn't about continuing traditions."

Her family spoke Mandarin Chinese at home. Now she speaks six languages, practices the martial art of Kali-Eskrima-Silat (knife-and-stick fighting), and plays the accordion.

When she was a child, she dreamed of becoming an actor but did not tell her parents. Instead, she went off to college, studying Asian languages and culture at the University of Michigan at Ann Arbor, earning a bachelor's degree.

Lucy began her acting career after auditioning for a minor part in a production of *Alice in Wonderland* during senior year and winning the lead role despite being an Asian. She says, "I thought there was a mistake, a big mistake. I kept following the name to the character. And I was in shock. Growing up as somebody from another country, really, not what you see on television, I never saw myself in the forefront, ever. Before that, I'd never seen myself as somebody who could be the lead because on television and film there was never anyone that represented what I thought I could be. So I thought, you know, 'Oh, I'll just always be somebody in the background.' And that's the first time I thought, 'Wow, I can do something and change how I perceive myself in the world.'"

Since then, Lucy has broken free of many of the stereotypes that are typically assigned to Asian performers, enjoying a successful acting career in film and TV. She has won numerous awards for acting and has also produced and directed. When she hosted *Saturday Night Live* in 2000, she became the first Asian-American female ever to do so. But she still says there is racism in Hollywood and stereotypes to break through. "I wish people wouldn't just see me as the Asian girl who beats everyone up, or the Asian girl with no emotion. People see Julia Roberts or Sandra Bullock in a romantic comedy, but not me. You add race to it, and it becomes, 'Well, she's too Asian,' or, 'She's too American. I kind of get pushed out of both categories. It's a very strange place to be. You're not Asian enough, and then you're not American enough, so it gets really frustrating."

Lucy is proud of her heritage but says, "My intention is not to represent Asian Americans but to be an Asian American who is working as an actress. People often confuse the two. When you are representing, you have the burden of some people projecting their hopes onto you. This can eventually lead to a certain amount of disappointment. I strive to not deny myself experiences that open up to me. I hope to live without looking back in regret."

She is also a talented painter and photographer who presents her artwork under a pseudonym, Yu Ling (which is her Chinese name). Her painting *Escape* was exhibited during the prestigious Art Basel Miami 2008. After an exhibit at a New York gallery, she won a grant to study art in China.

In 2004, she became an ambassador for UNICEF and a spokesperson for the Human Rights Campaign.

"My family had such a strong work ethic growing up," Lucy said. "So I never really stopped to think that (having a child) could help balance my life." That changed when her son was born via a gestational surrogate. "My life has opened up in a way that I never thought it could. Because the colors are just more rich; they're more bold."

Clearly, Lucy is a woman who follows her passions wherever they take her. She exhibits confidence and a willingness to try new things. No matter what stands in her way, she goes for it.

In *Think and Grow Rich*, Hill tells the tale of a great warrior who faced a situation that made it necessary for him to make a decision that would ensure his success on the battlefield. He was about to send his armies against a powerful foe whose men outnumbered his own. He loaded his soldiers and boats, sailed into the enemy's country, unloaded soldiers and equipment, then gave the order to burn the ships that had carried them. Addressing his men before the first battle, he said, "You see the boats going up in smoke. That means we cannot leave these shores alive unless we win. We now have no choice. We win, or we perish."

They won.

"Every person who wins in any undertaking must be willing to burn his ships and cut all sources of retreat," Hill said. "Only by doing so can one be sure of maintaining that state of mind known as a burning desire to win, essential to success."

What is your burning desire?

Hill suggests that you may as well know, right here, that you can never have riches in great quantities unless you can work yourself into a white heat of desire for money and actually believe you will possess it.

ASIAN VIEWS ON SUCCESS

There's a saying in China that it's better to be the head of a chicken than the tail of a phoenix. In other words, it's better to be overqualified than underqualified relative to one's surroundings. In Japan, they say it's better to be the head of a sardine than the tail of a whale.

For Asian Americans, success is defined as a combination of financial security (44 percent) and happy family life (47 percent), according to a 2018 survey conducted by Northwestern Mutual.[15]

Northwestern Mutual conducted the survey to learn how Asian Americans view success, how they define financial security, and the impact of finances on them as individuals and on their family lives.

To achieve financial security, Asian Americans cited the following as having the most positive impact: saving money (62 percent), spending wisely (58 percent), paying down debt (51 percent), and having a solid foundation of financial literacy/understanding (49 percent).[16]

Financial success is just one way to measure success; in this book, we're concentrating on building the solid foundation and understanding that will help you succeed, no matter what you strive to accomplish in life.

Researching this book, I found wildly differing studies, reports, and statistics about Asians as a group. Stereotypes are still prevalent and presented as fact by some researchers. For example, everyone knows that Asians:

- Have higher IQs
- Do well in school
- Push their children to study more
- Value higher education more
- Insist that their kids play piano or violin (and practice for hours each day)
- Are good at math and science
- Excel in tech and medical fields
- Are all hardworking

Do some research, and you'll find statistics and opinions to support all of these things as well as other hackneyed assumptions about Asians. However, you'll also find plenty of evidence that none of these stereotypes are accurate.

As Christina Ho says in her review of Ellen D. Wu's award-winning book *The Color of Success: Asian Americans and the Origins of the Model Minority*, "ethnic stereotypes have less to do with any innate racial or biological reality and everything to do with the political dynamics of the societies in which we live."

If you attribute your success thus far in life to above-average intelligence, a pushy mom, or your hard work ethic, great. If you have none of these "advantages," don't fret. It turns out humans are all pretty much the same, regardless of race. Yes, there are differences. These boil down to an individual's unique set of qualities, upbringing, and environment. So, if you got some of the "bad" stuff, you have just as much chance at succeeding in life as anyone else. The principles outlined in this book can help you get ahead in life no matter where you are starting from.

The first step to achieving success is developing a burning desire backed by action. "Every human being who reaches the age of understanding of the purpose of money wishes for it. Wishing will not bring riches. But desiring riches with the state of mind that becomes an obsession, then planning definite ways and means to acquire riches, and backing those plans with persistence which does not recognize failure, will bring riches," Hill writes.

Mental chemistry works magic, according to Hill, who explains, "I believe in the power of desire backed by faith because I have seen this power lift men from lowly beginnings to places of power and wealth. I have seen it rob the grave of its victims. I have seen it serve as the medium by which men staged a comeback after having been defeated in a hundred different ways."

Merriam-Webster says to desire is "to long or hope for."

Without longing or hoping for something, one cannot expect to have anything.

If you have not identified your personal burning desire, let this chapter inspire you to do so. Without a burning desire, there can be no success.

Success requires a definite goal backed by burning desire. This combination produces the motivation, drive, and stamina you need to create and execute a plan that will allow you to reach your goal.

Ilana Muhlstein is a registered dietitian who sits on the Executive Leadership Team for the American Heart Association and leads the Bruin Health Improvement Program at UCLA. She's a nutrition consultant for several companies, including Beachbody and Whole Foods Market, and she co-created a weight loss program called 2B Mindset. She's also a contributing writer for publications such as *SELF*, *Huffington Post*, and the *Journal of Obesity*. And it all started with a burning desire to lose weight.

"I was a very obese child and would eat anything in sight. I always wanted to be thinner and healthier, but it wasn't until I became determined to get to the bottom of what was causing my weight problem and out-of-control tendencies like volume and obsessive eating that things changed." As a teenager faced with health issues and embarrassment over her ballooning weight, Ilana had a burning desire to lose weight, which led to the decision to finally take matters into her own hands and do something about her weight struggles once and for all. Now she inspires others with everything she does and has grown a personal brand and business around her success.

In *Think and Grow Rich*, Napoleon Hill focuses the most on the burning desire to achieve financial wealth. He provides steps to turn your desire for wealth into financial reality. Hill refers to this early on in his book as "turning desire into gold."

TURNING DESIRE INTO GOLD

When I interview people, I always ask them, "Why are you here?"

Because I am in the financial services industry, the most common answer to this question is, "I want to make a lot of money."

The problem with this answer is that most people are not specific enough with their goals, or they are afraid to set the bar high in terms of cash flow. They want to make a lot of money, but they do not know why, or how much, or when. This is like tossing a ball at a target. Would it be easier if the target was still or waving around back and forth?

When your goals are firm, they are not paper targets flopping around in the wind. Firm goals give you something to focus on and a much better chance of hitting your target.

When it comes to your income, start by identifying how much money you need. What are your total monthly expenses? If you do not know, add them up! Once you find this, ask yourself questions like "When do I need this money?" Be specific. Do not say, "In a year." Say, "By August 31 at 5:00 P.M." The more specific you are about what you want and when you want it, the greater your chance of achieving your goal.

Hill's focus on money bothers some people. After all, we are all free to define success however we like. But being money conscious is never a bad idea. And once one has earned a sufficient amount of money, one can do more good works. Hill too turned his focus here when he discussed great leaders and what they give back to those around them, commenting, "You give before you get." It is a simple statement but also very accurate.

Raja Dhaliwal, financial guru, concurred when sharing his story with me. Born in Northern India in the state of Punjab to a middle-class family, he worked with his dad in the restaurant business until he married a Canadian girl and immigrated to Winnipeg, Manitoba, Canada. "I was a good student. Initially, I thought I would become a doctor or an engineer. After tenth grade, I became more interested in business. I always believed anyone can do anything if they put their mind to it."

Raja eventually got involved in the financial industry and built an organization of 4,600 licensed representatives that made over $70 million in compensation each year by helping hundreds of thousands of people. "I want to change lives and help foster hope in people. It's not so much about money anymore as it is about helping people. Some business owners have an employee mindset. Employees usually want to receive before they give. Treat your business right by giving first and then receiving."

A 2009 study by the Harvard Business School found that happier people give more and giving makes people happier.[17] Happiness and giving appear to operate in a positive feedback loop, with happier people giving more, getting happier, and giving even more.

Jack Ma, one of the most successful businessmen in the world, clearly knew this when he announced that Alibaba Group would devote 0.3 percent of its annual revenue to environmental protection causes. "Our challenge is to help more people to make healthy money, sustainable money, money that is not only good for themselves but also good for the society."

Award-winning DJ Steve Aoki, who has also been a guitarist in different hardcore bands, says, "The DIY lifestyle is what hardcore is all about. It's not about materialism and things that cost money. For me, the cool points were being productive in the community, doing something creative in that space, promoting it within the community. The community was not just Asians; it was white kids and all kids who were looking for acceptance too."

Steve is Japanese. He grew up in the predominantly white community of Newport Beach, California, and lived with his mom, whom he credits for much of his success throughout his adolescent life. "It was a 96 percent white population. I faced a lot of racism as a young person, but I am grateful for growing up and living in a racially ignorant place where I wasn't supported by the general status quo. If I had grown up somewhere different, I wouldn't have come out the same."

His father was Hiroaki Aoki, best known as Rocky Aoki, founder of the popular Japanese cuisine restaurant chain Benihana.

Steve chose not to follow in his father's footsteps. "From the beginning of my career, my first passion came from feeling as if I really fit in somewhere in a musical, cultural community called hardcore. It was more about the community of Asian kids who didn't really fit in elsewhere, not necessarily the music. At the time, I had been in physical fights with people who were outright racist. My mom would defend the bullies and apologize to not cause any problems. The Japanese culture is essentially to stay low, stay hidden, stay obedient. If you were rocking the boat, you were doing something wrong. That's why it was a life changer when I found a group that said, 'Hey, it's okay to be an outcast.' I learned how to make music, record it, and work with others in the same boat, giving back as soon as I absorbed."

He, like many successful young people, say that normal business and marketing channels have a culture and language that create an enormous obstacle to entry. "It forces us to be resourceful and creative; to start small, with the right message, with authenticity and passion, and take it to the right people. You must do the work, you must put in the time, form the habit and consistency of becoming better. This is burning desire and drive. It helped me find the people who cared about what I had to say."

"When you find your burning desire, you'll be even more focused on your goal, and you will know peace of mind," notes Justin Chon, an actor best known for his role in *The Twilight Saga* movies. He also writes, produces, and directs films.

Born in Garden Grove, California, he spent most of his life in Irvine, California. He has a younger sister who is a public defender. "She's married to a cop."

His father was a famous child actor in Korea in the sixties and owned a shoe store. His mom was an accomplished pianist. "My parents were more progressive than some parents. They allowed me to follow my path. They taught me to respect my elders, to have a good work ethic, and to understand that nobody will give you anything. Plus, they gave me a sense of community. My Asian heritage is part of my identity. My parents were not prejudiced and taught me to love others and love myself. My dad taught me to work hard and emphasized the value of a dollar."

Justin went to business school at the University of Southern California and studied entrepreneurship and marketing. "During my sophomore year, I enrolled in an acting class and discovered I loved it. I worked my class schedule around my acting class and practice sessions. I gave it my 'give it two years' philosophy."

An entrepreneur and judge on the hit television show *Shark Tank*, Kevin Harrington grew up in the Midwest in Cincinnati, Ohio. His father was in the restaurant business. "He controlled his own destiny," Kevin says. "Mom was a school teacher. Dad said, 'You need to own your own business,' and Mom said, 'You should be a doctor or a lawyer.' In a family of six children, I was the fourth of six. I have two older sisters. One is a doctor, and one is a lawyer, so that got me off the hook and gave me a chance to be an entrepreneur. I knew it would be hard. I grew up watching my dad work 60 plus hours a week."

Harrington is best known for infomercials and founded a company called Quantum International. His first big hit was Ginsu Knives. He was president of National Media and oversaw the launching of several successful infomercials. In 1994, he cofounded HSN Direct International Inc.

Harrington was one of the original panel members and investors on the ABC TV series *Shark Tank* and is the author of *Act Now: How I Turn Ideas into Million-Dollar Products.*

Kevin is obviously a man who believes in diversity and sees opportunities in many places.

Hill writes, "We who are in this race for riches should be encouraged to know that this changed world in which we live is demanding new ideas, new ways of doing things, new leaders, new inventions, new methods of teaching, new methods of marketing, new books, new literature, new features for television, new ideas for moving pictures. Behind this demand for new and better things, there is one quality which one must possess to win, and that is definiteness of purpose, the knowledge of what one wants, and a burning desire to possess it."

"I started off delivering papers and mowing lawns," Kevin shares. "I guess I started out in sales. My burning desire was to be a great salesperson. I saw other people in the neighborhood who were at the lower end of the spectrum. It made me want better for myself—to find a way to get these things on my own. Sales gave me the path and showed me how to be a successful entrepreneur."

Ray Parker Jr. grew up in a rough neighborhood too. "I grew up in Detroit. As a kid, I had a lot of encounters with police. But by my teen years, all I cared about was music and blues guitar. I met Stevie Wonder and decided that music was my path. But my dad worked in the auto industry and wanted me to become a white-collar worker in the industry. I couldn't see sitting in an office looking at the same picture for 50 years. Might as well shoot me now. I wanted to give the music business a shot and see where it went."

Ray's determination and desire paid off. He has written numerous songs for top stars like Johnny Mathis, Barry White, Chaka Khan, and Ann Wilson and has played with Dizzy Gillespie, Diana Ross, and other talented musicians. "Dreams are not born of indifference, laziness, or lack of ambition. I really love making music. I figured out there are two steps to life. You need to develop the ability to sustain yourself so you can survive and move forward without your day job. From there you can take it to the next level. Go with plan A and burn plan B. Tunnel forward and never look back."

Entrepreneur Shawn Villalovos said, "In the beginning, I didn't make any money in financial services. I was excited to be doing it, though I was living in my car. I saw what it did for people. My burning desire grew out of the process of helping others. I recognized my calling as I went through the learning process."

Growing up, Shawn didn't like numbers. He learned about finance through a job opportunity that was open to people with no financial background. "I saw how the people who were good at it had money. It was possible. So I took an interest. I always liked learning something new. I never was the kid who would go to school and get a degree in finance, yet I recognized the need in the US for someone like me. That got me started and motivated."

"In order to stretch our abilities, we next need grit, a combination of passion and perseverance," according to psychologist Crystal Lee.

"Grit is having stamina," explains professor and TED speaker Angela Duckworth. "Grit is sticking with your future day in, day out—not just for the week, not just for the month, but for years—and working really hard to make that future a reality. Grit is living life like it's a marathon, not a sprint."

Entrepreneur Jaime Villalovos was born in Venice, California, but moved almost immediately to a small, rural town in Montana that had a population of 325. "It was small in thinking and outlook on the world." Her dad was a Derrickhand in the oil fields. "It was a tough job. He broke almost every bone in his body." She grew up very poor. "Government aid, struggling to make ends meet, to buy food, provide basics like heat. There were six of us kids. I am the oldest. We lived in a broken-down trailer, huddling together in the bathroom with a space heater, doing our hair, singing songs. It's an emotional story. I knew I didn't want to be poor, and I wanted to lift my younger siblings out of poverty. I wanted to be an example to them that said it doesn't matter where you are from; it only matters where you are headed."

Jaime now has four children of her own. "After high school, I came out to California. I was going to pay my way to school and be an example to my sisters. My parents divorced when I was in second grade. They were hard workers, but they weren't passionate about anything and had stopped dreaming a long time ago. There was a lot of alcoholism in my family. This just motivated me to do more and not live that way. I was the first one in the family to go for a college degree."

Gregg Godfrey, the founder of Nitro Circus, an action sports collective created in his backyard and the focus of an MTV reality television program, grew up with an entrepreneurial mindset, thinking of stuff he loved and turning it into a business. He said he wasn't an academic kid. "I always wanted to be outside, climbing a mountain or riding a motorcycle. But I did go to college and graduated from the University of Utah. I was inspired by my dad, who was involved in the founding of

Bonneville Raceway. Nitro cars, funny cars influenced me. My parents pushed me to be creative. We weren't afraid of taking risks. By the time I was 14, I'd been in the ER 20 times."

Gregg was born in Draper, Utah. His father was a long-haul trucker, and his mother was a stay-at-home mom. After earning a degree in film from the University of Utah, he first worked as a stuntman for Disney but soon left to pursue his own film career. He made his first short documentary film, *Legacy*, in 1995.

He founded Nitro Circus in Utah in 2003. In November 2007, he won the Baja 1000, setting a world record for his 1,280-mile, 40-hour-and-22-minute solo motorbike run of the off-road race. On November 17, 2008, Gregg set the world record for the longest semi-truck ramp jump, the first of its kind, measuring 50 feet, 6 inches.

Passion is what motivates Gregg to continue in such a dangerous profession. "I enjoy the speed, the wind, watching other people be thrilled. This is my thing; I'm not good at a lot of things, but I am good at this. I love the combination of film, sounds, machines. It's a bizarre, beautiful monster!"

Gregg started by working for his dad, selling tickets and getting people excited. "Events, movies, and telling stories have always been in my blood. The first show I promoted in the University of Utah football stadium brought in 45,000 people."

As successful as he is, he always wants more. "I love it. I enjoy the process. Adventure really motivates me—anything that involves risk. It doesn't have to be a huge risk, but I do want to push the envelope a bit. My fix for adrenaline is what does it. It has cost me numerous broken bones, being knocked out, almost dead and out of body for minutes, and a torn femoral artery. I almost died!"

That's true burning desire.

Scott Williams's burning desire led him to Hollywood, where he became a television writer, working on *NYPD Blue*. "It was something I always wanted to do. I had an active imagination as a kid. My dad used to smack me in the head for daydreaming. Now I get paid for it."

His mom grew up one of thirteen kids in a bombed-out area of Edinburgh, Scotland. "My dad was from Brooklyn, very blue collar, worked two jobs his whole life. My mom had this attitude that there was a certain amount of nobility in poverty. I always had to reconcile this message that was drilled into me at a young age, with this suspicion that I was not deserving of success."

Scott remembers staring off at "that little TV in the corner of his mind" and said he was into sports in high school. "I went to college as a physical education major expecting to take a lot of sports classes. I was shocked when I needed to take biology, psychology, and sociology. I had a 1.9 GPA the first year. My father was heartbroken. Together we met with the dean, who pointed out that I'd gotten an A in English. So, I became an English major."

His father had been in the Air Force and had never attended college. "What will you do with that degree?" he asked Scott.

"It was hard, but I went to New York, determined to become an actor. Instead, I kicked off a 12-year bartending career. Then, I moved to LA and never looked back. I started off creating one-act plays—some successful. I was forced to create a short script and banged it out on an old IBM ball typewriter. By page two, I heard the applause in my mind. I worked it through with the group of actors, and it became a hit. This is where my career goal shifted from acting to writing. I landed an agent and an opportunity to write for Ray Liotta's company."

During the bartending years, self-doubt and doubters propelled him forward. "'I'll show you,' I thought. That little voice in your head that pops up is a powerful motivator and kept me going. It's a myth that once you've made it, you're good. You always must keep proving yourself. I think every project will be the one where I get found out!" he laughs. "I keep trying. As long as I keep going, I haven't failed."

Good thing Scott didn't quit. He writes and produces and has worked on the crime dramas *Brooklyn South*, *Third Watch*, and *NCIS*.

George Chanos, the chairman of Capriotti's Sandwich Shops, is also an author, the former attorney general of the state of Nevada, and the creator of the trivia board game *Notable Quotables*. He asks, "Don't we all want our lives to mean something? Isn't that the cornerstone? To do that, you have to have a commitment to something larger than yourself."

Julian Serrano is a restaurant entrepreneur from Madrid, Spain. He moved 300 miles away when he was 15 years old to go to culinary school. "Back then (45 years ago), it was like traveling 5,000 miles with the old-school travel around Spain; getting around was difficult. Now, it's much easier." Julian is a graduate of the Escuela Gastronomie P.P.O. hotel management school in Marbella, Spain. He spent time as a chef at Lucas-Carlton in Paris, France; Hôtel de France in Auch, France; Chez Max in Zurich, Switzerland; and L'Aubergine in Munich, Germany.

Once he arrived in the United States, Julian struggled. Finding a job was difficult during the winter. He felt he couldn't ask his mom for money, considering she hadn't wanted him to go in the first place. "This made me stronger, having to make my own way. I came to the US in the seventies, worked for Carnival Cruise Lines, and lived in Miami. I got my legal papers in Nashville because there were fewer foreigners there. I found a job and moved to San Francisco, where I lived for 30 years. I got married, had a daughter, and worked for a restaurant called Masa's. My family kept me going. Memories of the one I left behind—that inspires everything I do."

Penney Ooi emigrated from Malaysia. "I came from a small village. My mom was a housewife. My father was in the seafood business. Initially, my parents believed one day I would marry, have children, and live in the same village." She used to play basketball in her small village. "They discovered I was a good player and recruited me to play at a higher level. I started to realize that maybe I didn't have to live in the village. Maybe I didn't have to get married."

Eventually, Penney started to believe that better opportunities would be found in the city, and then in the United States. Her uncle sponsored her and helped her get to the States. "I decided to move to the United States when I was 21 to play basketball and study finance. I put together $16,000 to move and got into Southern Illinois University in Carbondale. I worked hard and finished my 4-year degree in 2.5 years, taking 24 credit hours a semester to save on expenses. My definition of success? If you are happy and feel fulfilled, you are successful."

Founder of LightSpeed VT, a training solutions company that focuses on repetition, practice, and accountability, Brad Lea grew up in the small town of Cottage Grove, Oregon. His dad was a millworker, and his grandpa was a logger. "My dad had an entrepreneurial spirit. He owned a local newspaper, pizza parlor, restaurant, and bar. I dropped out of high school in eleventh grade and decided I wanted to be a movie star. Along the way, I created LightSpeed VT. Back then, nobody had websites. I sold nine subscriptions before I even had the platform built. I was ahead of my time."

In the beginning, Brad said he would have sworn that in 90 days, he would be a millionaire. Ninety days later, he was just as convinced. "Breaking it down 90 days at a time helped me make it happen. First, figure out what you want and then put your head down for 90 days. Check in again and see where you're at, then go for another 90 days and regroup."

Building the company took a series of steps forward and backward. "I had to go out and get a job at one point to keep the dream moving. I worked as a sales manager and paid the bills for the company for one year to the day. Then, I went back to Lightspeed and never looked back."

Like many people, including several I've introduced to you already, clothing designer and entrepreneur John Ashworth's initial burning desire brought him to where he is now—living the dream in Oceanside, California. John's path to success was not a straight one, but golf always played a part in his dreams. "I was a golf geek in elementary school and wanted to win the

Masters Tournament. I became a caddy, played golf in high school, and won a scholarship to the University of Arizona. Though my degree is in agronomy (the science of turfgrass), I thought I'd get into golf course design or management because I knew I didn't have the game to become a pro golfer, but I wanted to be involved in the industry."

After school, John got a job as an assistant superintendent at a local golf course. A friend who was a pro golfer asked him to tour with him as his caddy on the pro tour. He observed what people were wearing and paid attention to fashion and design. "At the time, golf fashion was terrible—polyester and plaid. I found a partner and raised some money through friends and family, cobbled together a team of friends of friends who had some design experience, put together some samples, and went around trying to sell the ideas to small shops where there were no real major brands or variety. We made everything in the US out of cotton, not polyester." That company grew into Ashworth, a wildly successful golf clothing line.

"It is only work if you would rather be doing something else," John says, supporting Hill's ideas about desire and dreams being the foundation of success. "After we sold Ashworth to Adidas, I knew I didn't want to work for a giant corporation, so I moved to Scotland for a while to explore the roots of golf and figure out my next move."

Eventually, John and his previous partner started a retail company called Linksoul. "Great surfing and golfing was our goal. We run a golf course close to the office. I golf every day, and my partner surfs every day." John's new goal is to bring more people into the game of golf. "Great game. Great people," he said.

It is important to recognize that desires, like dreams, can evolve and change. They are unique to each individual.

"My burning desire is to help children. It's something that motivates me to keep going. Young children are our future. I want to fix the education system and have the curriculum adapt to the child so that children do not have to adapt to the curriculum. Either I will do it or I will inspire someone else to pick it up and make it happen."

Rock and Roll Fantasy Camp founder David Fishof's burning desire is to remain in good health and live a long life, though he is motivated by more than a desire for longevity itself. "I want to leave a legacy and change people's lives." David hopes his camp will become global and that rock and roll will change the corporate environment and culture.

I related to so much of what people shared with me while I was working on this book. Becoming a lawyer was never my burning desire, though I did it in honor of my parents and I have no regrets. Eventually, I realized my burning desire had more to do with making lots of money so I could provide a better life for my parents. They shared many stories about what their lives were like in Korea. When they came to the United States, they got our first home in Los Angeles, California. We lived in an area called the Rampart District. They worked so hard, working two or three jobs to make ends meet. I didn't want my parents to see only the hard life. That's what motivated me to make lots of money—so they didn't have to worry about it. When I told them I wanted to go into the financial industry, I was so worried they would be disappointed with my decision to go from law to financial services. At first, they said, "You're going to do what?" Now they refer clients to me.

I wanted to make my parents proud and reward them for the sacrifices they made coming to this country. They never got to do a lot of the cool things in life because they worked so hard with multiple jobs to put their children through school. I wanted them to know that their legacy would continue and their sacrifices were worth it, validating their efforts.

I also wanted to make a ton of money so they would not only remember the bad things in the world and struggles. I wanted them to experience the fruits of life while they were young enough to appreciate them. My mom had a heart attack in her fifties, and that created a sense of urgency in me to make money fast for them to have all of these good things while they were still alive and healthy enough to enjoy it. They got to see my success and travel the world, making my efforts pay off.

Now I desire to be successful in all areas of my life. I have a successful business that pays me well. I'm healthy. My wife and children are healthy. I know who I am spiritually. I believe in what I do and am happy and grounded. I'm proud of my contributions to society and my humanitarian efforts. I've given so much money to charities, speaking for free. I give to and help people in whatever way I can, making an effort and being open.

THE VALUE IN THE MOMENTS

One of my greatest desires is to find value in the moments that make up my day. I strive to maximize opportunities as they come up and take action whenever possible. When I set these intentions, I accomplish more, feel better, and consistently advance toward my goals. By breaking things down to this lowest common denominator and living life moment by moment, my life has changed for the better.

Without desire, shepherding an idea from development to the finish line is unlikely. Desire is a driving force. It stimulates our imagination and fuels us to move forward, to gather information, and to act.

Napoleon Hill was a master at explaining the basic principles of success. He surrounded himself with successful people, extracted their knowledge about success, and created a path for others to follow.

He recognized how negativity and the day-to-day struggle for survival can sap our energy and extinguish our desires. But he also saw how successful people funnel energy into success, achievements, and the pursuit of their dreams.

Like everyone, I don't enjoy every job I must do. But I do them anyway, having learned that even seemingly mundane tasks develop a work ethic that leads to more significant opportunities like my role as the executive producer of the movie *Think and Grow Rich: The Legacy*, a docudrama based on Hill's book.

My involvement with this exciting project started when I read the book, but it was my desire to do something more that led to this fantastic life experience.

Desire is the spark that ignites us and takes us from dreaming to doing. Desire is powerful!

Let's break it down.

D = DREAMS

All achievements are created twice. First, in the mind of the creator. Then, in tangible form.

A book begins as a collection of thoughts and ideas. A building starts as a vision in the mind of the architect. The Wright brothers dreamed of flying. Their desire to achieve something that everyone else thought was impossible helped them overcome every obstacle in their path. We all know how that story ended.

Embrace your dreams. Let your imagination soar. Dreams are the foundation of desire. In dreams, nothing is impossible.

E = ENERGY

Desire is such a dominant force because it contains energy. Energy has the power to move us. It has the power to uproot mountains, literally. Energy provides heat, light, and sound. It stirs the senses and touches our souls. It's like a magnet that attracts what we want if we are open to giving and receiving it.

S = SPIRIT

When you watch young children playing, you're witnessing pure spirit in action. Spirit is the carefree attitude that places you squarely in the moment without regard for what anyone else thinks. Spirit is your life force on display, a pipeline to your soul.

We desire things because they resonate with us, stir our emotions, energize us, and lift our spirits.

I = INDIVIDUAL

Every human being is unique, even identical twins. Every desire is also individual, though on the surface they may appear to be the same. You may desire a red Ferrari like the one your neighbor has, or a car like one you saw driving down the road, or a car you have on your dream board. Underlying your desires for this car are unique reasons why. Desire is personal and specific to the individual.

Be clear about the reasons why you desire something, and disregard all others. When you do, the intensity of your desire grows.

R = RICHES

What does being rich mean to you? For most people, it involves money. All the money in the world doesn't equate to happiness and is generally a poor measurement of success. Less is, quite often, more.

Richness may mean freedom, the flexibility of working for yourself or working from home. Riches could be a close family, being surrounded by people you love. Or pursuing your dreams, accomplishing your goals, knowing who you are, and being at peace with yourself. Or it could be money. Lots and lots of money. And that's okay too.

E = EXECUTION

All your wants, wishes, and plans are worthless without execution. Until you put the wheels in motion and begin creating a tangible version of your dream, it will remain locked in your mind. The tragedy is that unrealized desires don't benefit anyone, including yourself.

So, take that first step. Get in touch with your inner child, the kid who did everything with great enthusiasm and spirit! You can do it again.

Desire leads to a belief, which leads to action. It provides the necessary support to square off with fear and takes it down with a solid one-two punch. Best of all, clearly defined desire adds energy to your dreams and moves you toward them with clarity and conviction.

In *Think and Grow Rich*, Hill warns, "There is a difference between wishing for a thing and being ready to receive it. No one is ready for a thing until he believes he can acquire it. The state of mind must be belief, not mere hope or wish. Open-mindedness is essential for belief. Closed minds do not inspire faith, courage, and belief."

As science and technology deliver more options of time-saving gadgetry to choose from for every area of our lives, a new era of "First World problems" have taken hold. If what we want isn't delivered to our doorstep quickly or our needs are not satisfied within moments of us realizing we want something, our whole day can be thrust into a tailspin. We can make a phone call from practically any place on earth, yet if the connection takes more than a few seconds, we get irritated. "What, no signal?" Such tortures living in the 21st century!

What if you woke up every day with a significant disability? What if you couldn't walk or had no arms? Can you imagine the shift in your perspective caused by such a genuine challenge? When I met Jessica Cox, I experienced such a realization and transformation.

Jessica is an independent, dynamic woman with an infectious, positive attitude. Her list of achievements and successes is impressive. And she also happens to have been born with no arms. According to doctors, hers is a fluke medical condition that cannot be explained, though it doesn't appear to be genetic as she has an older brother and younger sister who were born without disabilities.

After graduating from high school, Jessica attended the University of Arizona, earning a bachelor's degree in psychology. She now works as a captivating motivational speaker.

Meeting her, I was inspired and humbled. I felt a twinge of shame recognizing how petty and insignificant my First World challenges are in relation to genuine obstacles many people face daily.

We all have people who inspire us and act as role models in our lives. The key is to be on the lookout for the little things they do that make a huge difference to the people and the world around them. Desire plays a role here because when you deeply desire something, your senses are naturally heightened. Your ability to see the good in people, places, and situations is magnified as a natural by-product of your own desire to achieve success.

For young people, especially teenagers, role models might be their parents. If you are a teenager, you know it's easy to jump on the bandwagon of hating your parents and blaming them for your troubles. Jessica could have easily gone down this road as a child. She was angry. She would ask her mom why God made her this way.

"Be patient. God has a greater plan for you," her mother answered.

"Some people say part of the drawback of being Asian is expectations from parents. Pressure to excel from the community and internally. But having high expectations is a good thing. Do well at whatever you choose to do," Jessica said.

Jessica's mom was born in the Philippines and immigrated to the United States when she was 20. While working as a nurse, she met and married Jessica's father, an American man, and they went on to have three children together, including Jessica, who was born in Sierra Vista in Southern Arizona.

According to Jessica, there is a strength among Filipino women like her mother and aunt that is comforting. Women seem to take on the role of the boss, conveying strong will, grit, determination, and perseverance. Her mom worked hard for everything and eventually rose to the position of assistant director of nursing in her field.

Developing a burning desire for what is important and meaningful to you is like flipping a switch on a powerful magnet. Answers to your questions are drawn to you with little or no effort. Resources appear when you need them like opening a faucet with an endless flow of energy.

Dwayne Johnson spent much of his childhood moving back and forth from California to New Zealand. His family was homeless for a time. After a string of money problems, which included his mother's car being repossessed, the Johnsons hit bottom. "We were living in an efficiency that cost $120 a week," he explains. "We come home, and there's a padlock on the door and an eviction notice."

The family's financial situation led to a destructive path as a teenager. He began robbing stores frequented by wealthy tourists, often landing in police custody. After one of these arrests, narrowly escaping conviction, he realized that one of the few things he could control in the world was his body and what he did with it. "What can I control with these two hands?" he asked himself. "The only thing I could do was train and build my body. The successful men I knew were men who built their bodies."

Attending one of several high schools in Pennsylvania, Dwayne met a man he said changed his life, and he began playing football. "My grades got better, and I started getting recruited from every college across the country," he says. "My thought process started to change. That's when I started thinking about goals and what I wanted to accomplish."

Johnson credits much of his success to his football coach. "I love that man. I'll never forget the impact that he had on my life," Johnson says. "My takeaway from that amazing relationship that I had was the empathy that he had for a punk kid who treated him so rudely and disrespectfully. He looked past that BS and said, 'I believe in you, and I want to turn you around.'"

Dwayne went to college on a football scholarship but began to develop depression. "I didn't want to do a thing. I didn't want to go anywhere." He struggled for years after his NFL dreams were crushed and the career he'd counted on disappeared. At one point, he only had $7 in his pocket. He looked inward and at his strengths, deciding to take up the family wrestling tradition, eventually becoming known as "The Rock." He dominated the sport for almost a decade despite a severely injured knee, winning the WWF/WWE championship belt eight times.

Despite his success, Dwayne had another dream. He wanted to be an actor. At first, Hollywood cast him as musclebound men with few lines, but his dogged persistence in going for other roles and pulling himself out of the ashes of failure when the box office was less than kind earned him the distinction of being among the top-grossing actors in all of Hollywood in 2015.

After a string of badly received kids' movies, it was thought that his acting career was over. He couldn't go back to football or wrestling. "Returning to wrestling wasn't an option because I didn't want to go back [as someone] deemed a failure." Johnson called a meeting with his agents and said he had a plan. He wanted to be Will Smith, only different and bigger. "I don't know what that means," he said. "But I can see it, and I have these." He held up his hands. "And I need everybody to see it with me." The silence was thundering. He got new agents, and now he has a career like Will Smith's—"only different and bigger."

"Regardless of what we achieve in life, we always gotta keep striving for more, staying hungrier than the rest and being grateful around every corner," Dwayne says.

The more I consider the power and importance of desire, the more I begin to see the connection between desire and experience. To develop a burning desire for something, you generally need a frame of reference or at least some understanding of what it is that you seek. For example, you might desire to become a pilot and plan to join the Air Force in pursuit of your dream. Throughout your life, you may have developed a deep interest in airplanes and aviation, and this passion has led to the creation of a burning desire to become a pilot. It's also possible that you've always known you would become a pilot from the moment you were born, although I find people who know their calling from a young age are more the exception than the norm.

The same is not always true for experience. Stuff happens, and it's not always desirable. We have dozens of experiences throughout the day that occur without our awareness—experiences that are seemingly insignificant yet make up the bulk of our day as we go through the motions of life.

What if we could amplify some of these moments and make them stand out?

By focusing on what you are doing while you are doing it, you immediately increase the quality of your experience. Your level of awareness is naturally heightened as you become more present in the moment.

Here is where I see opportunity—increase your desire for the little things in life. When you become more conscious, wouldn't you agree it's possible to increase our level of desire for the things we are already doing as we go through the motions each day?

How do we turn dreams, hopes, wishes, and burning desires into confidence? The next chapter will guide you through the process of visualizing and believing in the achievement of your desires, using faith.

THE BIG TAKEAWAY

You will become as small as your controlling desire, as great as your dominant aspiration.

WISDOM FROM THE ASIAN MASTERMIND

"Knowing is not enough; we must apply. Willing is not enough; we must do."

—Bruce Lee

"If one does not attach himself to people and desires, never shall his heart be broken. But then, does he ever truly live?"

—Jackie Chan, actor

"The successful warrior is the average man, with laser-like focus."

—Bruce Lee

"In America, nobody says you have to keep the circumstances somebody else gives you."

—Amy Tan, author

"The size of your success is measured by the strength of your desire, the size of your dream, and how you handle disappointment along the way."

—Robert Kiyosaki

"When you have a passion for something, then you tend not only to be better at it, but you work harder at it too."

—Vera Wang, fashion designer

"Without a strong reason or purpose, anything in life is hard."
—Robert Kiyosaki

"The key is to fall in love with something, anything. If your heart is attached to it, then your mind will be attached to it."
—Vera Wang

"Have a bias toward action. Let's see something happen now. You can break that big plan into small steps and take the first step right away."
—Indira Gandhi, India's third prime minister

"In the end, it's not about failure; it's about how much you love what you do."
—Vera Wang

GROWTH EXERCISES

Turn desires into gold.

1. Fix in your mind the exact amount of money you desire.

2. Determine exactly what you intend to give in return for the money you desire.

3. Establish a definite date by when you intend to possess the money you desire.

4. Create a definite plan for carrying out your desire, and begin at once, whether you are ready or not, to put this plan into action.

5. Write out a clear, concise statement of the amount of money you intend to acquire, the time limit for its acquisition, and what you intend to give in return for the money. Clearly describe the plan you will execute to meet this goal.

6. Read your written statement aloud, twice daily, once before retiring at night and once after arising in the morning. As you read, see and feel and believe yourself already in possession of the money.

Imagine you are a millionaire.

"Can you imagine yourself a millionaire?" Hill asks. "The steps call for no hard labor. They call for no sacrifice. They do not require one to become ridiculous or credulous. To apply them calls for no great amount of education. But the successful application of these six steps does call for sufficient imagination to enable one to see and understand that accumulation of money cannot be left to chance, good fortune, and luck. One must realize that all who have accumulated great fortunes first did a certain amount of dreaming, hoping, wishing, desiring, and planning before they acquired money."

Journal your vision of what being a millionaire looks like. Make it detailed and personal.

"Both poverty and riches are the offspring of thought. There are no limitations to the mind except those we acknowledge."

—NAPOLEON HILL

FAITH

Visualization of, and belief in,
the attainment of desire

What do you think when you hear the word *faith*?

Napoleon Hill believed faith, or the lack of it, controls your destiny. He said faith stimulates your subconscious, while a lack of faith creates negativity. Optimism combined with faith forms the foundation of success.

Merriam-Webster defines faith as "something that is believed, especially with strong conviction; especially a system of religious beliefs."

Hill saw faith as potentially more than one's relationship with any God or religion. "Faith inspires action," he said.

FAITH AND ASIANS

The Asian culture is so diverse. About the only thing one can say with any authority is that Asians, as a group, identify less with specific religions than any other group. Research uncovers a wealth of information on religious faith but only the broadest statements on belief in oneself or the universe.

Perhaps the culture is too diverse to make any authentic claim, though we've all heard stories about the belief in luck and fate in Asian lore. This may or may not hold true for Asian Americans today, though Kristi Yamaguchi wore a Chinese luck charm her grandmother gave her when she skated in the Olympics.

"Luck is in every part of China. Many Chinese stores and restaurants have the word *luck* in their names. The idea is that just by using the word *luck* in names of things, you can attract more of it. I think that's true in my life as well. You attract luck because you go after it," explains author Amy Tan.

Hill said, "No one is doomed to bad luck. The subconscious mind will translate into its physical equivalent a thought impulse of a negative or destructive nature, just as readily as it will act upon thought impulses of a positive or constructive nature. This accounts for the strange phenomenon which so many people experience, referred to as misfortune or bad luck."

Although Hill could be right and there is no such thing as luck, there's nothing wrong with having a little faith mixed in too. You never know. Just don't put all your hopes and efforts into luck or buy lottery tickets to solve your financial problems! Do as Kristi did and work like an Olympian for your goals too. You will likely find that the harder you work, the luckier you get.

Motivational speaker Jessica Cox always felt blessed and supported by her parents. Growing up without arms presented unique challenges. "As a role model, my mom helped me develop my faith that I could accomplish anything. Throughout my life, I have never come from a position of sadness; it was more anger and frustration, not understanding why I was different. No one seemed to be able to provide a satisfying answer. My mom helped by providing channels and outlets for this anger and frustration."

At a young age, Jessica used to kick her brother and sister a lot. Because Tae Kwon Do is one of the martial arts that emphasizes kicks, it was a great way to channel frustration and anger into a positive outlet. At the beginning of her practice, Jessica used to look down much of the time. "My instructor helped me bring my eye level up consistently, which helped me become more confident and earn my black belt. He helped me find faith early on in myself." At the age of 14, Jessica earned her first black belt.

"Life is a journey of ups and downs. We have to learn as we go and use our experiences to help other people learn to have faith too," she said. "I believe God gave me many gifts. Some I don't even know about yet. Being an advocate for others, writing a book, talking to people—I'm open to new opportunities and a constantly evolving purpose."

"In the music business, the odds are stacked against you even more than opening a restaurant. You must really love what you do and manage your expectation on how you will survive financially. Many artists have two or three jobs. Faith helps a lot when adversity comes," said DJ Steve Aoki. "A lot of challenges happen in your earlier years when the future is a massive question mark and all you have is faith and desire."

Shark Tank judge Kevin Harrington was taught a strong foundation in religious faith. He was raised Catholic and went to an all-boys Catholic school. "They taught me values, putting others first, the foundation of faith, doing the right thing, asking people I meet how I can help them. Later, I learned the more successful you are, the more people you can help. It became my driving force and purpose in life.

"I read *Think and Grow Rich* when I was a teenager. It supercharged my thinking and beliefs and planted the seed that I could become a powerful young man and entrepreneur, the belief that I could achieve everything I wanted," Kevin says.

Shawn Villalovos found *Think and Grow Rich* when he was a teenager too. "I didn't want to have a boss, and I didn't like my parents bossing me around. I remember reading the part about what you'd be willing to give in return for the money you desire. I thought, 'I could live without a house, no rent, cut out expenses,' and I just started doing it. I believed I could do it, so I did. I joined a gym for $7 a month for life and would work out every day and then shower. I lived in my car for about six months. The toughest part was not knowing where you would park your car, looking for dark streets, parking lots. I had my story down. I used to park near the freeway. 'I was tired and just pulled off to sleep,' I'd tell cops. You have to have faith it will all work out, living like that. Be willing to try anything. I'd hang out with friends and offer to be the designated driver. I didn't have money to party, but I would drop people off and hopefully crash at the last person's place.

"That seems like a long time ago. In business, it's other people, adversaries. Lying and stealing from you. 'Why is God letting this happen to us?' You don't let it keep you from moving forward. Just stay the course. God has his way for them and places for them. Just move forward and have a broader view so you don't get stuck. Have faith," Shawn advises.

A former NFL football player for the Seattle Seahawks and the Detroit Lions, Lawrence Jackson found faith at a young age when he learned to master his breath to overcome a speech impediment and control his asthma. "I became very close with my internal voice and used to meditate for hours. It gave me a mentally strong approach to life and shaped me into a unique person. I feel like I could have messed up at any step along the way, but faith and learning to listen to myself made a difference."

Nitro Circus founder Gregg Godfrey didn't always have faith that he could reach his goals or be successful. "There was a lot of coordination, permits, and substantial investments. My faith was challenged at times, but I was always willing to go for it."

As George Chanos says, "To be successful, you must have faith in yourself and believe in yourself. I've always had an intense belief in myself and my purpose. I know I'm here to do something more than occupy space. I've never had a doubt. Success doesn't require an absence of fear. It requires you to overcome your fears and move past them. With each step, you will either succeed or fail. They are both good. From success, you move forward and make progress. From failure, you learn. Maybe you start a business, and it fails. Some of the people you meet along the way may present other opportunities."

That's exactly the way it worked for financial guru Raja Dhaliwal. "When I moved to Canada, I worked in a factory for six months. Then, I worked as a gas station attendant for three years. I began wondering what it all means. I'd come here for a bigger purpose. I was driving a taxi when I started looking for other opportunities. Eventually, I moved and got involved in the construction business for a while, but I was concerned about putting all of my energy into the real estate market. Then, I met a person who introduced me to the financial services industry."

His religious background and spiritual beliefs taught him to learn something new every day and have always given him strength. "My parents lived paycheck to paycheck. I wanted to do something very big with my life and not go down the same road." He was a big thinker from the beginning. "I understood a long time ago that we all come from one foundation, one God. God gives me endless hope and unlimited belief and opportunities."

He also believes that finding your purpose can be helped along by mentors and parents. "We are all born with a purpose, though it is difficult to understand with your mind, thinking, and analysis. You need to get out of your head and connect with this greater purpose, take control of your mind and not let your mind control you." This faith in himself and in a higher power saw him through as he found his way in the world and realized his true purpose. To find yours, he advises, "Sit down and ask yourself some questions. Find the reasons. Find your dreams and list your dreams. Go with the flow."

Charles Darwin said, "It is not the strongest of the species that survives. It is the one that is most adaptable to change."

Failure is not the reverse of success; failure is the central part of meeting our goals.

Growing up, we learn through trial and error, making mistakes, eventually learning to walk, talk, and develop into adults.

We are designed to transmute weakness into foundations of strength. Failing teaches us what we need to do to adapt and grow.

"Failure is an opportunity to learn and grow," says psychologist Crystal Lee. "Failure is an opportunity to be embraced, analyzed, and picked apart, rather than something to run away from. Having psychological flexibility lets people think outside of the box and be creative when confronted with an obstacle. It also allows a person to change course as needed if what [they have] been doing hasn't been working."

Failure is not permanent. Successful people know this, believing in themselves and seeing failures as opportunities.

Scott Williams paid his dues, writing and getting rejected, years after college ended. "I figured I'd break through eventually. Then, my wife, Catherine, and I had a son, Shane. He was born with a rare disease called spinal muscular atrophy. The greatest day of my life was also the worst day. My sister said, "What's the problem? Just put ramps around the house.' Her perspective snapped me out of it. Suddenly, I had to make enough money to support the medical expenses. I'd have to put my writing on hold. But the next day, I got a call from my agent, who said they wanted me to write for *NYPD Blue*. Television writing! A steady gig. The timing was so profound. There must be higher forces, angels, at work."

After Shane passed away, Scott fell into a depression. "I was glad my car knew the way to work. I was on autopilot. But then, my sister sent me an article about a playground built in New York in honor of a child who had died from the same disease Shane had. My wife is very philanthropic and an angel to many people.

'Let's do this in Shane's memory,' she said. We put a phone line in Shane's empty bedroom and got started. Pretty soon, I was coming home asking, 'What miracle happened today?' We were building playgrounds for children with all abilities but accessible to children with disabilities that allowed them to get into the playground and actually be able to play. To date, we've built 70 playgrounds all around the world."

"It wasn't until later that I realized it had taken Shane to show me what success was. He gave me something else to focus on, which gave my life more meaning, inspiring me to reach for success like I never had before."

He demonstrated what Hill put forth this way: "It is essential for you to encourage the positive emotions as dominating forces of your mind and discourage and eliminate negative emotions. A mind dominated by positive emotions becomes a favorable abode for the state of mind known as faith. A mind so dominated may, at will, give the subconscious mind instructions, which it will accept and act upon immediately."

Julian Serrano, who currently owns four restaurants, says, "I was always business-minded. Even when I was 15, I thought I'd be successful because I was street smart and confident that I could take care of myself."

But it wasn't always easy. "Being alone, coming to the US by myself was difficult. Back then, I figured I'd be okay, but I had no idea what I wanted to do at first. I just knew San Francisco felt right to me and took the rest on faith." His faith paid off. Julian is now a two-time winner of the prestigious James Beard Foundation Award and the executive chef of Picasso at Hotel Bellagio in Las Vegas. The two Michelin star restaurant has won the AAA Five Diamond Award every year since 2002, and its wine list has received the coveted Grand Award from *Wine Spectator* magazine. His latest creation is at the ARIA hotel in Las Vegas, Nevada, where he shares the secrets of his own Spanish cuisine. In 2010, *Esquire* magazine named the restaurant one of its best new restaurants of the year.

Penney Ooi also held onto faith through the adversity of growing up poor. "We had to survive on minimal means. In college, I stayed on campus the first year, then rented a small house with a roommate in the following years. We used to go to the flea market to buy used furniture and go to the supermarket at night to purchase baked goods that were marked down. Some people say money is the root of all evil. This isn't a true statement. Evil is the love of money, not the money itself. It's losing sight of what is important. Having money allows you to do a lot of good things for a lot of people."

Brad Lea always believed his company would be a success. He was only surprised by how long it took. "Eventually, when you are born, you will get a Social Security number and a Lightspeed password." He laughs, but I get the feeling he's serious. "You've got to have faith. Originally, I found a guy who told me it couldn't be done. Then, I found my partner, who helped me build the first version of Lightspeed. He was working on his own venture, building software systems for housekeepers and the service industry. I offered him a piece of the company and all he cared about at the time was what he'd be doing. He never doubted we'd be successful; he just wanted to make sure he was a good fit and would be happy for the long haul. He's still part of it."

Faith creates a positive attitude and is an essential ingredient in success, as shown by everyone who shared their stories about faith and how it carried them through uncertain times in their lives.

Hill said that positive thought impulses, stated in writing, memorized, and repeated until they become a part of the working equipment of the subconscious mind, will create and build self-confidence and faith in your abilities to achieve whatever you've set your mind to.

THE SELF-CONFIDENCE FORMULA

Hill said to write out the following sentences, memorize them, and repeat them until they are part of your subconscious mind:

1. I know I can achieve the object of my definite purpose in life. Therefore, I demand of myself persistent, continuous action toward its attainment, and I here and now promise to render such action. (I know I can do it, and I will do it.)

2. I realize that dominating thoughts of my mind will eventually reproduce themselves in outward, physical activity, and gradually transform themselves into physical reality; therefore, I will concentrate my thoughts for thirty minutes daily upon the task of thinking of the person I intend to become, thereby creating in my mind a clear mental picture of that person. (I will meditate for thirty minutes every day and visualize my dream.)

3. I know through the principle of autosuggestion, any desire that I persistently hold in my mind will eventually see expression through some practical means of attaining the object back of it. Therefore, I will devote ten minutes daily to demanding of myself the development of self-confidence. (I will work with autosuggestion for ten minutes each day.)

4. I have clearly written down a description of my definite chief aim in life, and I will never stop trying until I shall have developed sufficient self-confidence for its attainment. (I have a clear, written-down dream and will not stop until I reach it.)

5. I fully realize that no wealth or position can long endure unless built upon truth and justice. Therefore, I will engage in no transaction which does not benefit all whom it affects. I will succeed by attracting to myself the forces I wish to use and the cooperation of other people. I will induce others to serve me because of my willingness to serve others. I will eliminate hatred, envy, jealousy, selfishness, and cynicism by developing a love for all humanity, because I know that a negative attitude toward others can never bring me success. I will cause others to believe in me because I will believe in them, and in myself. (I will be a good person.)

6. I will sign my name to this formula, commit it to memory, and repeat it aloud once a day, with full faith that it will gradually influence my thoughts

and actions so that I will become a self-reliant and successful person.

We often find that we end up where we chose to be. Faith gives us the courage to make necessary changes in our lives and inspires us to keep reaching for our dreams.

Growing up, my parents always told me I could do anything I wanted. "You're a great singer, a great dancer," they'd say. I actually believed those things! These infusions of faith in me at a young age changed my life. Now, whenever I encounter a new challenge or an unknown, my first response is, "I can do it," not fear and resignation.

I believe we all can instill faith in others through our words of encouragement and acts of support. There are times when a friend or family member may be struggling and needs a boost of confidence and reassurance. This is when you deliver enough faith for the two of you.

I believe what Hill said when he stated, "Faith is a state of mind which may be induced by autosuggestion. It is a well-known fact that one comes, finally, to believe whatever one repeats to oneself, whether this statement is true or false. Thoughts which are mixed with any of the feelings of emotions constitute a magnetic force which attracts other similar or related thoughts."

"Riches began in the form of thought!" Hill declares. "The amount is limited only by the person in whose mind the thought is put into motion. Faith removes limitations."

In the next chapter, we'll dive deeper into the way autosuggestion works and how you can apply it to your own life.

THE BIG TAKEAWAY

Faith is the "eternal elixir" that gives life, power, and action to the impulse of thought.

WISDOM FROM THE ASIAN MASTERMIND

"We dream to give ourselves hope. To stop dreaming, well, that's like saying you can never change your fate."

—Amy Tan

"If you want to be rich, you need to develop your vision. You must be standing on the edge of time gazing into the future."

—Robert Kiyosaki

"Choose the positive. You have a choice; you are master of your attitude. Choose the positive, the constructive. Optimism is a faith that leads to success."

—Bruce Lee

"Hoping drains your energy. Action creates energy."

—Robert Kiyosaki

"Things that came before, people and things and experiences, that does mean something to me. It doesn't mean I don't embrace the new, but I don't forget the past either."

—Vera Wang

"If you want to be financially free, you need to become a different person than you are today and let go of whatever has held you back in the past."

—Robert Kiyosaki

"No matter how tough the chase is, you should always have the dream you saw on the first day. It'll keep you motivated and rescue you (from any weak thoughts)."

—Jack Ma

"Don't be afraid to be ambitious about your goals. Hard work never stops. Neither should your dreams."

—Dwayne Johnson

"Start small and dream big."

—Robert Kiyosaki

"It's very difficult to know the outside world, but you know yourself. You know your need and what you want. If I know myself better, I can change myself to meet the outside world."

—Jack Ma

"The first step to achieving your goal is to take a moment to respect your goal. Know what it means to you to achieve it."

—Dwayne Johnson

"Faith, not facts, moves mountains."

—Guy Kawasaki, American-Japanese marketing
specialist, author, and Silicon Valley venture capitalist

*"In 1995 I had $7 in my pocket and knew two
things: I'm broke as hell, and one day I won't be."*

—Dwayne Johnson

GROWTH EXERCISES

End your day sans screens.

As you fall asleep, ask yourself, "What am I proud of
today? Who inspired me today? What will I accomplish tomorrow?" Spend a few minutes immersed in your
dream. Picture it. Feel it. Be it. This is a wonderful way to
fall asleep.

**Instead of thinking about what you get from your job or
business…**

ask what you can give. What can you do to make your
job more fulfilling? When you see opportunities to create
value, the world around you becomes clear and welcoming.

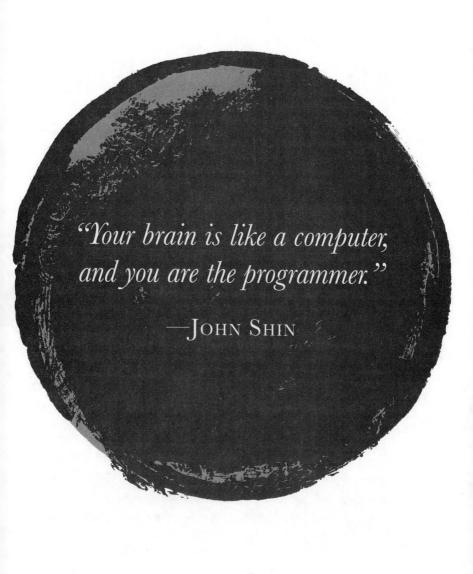

"*Your brain is like a computer, and you are the programmer.*"

—JOHN SHIN

AUTOSUGGESTION

The medium for influencing the subconscious mind

Do you talk to yourself? Most people do.

What do you say when you talk to yourself? Have you ever criticized yourself for something you've done or said? When you look forward to your day, do you imagine it will be a positive or negative experience? Have you ever dreaded a social event and listed all the ways you will have a miserable time? Do you pump yourself up before a meeting or speech or big event, using reminders of past successes or images of the outstanding results you would like to have?

Of course you have. We all talk to ourselves, all day long, thinking as many as 70,000 thoughts per day. But have you paid attention to the quality of your self-talk or thought about its power over you? Have you taken the time to note your results when your self-talk is negative versus positive?

Self-suggestion is one of the only things we have 100 percent control over in our lives. We decide whether to dwell on positives or negatives, to tear ourselves down or lift ourselves up. Awareness is the first step to harnessing this powerful tool.

Hill calls self-suggestion, or autosuggestion, "the agency of control through which an individual may voluntarily feed his subconscious mind on thoughts of a creative nature or, by neglect, permit thoughts of a destructive nature to find their way into this rich garden of the mind."

Merriam-Webster defines autosuggestion as "an influencing of one's own attitudes, behavior, or physical condition by mental processes other than conscious thought: self-hypnosis."

Some people view autosuggestion or self-hypnosis as New Age mumbo-jumbo. But whether we're conscious of them or not, research has proven that our thoughts and suggestions to ourselves influence how we feel, what we believe, and how we respond to any given situation.

Statements like "I am a smoker," or "I am nervous," or "I will make a difference today" are almost certainly true because you believe them. The more you believe something, the truer it is for you and the harder it is to break free from thoughts that limit your progress in life.

In Western cultures like America, if a person is not good at something in the beginning, like playing chess, they often will stop doing it and find another task at which they excel. Asians, on the other hand, often view poor performance as a challenge to try harder.

There's tremendous power in self-belief. People who say, "I can't do it," usually don't even try; that's how powerful thoughts are—they can literally stop us in our tracks.

"Any excuse, no matter how valid, is still an excuse. It weakens your character. You need to review and re-energize your goals and make them happen. Life happens. All these other people had hard times and still made things happen," notes football player Lawrence Jackson.

You may be tempted to look at a goal and think, "There is no way that's going to happen" and want to change your goal to make it easier. The process of setting goals should incorporate making them the right size to start—attainable and believable, yet challenging enough to make you stretch. This keeps you on track, moving forward, and helps you avoid excuses or the temptation to start changing things as you approach the deadline.

Positive self-talk works to eliminate negative self-talk too, because our brain can't process both positive and negative thoughts at the same time. Negative self-talk sabotages us like nothing else can.

Brad Lea says, "Most people fail as soon as they input poor information into their minds. Bad inputs lead to limiting beliefs. Old sayings become our limiting programs. For example, someone might say, 'Money doesn't make you happy,' but I disagree. If you gave me a million dollars, I would be happy, not because of the money but because of what I could do with the money. Money buys you freedom. Some people let limiting beliefs sink in and get stuck. They become excuses. Limiting beliefs run the show in the background."

Autosuggestion erases doubts, fears, and excuses, making room for positive thoughts and ideas to occupy previously wasted space. You are fully in control over what fills this space when you practice autosuggestion and self-talk. Your brain is like a computer, and you are the programmer.

"Your mind is a stage. Only put into it what you want to get out of it. If your mind is a stage and you allow yourself to be bombarded by things you don't want in your life, that's what you will get. If you want to think and grow rich, you need to put that in your mind. It's so simple: what you put in is what you get out—your habits, what you think, what you do," Gregg Godfrey says with conviction and powerful imagery.

Limited expectations will prevent you from reaching the highest levels of success, while expanded expectations open pathways to achieving any goal. Hill takes this a step further when he talks about demanding and expecting your subconscious to hand over the plan or plans you need. When he speaks of demanding and expecting, he emphasizes how decisiveness and commitment enable autosuggestion to work at its fullest capacity to help you achieve remarkable results.

The body is the servant of the mind. It obeys the commands of the mind, whether they are deliberately chosen or automatic. Until thought is linked with purpose, there is no accomplishment.

Raja Dhaliwal says, "The biggest talk you do is to yourself. My self-talk is always positive, on the solution side, not the problem side. I look at possibilities, not impossibilities." He believes he is winning the game in his mind before it happens. Initially, his self-talk happened consciously, but now it has gone to the next level, where it happens all the time without thinking about it.

"I pay attention to the words I speak, and I feed my mind positive words and phrases while eliminating negative words and phrases from my vocabulary." He also meditates every morning and evening. "I do Nitnem, a daily spiritual meditation from the Sikh religion which goes through the five teachings of the Guru."

Practices like meditation can help calm the mind and direct our focus to positive messages, jumpstarting everything else we do. Religion doesn't have to be a part of it.

Life coach and author Dr. Marissa Pei wakes every day and lists eight specific things she is grateful for. "I learned this from Dr. Wayne Dyer, who said to list five things, but I am an over-achiever, so I do eight. Eight is my lucky number and a lucky number in Chinese. Focusing on gratitude stops the critic from starting in right away."

Marissa takes the power of autosuggestion into her day by asking herself how prosperity shows up in her day; how joy, peace, and love show up; and what she can do to make room for them. "I look for opportunities to make wishes and to dream." She ends her day by listing another eight specific things she is grateful for. "I pay the most attention to the things I did get done, not what I didn't get done."

One of the things I routinely encourage people to do is to dream big. Push past what feels comfortable and shoot for the stars. The only thing holding you back is your own thinking.

I know people who routinely, almost enthusiastically, claim to be terrible with names. As the saying goes, "Argue for your weakness, and it's yours." They might argue that some people are blessed with an excellent memory while they, unfortunately, are not.

Pay attention to the words you use when talking to your-self and others about your abilities. For example, if you say, "I'm terrible with names," chances are good you will have a problem remembering names. Better to say nothing. Best would be to say, "I have a perfect memory. His name is Bob." Reinforce the positive.

"I don't have money to invest." I hear this all the time and know these people are overlooking the "latte factor": when you consider the amount of money you spend each week on lattes, coffee, and other beverages or snacks, it adds up. This money could be used for investment and early retirement.

Let's face it, life is expensive. Sometimes there's money to save, and other times there's not. Income is a roller coaster ride for many. I recognize there are exceptions and temporary setbacks in our lives. For the most part, limiting statements are about perception. Illusions. Beliefs. Poor habits. Excuses, plain and simple. Harsh? Maybe. Maybe not.

But definitely, negative self-talk is something you can live without and something that should be replaced by higher levels of calm and satisfaction, making for a happier you.

The more you believe your own stories, the higher the chances they will become your reality, good or bad.

"How about victim mentality?" Penney Ooi asked. "Some people have been given things. An entitlement mentality forms, which leads to a victim response in difficult situations. Staying in a victim situation keeps you stuck your whole life. You will expect things to be handed to you always."

What about the stereotypes associated with statements like "I'm black," "I'm Asian," or "I'm overweight"? According to musician Ray Parker Jr., these are nothing more than excuses.

"You are born with a whole set of circumstances; these are your cards, and you can't change them. What seems to be negative at first could become an asset. You just don't know. Put your excuses aside and focus on who you are and what you are passionate about."

I feel the positive influences of autosuggestion when I am driving by myself. That's when my mind gets creative. No one is watching or distracting me. I'm in a cozy, private bubble in my car, free to let my thoughts wander or to direct them to where I want them to go. Every time I drive to a client's house, I hold a similar conversation in my mind.

I ask, "Why am I going here?"

"I'm going to help them," I reply.

I reinforce my purpose by asking, "How?"

Positivity enters the mix when I remind myself of my ultimate purpose. "So their family is protected, and they can retire in dignity." This thought makes me happy and fills me with pride and eagerness to be of service to people. Therefore, I always walk into every appointment filled with positive energy and the belief that I will make a difference in someone's life, whether I sell them something or not. In my experience, this positive energy and quiet surety of purpose rubs off on clients, making the whole experience of talking about their financial goals enjoyable and positive.

Actor and producer Justin Chon uses a similar process before going into every casting opportunity. "I think about what the agent wants and examine how I will fit into the project overall. I visualize the kind of person people want to work with and make sure to communicate an easygoing style of someone who is a pleasure to be around. I figure I get paid to do all the other things that surround acting—dealing with the press, being on the set, being patient, polite, and professional. I act for free; the rest is the job."

Weight-loss expert Ilana Muhlstein says her teachings work because they rely more on a person's mindset than on what they eat or how much they exercise. "I developed many sayings that helped me succeed. I agreed with myself to lose two pounds at a time and included positive thinking in my plan." Her self-talk included "Get on the scale and subtract two pounds. You can do that. Small increments"—productive, not destructive phrases—"Dinner and done," "One bite to taste."

According to Ilana, "These positive mantras led to gradual, consistent weight loss. When you focus on being healthier and happier, life will keep getting better and easier as you go. Focusing on mental improvements will support the consistent efforts and small increments that will keep you heading in the right direction."

Another one of her favorite mantras is "It's never too late to get your act together." She reminds people in her programs to start believing their best is yet to come and teaches them to focus on developing positive mindsets and perspectives. "Positive reinforcement and focusing on you, not on what you shouldn't be doing or what you should be avoiding, works. But some people are stuck in their current state of negativity. They say things like 'I'm fat, so what's the difference?' and 'I don't care.' Surrounding yourself with the right people helps to reinforce the positive. Positive people and a positive environment lead to positive weight loss."

Chef Katsuya Uechi, the owner of multiple Katsuya restaurants, has catered to some of the most iconic celebrities in Hollywood. He was inspired to cook by the positive example of his mother, who owned a restaurant when he was a boy. Unwittingly, he used autosuggestion to shape his dreams. "I wrote in my journal when I was in my late twenties that I wanted to own a restaurant, buy a house, give a good education to my kids, and become a great, famous chef." When his sons were young, they were involved in karate. Because he was busy running his business, he didn't have time for that. "One of the last things I wrote in my journal was to one day open a karate school, which I have done. Everything I wrote became true. Except for one thing—grow my hair!" Katsuya laughed, sharing this last tidbit.

One of the chief foundations of success is belief—in your dreams and in yourself. When you don't know how you'll accomplish your dreams yet, believing you'll find the answers separates you from the masses. Dreaming of certain things means you believe you can have them. This is huge!

PUT AUTOSUGGESTION TO WORK FOR YOU

Everyone can consciously change their circumstances or attitude by intentionally concentrating on positive actions and thoughts to influence their subconscious. Magic happens when we focus on achieving positive outcomes and we have a clear vision of what we want to receive, as well as what we are willing to give in exchange for receiving it.

You seldom get something for nothing, and your mind knows this. Thinking your vision through solidifies your plans for attaining success and eliminates the potential for scoffing at autosuggestion, because you know you can't merely wish for a Porsche and have it pop up in your driveway. Giving something in return for what you gain is crucial.

Hill emphasized the need for exchange, saying, "When visualizing the money you intend to accumulate, see yourself rendering the service or delivering the merchandise you intend to give in return for this money. This is important!"

Note the three parts necessary for this process to work: visualization, focus, and exchange.

Overlaying all of this must be desire. Without it, direction and surety of purpose are difficult to find.

ADD EMOTION

Hill explains that reading positive words and reviewing goals is of no consequence unless you mix emotions or feelings with your reading. Your subconscious mind wakes up and receives the message that it needs to act only when thoughts are combined with emotions or feelings.

Your brain is tuned in to pain and pleasure, things that could hurt you or that have the potential to make you feel happy. This is one reason why we tend to remember traumatic or extremely joyous events in our lives in vivid detail. The emotion makes the memories stick.

Hill explains, "Your ability to use the principle of autosuggestion will depend, very largely, upon your capacity to concentrate upon a given desire until that desire becomes a burning obsession."

Focus and clarity, therefore, are essential foundations for the successful use of autosuggestion. Hill recommends that you "hand over the thought suggested to your imagination and see what your imagination can or will do to create practical plans for the accumulation of money through the transmutation of your desire." Transmutation refers to the act of transforming one state of being into another—in this case, your thoughts (desire) into reality (money).

It is important to trust what your mind tells you when you turn your thought process over to your imagination. Be on the lookout for sparks of inspiration, ideas, and hunches. Record these gifts from your imagination and act on them immediately. Acting can be as simple as plotting steps or fleshing out your idea once you've written it down.

STRENGTHEN YOUR FOCUS AND VISUALIZATION ABILITIES

Hill writes, "The subconscious mind takes any orders given it in a spirit of absolute faith, and acts upon those orders, although the orders often have to be presented over and over again, through repetition, before they are interpreted by the subconscious mind."

The easiest and most enjoyable ways to feed your mind are reading books, listening to educational audio programs, watching instructional videos and inspirational movies, and surrounding yourself with people who share similar interests. These activities enable you to change your self-talk station, feeding your brain a steady stream of positive, healthy, motivating information that gets you fired up and that communicates your strong emotional desire to your subconscious mind.

Thinking on a deep level and investing time in personal development take energy. It can be challenging to focus on something for more than a few minutes. At the end of an exhausting day, the last thing we want to do is think about goals.

If you suffer from a lack of confidence, fear, or poor habits, you might take the easy route and stick with what's comfortable and familiar. You might binge-watch the entire Netflix catalog or spend all your free time gaming and playing Fortnite. Let's face it, some of us are just plain lazy, and we all fall victim to this potentially enjoyable bad habit from time to time. We slack off.

Although many things can keep us stuck, what's most interesting is how much time and effort we invest in excuses for staying where we are—stuck—doing the same things we've always done and remaining in our comfort zones.

If we applied that negative energy to setting and achieving our positive goals instead, we would soon be miles ahead. So, start managing your inputs. Take charge of your programming, your thoughts, and direction.

Knowing where you are headed and why you are going there is vital to getting what you want out of life. The easiest way to get moving is by recognizing you are in charge and flipping the channel, picking better inputs in an instant.

Read more. Listen more. Be selective about what you allow in and how much time you spend watching television, playing games, browsing the Internet, and wasting time on social media.

Take a close look at your friends. If they are on the road to nowhere, you are along for the ride. Spend your time thinking, dreaming, planning, and executing your next steps on the road to success. Surround yourself with good people. And remember, if the song list for your life doesn't move you, change the station!

REFRAME

So, what do we do to get rid of negative, limiting thoughts? We reframe them. Change our viewpoint. Rewrite our stories. Change our words.

Start by looking at problems as challenges. Then, replace those challenges with opportunities. With every opportunity, there is possibility. And with every possibility, there is hope.

Motivational speaker Jessica Cox firmly believes in the power of positive thinking and self-confidence, saying, "The hardest thing I've had to accomplish, more so than learning to fly a plane, was becoming confident in my own skin. It hasn't been easy being born visually different. Communication is more than verbal. Carrying myself with confidence, smiling, and giving off positive energy helped others embrace my differences, which transferred to me."

Jessica found a way to change the most difficult thing in her life into amazing accomplishments that many people would have believed were impossible, spreading hope and inspiration wherever she goes. "I love what I do," she declares.

"I don't work; I play. I get paid to play." Saying this keeps Ray Parker Jr. motivated to look at things in a positive light. "What do you say to your inner self? Grab a mirror and look at yourself. A good talk in the mirror and repetition will work wonders. Keep building until you build confidence. Don't say 'I can't.' Those words can live forever. Think positive and believe you deserve better. You must believe," he said. "Your subconscious and ego can grow if you believe."

Ray learned valuable lessons at an early age from his father. "My dad told me to take all my money and put at least 10 percent of it away. Even if you make $100, you put $10 away; every year you're worth more. Your subconscious sees you are moving forward. It's not about how much; it's about you. If you have trouble saving, remember that the most important vendor is you, not the phone company, not the bank. Pay yourself first," he advises.

Ray takes responsibility for his results by holding himself accountable and treating himself as a top priority in terms of importance. Our subconscious is always listening and paying attention to our actions.

Shawn Villalovos's mom and grandma always reinforced his positive qualities, building his confidence as he grew. "They'd say, 'You're so handsome! You're good at this or good at that.' I do doubt myself sometimes. I just don't stay there long. I have to speak to small and large groups for business, which is not natural for me at all! A real struggle. Even this interview is a little awkward. I'm usually soft-spoken. It feels like I'm yelling when I speak into a microphone or in front of an audience. I used to sweat uncontrollably and had to give up wearing colored shirts. I'm still embarrassed when I think about it. My hands and feet would feel frozen. At some point, I just accepted that I would have to be embarrassed all the time and started focusing only on what would happen when I finished speaking—on the results and how good it felt afterward hearing that I had inspired people and changed their lives."

I've given thousands of talks throughout my career. What has made a huge difference in my results, self-confidence, and nervousness before getting on stage is shifting my focus to my audience. Who are they? Why are they here? Why should they care? Answering these questions up front is a classic example of autosuggestion and self-talk.

Jaime Villalovos said, "If I just do the right things long enough, there will be a huge explosion. I tell myself all the time that I am the hardest-working superstar. I read affirmations and my goals regularly. I say, 'It's right around the corner.' I remember standing in my closet and saying out loud, 'I deserve to win.' From that moment, things began to change. My income began to climb, and success started to happen."

Boosting your subconscious mind starts by understanding and embracing the power of your conscious mind.

As Lawrence Jackson says, "Inhibitors, anxiety, stress, worry, fear, learned behavior, your outlook on life, the impact of your family, and the people around you—everything that impacts your conscious mind affects your subconscious mind. You have to load your conscious mind with positive thoughts, feed it constantly so that it is available to the subconscious mind when you need it without even having to pay attention to it. My whole success lies in the way I think. Who you are today is a result of your thought process. The minute you think bigger, you become bigger. When you think smaller, you become smaller. Big goals always encounter adversity. But it's something I need, a lesson

I need to learn so I can grow. How to handle adversity? Be prepared, have cash saved, stay on track. The rule is no excuses."

George Chanos agrees, saying, "Talking to yourself and controlling your thought process is essentially programming your brain. You build confidence by reinforcing and reviewing your goals and dreams. It works both ways, and if you program your thoughts with negative stuff, they will go there too. We control our brains; they don't control us."

I mentioned the victim mentality earlier, and George's comment echoes the sentiment that we are in control. What we feed our body and mind is a choice we make daily.

A first-generation immigrant from Malaysia, Penney Ooi knows adversity. "Not having a job was huge at first. If I can't work, I can't get a Green Card. Mom spent so much money for me to come here. I could not fail. All the companies that would hire a finance major required someone with a Green Card. A Chinese proverb says, 'Where there is adversity, there is opportunity.' This is when the testing comes, and you need to shift your focus and make changes."

Penney has developed exercises to focus her mindset and compartmentalize emotions when she has to. "I do things to change my environment and state of mind. If you want to be happy, you cannot listen to sad songs all the time. If I am angry, I pray. It calms my emotions. Instead of being angry for being pulled over, I reframe the experience and am thankful for the police who might have saved my life by stopping me. I say 'thank you' and let them know I am grateful for their service. Sometimes, they let me go. If not, I feel more positive anyway.

When I get angry, I shift from blame and anger to appreciation and gratitude. When I do, the whole world changes."

It's not always easy to focus on the positive. That's one of the chief issues some people have with positive thinking as a tool to a happier, more fulfilled, and more successful life—it requires effort at times. As with most bad habits, the more you think negatively, the stronger your habit becomes, which in turn makes negative thoughts easier and automatic.

To get the most out of life:

- Dream big.

- Be clear about what you want.

- Be willing to do whatever it takes to succeed.

You'll notice that all three of these elements are internal and require introspection and determination on your part. You may not know what you want and perpetually search for answers. Perhaps you know but are unsure how to get there. That's okay. In both cases, changing your inputs will offer new perspectives. New ideas open doors just as surely as negative self-talk closes them.

THE BIG TAKEAWAY

It is possible to change your life and achieve anything you desire if you identify your burning desire, have faith in yourself, and practice autosuggestion.

WISDOM FROM THE ASIAN MASTERMIND

"The more man meditates upon good thoughts, the better will be his world and the world at large."

—Confucius,
Chinese teacher, editor, politician, and philosopher

"The most life-destroying word of all is the word tomorrow."

—Robert Kiyosaki

"I'm optimistic, and I have a lot of goals. And I obey the laws of nature: I eat, exercise, and rest properly. But mostly, it's about keeping the mind engaged."

—George Takei, actor

"If you can't change your fate, change your attitude."

—Amy Tan

"I think being optimistic is ensuring your success. If you start out saying, 'I've got this problem' or 'I'm angry at that,' you will not succeed."

—George Takei

"It's not what you say out of your mouth that determines your life, it's what you whisper to yourself that has the most power!"

—Robert Kiyosaki

"Peace in, peace out."

—Dr. Marissa Pei,
the "Asian Oprah" and author of
8 Ways to Happiness: From Wherever You Are

GROWTH EXERCISES

Walk.

Go for a walk. It's that simple.

Meditate.

Schedule meditation like you would any other important activity. Set aside ten minutes. Morning or evening is best.

1. Get comfortable somewhere quiet where you won't be disturbed. Sit or lie down. Do whatever it takes to be comfortable and supported so you can relax. Turn off the lights or draw the shades.

2. Use your five senses. What do you hear? How do you feel? What are you thinking? Get it all out so you can put it aside for a time.

3. Notice your breath. Breathe in through your nose and out through your mouth. Notice the rise and fall of your chest. Feel the air moving through your body.

4. Survey your body, taking note of how each part feels. Start with your toes and work your way up. When your mind wanders (it will), focus on your breathing, directing it to areas of your body that ache or feel tense.

Practice yoga.

Take a class at that cute place you drive past all the time. Get a DVD or catch a televised yoga class On Demand. Check out yoga on YouTube or get a subscription to a yoga website. Yoga. It's everywhere. Try it.

Do these things all at once or spread them out, trying one new thing a week (walking, meditating, or doing yoga daily for one week, then switching to something else). Observe how you feel. Schedule more of the activities you enjoy.

Try a fast from complaining.

"When you are in the habit of looking for what's wrong, you cannot see possibility. You want to open up and see opportunity and begin dreaming. Don't close yourself off with complaining," instructs Dr. Marissa Pei, who shared this exercise.

For 21 days, do not complain about anything that happens. Instead, say, "All right, I can't wait to see what good comes of this!"

"Be very careful on day 20," Marissa advises. "If you catch yourself complaining, don't beat yourself up. Forgive yourself and start over at day 1. Day 1 is my favorite because I can keep starting over and get it out of my system!"

Here are some additional guidelines for your fast from complaining:

1. A statement or observation like "He didn't call" isn't a complaint, but if you tack on "as usual," it is a complaint.

2. If the complaint is in your head and it doesn't make it out of your mouth, it doesn't count against you (but try not to have anyone around witness your facial expressions).

3. If you are with people who are complaining, you don't have to start over unless you are nodding your head vigorously in agreement.

4. If you are reasonably self-aware, you are the one who makes the ultimate call on whether or not you have to start over.

5. If you are married and doing it together, be nice to each other.

6. If you say something like, "I hate it when…," or "It drives me crazy when…," or "It bugs me when…," there's a 99.999 percent chance you just blew the fast.

"The best *Take My Advice, I'm Not Using It* tip that worked for me while doing this exercise (and in general) is to never miss an opportunity to keep your mouth shut!" says Marissa.

"*Every adversity, every failure, and every heartache carry with it the seed of an equivalent or a greater benefit.*"

—NAPOLEON HILL

SPECIALIZED KNOWLEDGE

Personal experiences or observations

How much value do you place on knowledge?

We all need to learn many things to function in society as adults. But did we really need all those algebra and biology classes? If you're going into a career that doesn't require math or science, maybe not.

In some countries, tests determine college entry, and people who do not show an aptitude for professions requiring a college degree go into the trades. They apprentice with experts to learn skills on the job. Their education is in depth and focused.

Hill points out how many people had minimal formal schooling and still managed to achieve great things. He discusses this without downplaying the value of education, especially for highly specialized fields like medicine and law. Many young people today seem to embrace Hill's examination of the need for higher learning, electing to travel instead of attending college or skipping it in favor of on-the-job training and experience. As the costs of a college education rise, this trend will continue.

Hill states that "knowledge has no value except that which can be gained from its application toward some worthy end."

In business, I would agree with Hill that action and application are what make the difference. I can also appreciate the value of curiosity and learning about the world around us. Personal satisfaction and the pleasure of knowing things have intrinsic value. They remove barriers and facilitate conversations with people.

Hill breaks down knowledge into two types: "There are two types of knowledge. One is general, the other specialized. General knowledge, no matter how great in quantity or variety it may be, is of little use in the accumulation of money. Knowledge will not attract money unless it is organized and intelligently directed, through the practical plans of action to the definite end of accumulation of money. Lack of understanding of this fact has been the source of confusion to millions of people who falsely believe that knowledge is power. It is nothing of the sort! Knowledge is only potential power. It becomes power only when and if it is organized into definite plans of action and directed to a definite end."

So, knowledge is not power. Knowledge is potential power. One must learn how to organize and use knowledge once it is acquired. For this, critical thinking skills must be applied.

In the world we live in today, knowledge is available at our fingertips. From YouTube videos to Google searches and whole books available to read online; from workshops and webinars with people doing what you want to do to online classes—there are many ways to source information and learn. Can you imagine what inventors of old would have accomplished if they would have been able to research what was happening in the world and share their experiments with others?

Dialing into your interests and attaining specialized knowledge has never been easier. You can get all the knowledge you need, said Hill. "Successful men, in all callings, never stop acquiring specialized knowledge related to their major purpose, business, or profession."

In the Asian-American community, education is highly valued. Although younger people are pulling away from higher education, the teachings of their parents still have a firm hold. This can lead to problems as we enter a tipping point in the way the world views education today versus how older-generation parents do.

As evidenced by the statistics I shared in the preface, Asians are ahead of the game when it comes to formal education. Strong ties to their community and elders they can learn from, coupled with a continued emphasis on earning a college degree, propel them forward.

In areas outside the formal education circles, many young Asians are picking up the slack by combining several sources of education, technology, and learning, seeking out mentors, role models, and business networks to finely tune the information and education they receive.

The trick is to begin with passion and focus, develop your burning desire, and then be flexible when it comes to education, taking advantage of different avenues to gain the most knowledge and experience for what you want to do.

Motivational speaker Jessica Cox did not go to pilot school. She learned to fly a plane from an Air Force pilot. "After my first public speech, an Air Force pilot came up to me and asked if I'd like to go up in a small plane. I'd always had a fear of flying, especially in a small aircraft. I'd been in commercial planes before but not in a small plane. My dad jumped in before I could answer and said, 'She would love to.' After my first flight, I decided I wanted to become a pilot. Overcoming my fears was fast. Logistically, it took longer. I learned in a 1940s-era Aircoupe. The ailerons and rudders are interconnected, requiring only two limbs to operate. The lower-tech set-up worked perfectly for me."

Jessica had to find the right instructor, someone with this rare aircraft experience. She did some digging, finding groups in *Aircraft Owners and Pilots Association* magazine. "The March issue had that plane on the cover. I contacted the owner through the magazine. The next hurdle was a license to fly. The FAA offers a sport-pilot certificate, allowing anyone to begin training without a medical evaluation with only a driver's license. I was in!" She earned her license and a Guinness World Record for being the first armless person in the world ever to have obtained a pilot's license in 2011.

DJ Steve Aoki gained more than formal education in college; he learned the value of experience. "Back in college, I used to be in screaming hardcore bands and would sing and scream with no warm-ups. We were giving it all our passion and heart with no additional training. Twenty years later, I'm paying the price. Now, I realize the DIY mindset helped me get started and moving, but I should have taken better care of myself and learned from the pros. Early on, my attitude was all about me. I was going to do this myself. I didn't need any training. I communicated with everyone who came out to see me, not like professors in a large classroom who connect with only the people in the front row taking notes. Teachers don't reach or convert those who are in the back, dozing off. I try to reach people in my audiences and move them with my passion. 'That was a Steve Aoki experience, and that's an experience I'll never forget' is what I like to hear when I do a show.

"Education is important," Steve says, "But kids need to get out there and experience life to find out what is going to work for them. They need to form organic connections with other people that don't exist in front of a computer.

"I was really inspired by Bruce Lee too. His mystery. His philosophy. He was one of the first to break through and one of the only Asians to be recognized on a world stage. He was a great philosopher who spoke things you would want to sit up and apply to your life. Now there are many more Asians out there speaking their minds. Chad Hugo from the Neptunes; Ken Jeong, the famous actor, comedian, and former doctor; Steven Yeun from *Walking Dead;* David Choe, one of my favorite artists of all time; Michio Kaku, the Japanese scientist—they are all doing a great job representing Asians!"

Actor Justin Chon admires people who go their own way too. "Sean Baker made a film on an iPhone called *Tangerine.* Though Sean has a degree in film, his success isn't about the education or the tools; it's what he did with them. The messages he brought forth. You can have all the best contacts, equipment, and education, but if you don't know what to do with them, you're out of luck."

Justin echoed something Hill discusses several times in *Think and Grow Rich*: one doesn't have to start at the bottom or follow a road set up by someone else. College doesn't have to be part of the equation for success. "Go to college or not? Depends on what you want to do. If you don't know for sure, perhaps college is a good route. Figure it out. If you are passionate about what you want and know for sure, go for it. College is a tool that can help you. No right or wrong, but think about why you are going. It's too expensive to take lightly."

Team USA Olympic hockey player Hannah Brandt said something similar: "Education is important, but success is not necessarily something that requires a degree, unless you want to become a doctor or lawyer. Success is more about knowing yourself and having a passion for what you want to accomplish. It's about your work ethic and the people you surround yourself with. It comes down to knowing who you are and what you want."

According to Hill, "The idea of starting at the bottom and working one's way up may appear to be sound, but the major objection to it is this: too many of those who begin at the bottom never manage to lift their heads high enough to be seen by opportunity, so they remain at the bottom."

He goes on to discuss getting into a rut, which is something I believe happens to everyone from time to time. How long you remain in the rut is what makes all the difference. When we fall into a rut, it's easy to get comfortable within the boundaries we create for ourselves. Habits begin to form that can become so strong we accept them as what's normal and stop reaching higher and seeking to improve our situation.

"And that is another reason why it pays to start one or two steps above the bottom. By doing so, one forms the habit of looking ahead, of observing how others get ahead, of seeing opportunity, and of embracing it without hesitation," writes Hill.

Entrepreneur Kevin Harrington reads five newspapers a day to keep up with what's going on in the world. "The first self-help book I ever read was *Think and Grow Rich*. It reinforced my decision to be an entrepreneur when I was a young boy."

As a young entrepreneur, Kevin said he used to think he should know everything. "I found out fast that was not possible." He brought in experts to help with things like finance. "I created a dream team of people who follow me around and zip up the deals. It's essential to have experts to get the job done. And you can learn from them as you go. The more you learn, the more gears you have available to move forward into the next 30 years of life."

Often the challenge facing millennials and young people today is getting started. Kevin wrote a book called *Act Now* to address this issue. "It's all about having an idea and making it happen now. Be persistent. If you've had an idea for ten years, what are you waiting for? Be persistent until you find the right partner, association, alliance. There are many people out there seeking you."

Kevin has two boys. The oldest went to Penn State and loved it. "He got a degree in finance and runs operations for me now. My younger boy is waffling about whether to go back to school. He's not sure it's the right fit for him. But he'll find his way. Some people are perhaps too young to quit school and are not ready or motivated to go out and build a business. It depends on the individual."

Musician Ray Parker Jr. thinks some millennials have an entitlement problem. "You've got to get out of your comfort zone and step into the real world. If you know you are going to be a doctor or have no clue whatsoever what you want to do with your life, go to college. Otherwise, it's not necessary. If you are talented and believe in yourself, you've got to go for it. Don't follow the crowd. Go your own way."

Shawn Villalovos rereads *Think and Grow Rich* a few times a year. "I'm constantly reading books and listening to podcasts and interviews, always some sort of audiobook or training program. Two, three, four books a month, about thirty or forty per year. I enjoy the stories in *Think and Grow Rich*. They are powerful and demonstrate how all families struggle. They make me appreciate what others have gone through to get to where they are, how they overcame challenges. I also like autobiographies because they are relatable and powerful."

Entrepreneur Raja Dhaliwal increases his knowledge by reading books and studying others. "I'm a visual learner, so I observe and study other successful people by watching videos of thought leaders and great speakers of the world." He counts *Think and Grow Rich* as one of his favorite books and also regularly reads *Guru Granth Sahib*, considered one of the world's greatest scriptures.

Lawrence Jackson also loves the written word and studied business before he got into football. "*Entrepreneurship, Mississippi*, and *hippopotamus* were words that blew my mind in fourth grade. I remember we had a career day and Leslie Sykes came to school and talked about entrepreneurship. I knew I wanted that and began to look for opportunities to sell things. I contacted Nike to see if I could rep their shoes. As a kid, I had no fear.

"I ended up going to school, building character, staying out of trouble, playing football. Football is like an interactive version of chess where I was making my own moves within the game. Football was the best shot I had to build upon, and I saw it as a lever to move on to greater things. College teaches you discipline, teaches you focus. You don't have to go to college to be successful. It does give you access to philosophy, science, math, cultural studies. It's more important what you do with the knowledge you gain in college."

Multimillionaire business mogul Jaime Villalovos said it's all about putting yourself in a position to win. "You have to find the best people, who want to help you and are already where you want to be. I'm extremely coachable and surrounded myself with mentors, putting myself at their mercy, at their feet. I did whatever they said. Want me to wear purple? I'll wear purple. I listened and followed their lead. All of them recommended reading *Think and Grow Rich*, the first book on success I read. I have a strong desire to learn, but what makes it work is the willingness to change, to do whatever it takes to succeed.

"I learned three major things from *Think and Grow Rich*: desire, persistence, and associations (with people). People want things, but not deeply enough. When the wind blows and adversity strikes, the tree tips over because the roots aren't deep enough. There was a point when I wanted to quit. I went to bed that night and heard my mentor speak to me, reminding me that my desire was so deep that I couldn't quit even if I wanted to. I got up and read my goals out loud. That night, I applied persistence and an honest assessment of my associations," Jaime said.

Learning and motivation, then, is an ongoing practice, best absorbed from, and shared with, many sources. As Jaime said, "Motivation wears off quick. On their best day, a speaker can only heat you up. The sun will heat you up too, but even on the best day, if you put a pot of water on the ground, the sun won't make it boil. You must put a fire under it. I light my own fire, reviewing my plan daily, not just once a year after New Year's. Your plans must energize you. What lights a fire under your rear end may be different than me. When I am working with others, I ask them about their lives and keep digging until they get emotional. I tap into those roots and dig and dig. Keep reviewing goals to keep moving. Once you hit a goal, your comfort zone becomes a new comfort zone. You've got to keep digging, reviewing, resetting."

John Irving wrote *The World According to Garp*, which impressed upon Scott Williams that anything can happen to you in life. "I remember reading it on the subway, and it moved me. The only failure you have is not trying. And trying takes many forms. 'They are paying me a lot of money for a script I am writing for Ray Liotta,' I might think. But no, they are paying me for all the kegs I changed tending bar, dues I've paid, and work I've done in my life to get to this point. The script is free. It came after the work I put in. I remind myself of this when I need help getting past the 'I'm not worthy' block."

Capriotti's Sandwich Shop Chairman George Chanos's parents divorced when he was only one. "They were loving but lived on opposite sides of the country. I turned this challenge into an opportunity. Transferring in Chicago at O'Hare when I was eight years old, I learned independence, exploration, and a sense of confidence. In college, law school, and my law practice, I took challenges and used them to make myself stronger."

George runs turnkey operations. "Everything is designed for you. When you follow the process, you will succeed. It's very specialized knowledge, but everything is provided for you."

George's company grew in large part due to a viral fan following. "People equate their first sandwich to the first time they fell in love. Our raving disciples set us apart, driving twelve hours, across four state lines, to get one; then filling their trunk with a week's supply; and then saying a week-old Capriotti's is better than a fresh sandwich from someone else. The recipes date back to the founding of the company. They are protected and not changed or altered. Today, we are the stewards of the founder's wishes."

Specialized knowledge played a big part in George's success. He credits hiring the right people as a significant element to the Capriotti's formula for success. "We're in 19 states and expanding. The model is so successful, we're able to command $250,000 to $450,000 per franchise, depending on the size of the buildout, drive-through, flat-screen televisions, etc. Once you set it up and put in the right manager, you work there to get things going, and then move on to the next one. Ultimately, you hire an area manager to do what you were doing, while you step back and let them operate on their own."

We can learn anything. We decide whether we want to or not. "Look at guys like Andrew Carnegie. He came here with nothing and became a self-made business mogul. The resources were there. They still are. People are not always resourceful, but you can learn to be," says George.

Julian Serrano has learned the most from his partners, on the job, and in the kitchens and restaurants. "I was never too interested in becoming an owner. I enjoyed being a chef and made good money. I passed up many opportunities to go into business with partners along the way. The owner of Masa's wanted to partner with me but wanted to do it all his way. I passed. In Vegas, my partner is MGM, which is great because they let me do what I want. When evaluating opportunities and potential partners, interview them like they will become your employees. I need to feel good about what I am doing and feel good about the people I work with. It's not so much about the money as it is about the reputation and people having a good experience in my restaurants. I must be able to trust people to run the kitchen and the dining room. It's a difficult business, and if you don't have a passion for what you are doing, you will not succeed. You have to love what you do, or you will fail.

"I learned a lot from my mistakes and always listen carefully to what the customers say. It's like sales—we're selling what we do in terms of the food and quality. How the customer feels is critical to success in the restaurant business. The best feedback comes when someone is honest about not liking something, which helps me make changes and grow," Julian says. "No matter what the complaint, I'm always interested in what is going on. It's the best specialized knowledge there is."

He also learned from his fellow chefs and restaurant owners along the way. "Most chefs succeed or fail because they arranged a bad deal, not because of their cooking abilities. One of the best things I've done is to observe other people and chefs who have failed and learned from them—learned what not to do and how to do things differently. I also hired a good attorney to make sure my interests are protected."

Specialized knowledge also helped restaurateur and chef Katsuya Uechi. Born in Okinawa, Japan, in 1959, he dropped out of high school. "I caused a lot of problems and hung out with bad people before moving to Osaka when I was 18 to go to culinary school for one year." After culinary school, he moved back to Okinawa and worked in several restaurants and hotels as one of the chefs, learning from those around him.

Katsuya moved to the United States in 1984 with $400 in his pocket and his bag of knives. "I worked for next to nothing, 7 days a week, 15 hours a day! I knew very little about the country or what I was doing and spoke little English." Eventually, after a few years working in the business and feeling the community seemed to be unfavorable toward him, he returned to Japan for three years to study and develop his skills further. "I was hungry for knowledge and wanted to learn more about cooking and being a chef. To be a good sushi chef, you need to have a good eye to pick the right fish, technique, and good rice-making skills," he said.

Penney Ooi sees learning as a proactive exercise, no matter how you acquire it. "When I was younger, I reacted to things. Then, I decided to study finance and became skilled in this area. I learned it was important to leverage other people's time and money. I used to be a loan officer, but I saw that the broker made more money and had a better life, so I paid attention."

Today, Penney teaches others. "Getting inside their minds and hearts is important. Ninety percent of success in business is me; only 10 percent is skill. When you can get into people's hearts, you can get into their minds. If you can change their mindset, they can run a system. College may or may not be useful. You can learn a lot on YouTube." She laughed: "I had an agent who joined my business when she was 18 years old, right after high school. Her father was a successful engineer who got laid off, and she was impacted by the stress and depression he went through. She saw her friends who didn't go to school already building their resume. Because going to school was not essential to her, she decided that she could learn just as much through experience and getting a job would give her the skills to build a business."

Penney said school and education never stop. "Education is forever, a lifetime. Being around other successful people helps me grow too. If I need vision, I may borrow a vision or borrow a belief. If nobody is around, I grab a book. Leaders are readers.

"Follow the principles of success, practice them, and find a mentor," Penney advises. "You have to practice and apply feedback. Practice doesn't make it perfect. Practice, along with feedback, makes it perfect."

Brad Lea is a believer in the school of hard knocks too. "I feel like I learned everything I needed by the eleventh grade. I dropped out and developed an advantage by learning about the world, the streets, what it takes to survive. My friends went on to college and didn't have this experience for another five years. I was already weathered and worn."

Brad's industry is undergoing massive shifts in knowledge. "AI, robotics, and technology are coming in all areas and taking over in certain things faster than others. I see it happening more in voice recognition than in virtual reality. There's a lot to learn all the time to stay on top of it.

"If someone came to me and asked if I thought they needed to go to college to be successful, I would say, 'No. Focus on building relationships and gaining experience,'" Brad says.

Like many of the successful people who shared above, I read books, listen to audiobooks and podcasts, and go to conferences. But I learn the most from the people I meet.

A while ago, I was supposed to have dinner with a guy who canceled, so I went by myself. While I was enjoying my solo dinner, I overheard a couple of younger guys at the next table talking about social media. I turned to them and said, "I overheard your conversation and have a bunch of questions to ask you. Would you mind helping me out?" I started asking them questions about social media and wound up spending three and a half hours talking about SEO, retargeting, and redirecting strategies, a wealth of information I previously knew nothing about! I went home and did more research into the night.

I'm a big fan of research and asking questions. This is a skill you can easily develop, and it will open many doors for you. The secret to asking questions is remembering that most people love to talk about themselves and share their ideas. By asking questions, you are setting the stage for them to shine.

THE THREE COMPONENTS OF SUCCESS

If you are just starting out, you might perform poorly at first. You might be awkward, clumsy, and prone to making mistakes. I've had my share of these awkward first moments. We've all been there—walking, riding a bicycle, driving a car, giving a speech. At some point in your life, you experienced a first time with everything. Hopefully, you received some uplifting praise for your efforts from someone who encouraged you to keep trying.

Praise is about approval and admiration—not so much that you did it right; it's that you did it at all. Praise lets people know that you are proud of them for trying and for pushing past the fear of the unknown. I admire people who are willing to look foolish and perform poorly at first because they will improve if they continue to try.

Part of the process of learning new skills and developing our sense of selves is spending time in a structured academic environment. Arguably, a more important aspect of life is hands-on experience, combining theory with real application and practice. Developing these subtle nuances of daily living and social development goes beyond the basics of reading, writing, and arithmetic. These components of human interaction run much deeper than theories found in textbooks in school.

For example, it is possible to read about playing baseball, study the game, and watch it on TV. We can take our children to a batting cage and let a machine throw a perfect pitch over and over while they develop their timing and batting skills. But what about a curveball or a changeup? What about the pitcher's delay tactics and timeouts designed to throw off our batting rhythm? When facing a human being on the pitcher's mound during a game, the skills learned in the batting cage do not provide these emotional components. How do we read what he or she is thinking or handle our own emotions while we wait for the next pitch?

If the secret to championship success were available in a bottle, then every team would be a contender and take a shortcut to victory. But life doesn't work this way. Not in school, not in sports, not in the workplace, and not on the playing field of life. Success is a combination of book smarts, street smarts, and emotion. Life is a hands-on experience, combining all three elements.

Jack Ma, one of the richest men in the world, has a degree in English, yet he runs an Internet-based commerce company. In early 1995, he heard about a new technology called the Internet, but he wasn't able to access it until he took a trip to the United States, where he discovered information about beer from many countries but very little about China. Prompted by emotion and pride as well as interest in this new technology, he and a friend created a website about China. Within a few hours of the site's launch, Jack received e-mails from Chinese investors wanting to know more about him. His imagination and persistence created waves in the universe that led to China Pages, a company he formed with his wife that made websites for business owners and companies in China. Ma later revealed that he never actually wrote any code or made a single sales call to any customers. He didn't even own a computer until he was 33. None of these things held him back, though they could easily have been a game changer for anyone else starting off in business.

Jack recognized that something bigger was at work here and that he had skills that would help him achieve his desires—with the help of others who had more specialized skills.

Jack knew that what separates the champions from the masses are the intangibles—our emotional connection to people and a deeper understanding of ourselves. Why do we do the things we do? What are our true intentions? How do these subtle nuances impact our performance, relationships, and the big picture? These intangibles are what we develop during the hands-on learning experiences throughout our life.

Using our baseball analogy, there is a depth of character that develops in the backyard while playing catch with Mom or Dad. A level of confidence is formed during the moments when nothing is being said. You both learn something in the process. When you drop the ball or throw a wild pitch and must chase it, you learn humility. We all make mistakes, and that's okay. We're all fallible and human. Life is not something you learn in a textbook or at the batting cage.

THE BIG TAKEAWAY

Success and failure are primarily the results of habit. Opportunities for education and specialized training are everywhere and will give you an edge now and in the future. Be curious, ask questions, and always keep learning.

WISDOM FROM THE ASIAN MASTERMIND

"Real knowledge is to know the extent of one's ignorance."

—Confucius

"In the real world, the smartest people are people who make mistakes and learn. In school, the smartest people don't make mistakes."

—Robert Kiyosaki

"Don't be afraid to take time to learn. Working for other people is good. I worked for others for 20 years. They paid me to learn."

—Vera Wang

"Self-knowledge involves relationship. To know oneself is to study oneself in action with another person. Relationship is a process of self-evaluation and self-revelation. Relationship is the mirror in which you discover yourself."

—Bruce Lee

"The most successful people in life are the ones who ask questions. They're always learning. They're always growing. They're always pushing."

—Robert Kiyosaki

"Learning without thought is labor lost; thought without learning is perilous."

—Confucius

"The most successful people are mavericks who aren't afraid to ask why, especially when everyone thinks it's obvious."

—Robert Kiyosaki

"Success isn't about the end result; it's about what you learn along the way."

—Vera Wang

"You will make some mistakes but, if you learn from those mistakes, those mistakes will become wisdom, and wisdom is essential to becoming wealthy."

—Robert Kiyosaki

"I go to the past for research. I need to know what came before so I can break the rules."

—Vera Wang

"Even for charity, I always give priority to education because I always teach young people that knowledge is your real companion, your lifelong companion, not fortune. Fortune can disappear."

—Stanley Ho, casino tycoon

"We learn to walk by falling down. If we never fell down, we would never walk."

—Robert Kiyosaki

"In the early days, I really felt the pain of not being able to find information easily. I guess that helped me to develop an urge to write things like a search engine."

—Robin Li,
Chinese Internet entrepreneur, cofounder of the search engine Baidu, and one of the richest people in China

GROWTH EXERCISES

Reflect on past wins.

Think about one or more of your past successes. Was the driving force behind your success related to luck or chance? Likely not. And even if it was, I guarantee that you thought about it and took some form of action before that lucky event. Everything we do, have ever done, and will ever be is preceded by thought. Our thinking led to a belief that was blended with persistence, determination, and action. What's encouraging is it works. And it will work again. You have control over your destiny.

When you reflect on past success, see if you can pinpoint the choice you made at the root of it all. That decision, and the ones you make throughout your life, directly affect your results. Too often, we get bogged down with mental static. Excuses. We feel we need more training, knowledge, education, or experience before we can make a move. This is backward. The crucial first step toward success in any area is to decide. Make a decision; then get behind it. The "how" will fall into place almost magically when you do.

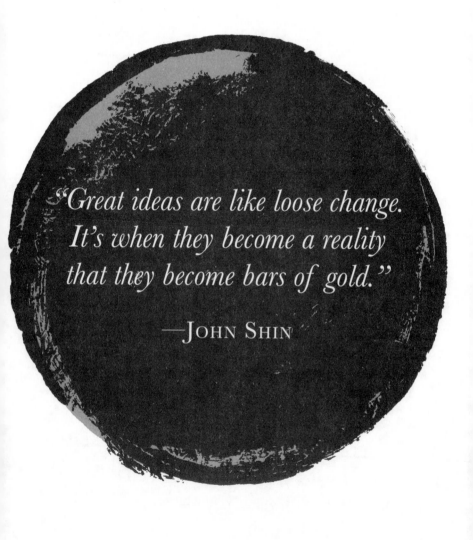

"*Great ideas are like loose change. It's when they become a reality that they become bars of gold.*"

—JOHN SHIN

IMAGINATION

The workshop of the mind

I magination is the lifeblood of every successful business, and new ideas are the starting point of all fortunes. Ideas are products of the imagination, and most new ideas start out sounding a little unusual. History often reflects that the more unusual and bizarre the idea, the greater the fortune that follows.

People frequently tell me that they think I'm a bit crazy. I attribute this to my willingness to allow my imagination and dreams to run wild. Everything seems possible to me mainly because I am willing to go beyond the limits that most people set for themselves. I owe this in large part to my parents.

Throughout my childhood, my parents supported me and all my interests. Regardless of how unusual or extraordinary they might have been, my parents consistently expressed words of encouragement as if I were already a world-class performer or talent in whatever endeavor I chose. My imagination bloomed vibrantly as a result.

This didn't mean I was always free to do whatever I wanted. I may have been told I was a great dancer or fabulous singer by my mom, but this didn't change her conviction that I was still becoming either a doctor or a lawyer! Our Asian heritage and Korean family roots run deep. "We didn't come here to mess this up" is an expression from my parents that is forever tattooed on my brain.

Some Asian parents still exercise tight control over their children regarding career choice and freedom of expression. Breaking generations of tradition and rules surrounding achievement, success, financial security, and academic performance is not easy. I believe this is an area where tremendous opportunity exists in the Asian family to promote imagination and creativity. Loosen up and let your children spread their wings a bit. Let them figure things out for themselves. My wife, Arlene, and I do this regularly with our children, and it has brought us closer together as a family. The process has also been a positive exercise for me, developing an even more outrageous imagination!

Healthy use of the imagination can be big or small. A modest use of mine was an idea to add fun to our weekly sales meetings by having a wheel of fortune. Team members spin it for a chance to win bonuses. On a larger scale, I can picture a day when all my associates will be driving Ferraris or Lamborghinis. When we have our day out together, there will be hundreds of cars following each other, like a Ferrari club. Parents walking with their kids will say, "I think there's a Ferrari or Lamborghini club day today." And the kids will say, "No, Mom, those are John Shin's associates." I imagine we'll all own airplanes and go to dinner in other states, returning in the same time a typical dinner outing would take. Or perhaps, we'll all own yachts and set sail together to a weekend retreat in our own company fleet.

How do you use creativity to solve problems, big and small, and pursue your dreams? How do you encourage your imagination to bloom?

In *Think and Grow Rich*, Hill says, "The imagination is literally the workshop wherein are fashioned all plans created by man. The impulse, the desire, is given shape, form, and action through the aid of the imaginative faculty of the mind."

Hill goes on to say, "Man can create anything which he can imagine…and the only limitation, within reason, lies in his development and use of his imagination."

Somewhere between childhood and adulthood, many of us lose touch with our imagination. As children, our imaginations are boundless. We love fairy tales and picture books of fantastic places and have no trouble believing in the creatures that inhabit them. As we grow, we begin to acquire knowledge that tells us some of the things we once believed are impossible. Soon we begin to say that we'd like to spend more time on creative pursuits but don't have time for them.

In the Asian culture, it is not uncommon for our imagination to be discounted in favor of education and the "practicalities" of success. This is usually the result of our upbringing and parents' beliefs. Even in areas within the creative arts like music, for example, Asian parents often focus more on technical education, lessons, and a regimented practice schedule over free-form expression, playing by ear, and creating original music.

TWO TYPES OF IMAGINATION

In the original *Think and Grow Rich*, Hill discusses two types of imagination: synthetic imagination and creative imagination.

Synthetic imagination is the use of the knowledge that we already possess or have access to, rearranging it to find solutions or create new ideas based on old ones. This is where the voice of your parents can usually be heard.

Creative imagination is free-flowing and encourages hunches, inspirations, and "crazy" ideas. This is extraordinarily powerful in groups when many minds are all brainstorming on a similar wavelength. A pitfall of free-flowing creativity is stepping out on a limb with a new and previously unheard-of idea. This can be a bit scary, as others might try to discourage you because they do not have the vision or the courage to take risks on their own.

Some people don't let what others think hold them back. They realize the most magnificent achievements started off as only a dream. They pursue their goals with burning desire and faith in themselves. They let their imaginations work for them and can see themselves in the spotlight, successful. And they are willing to blaze a trail into the unknown where no one has gone before.

Like entrepreneur Kevin Harrington, who realized that the Discovery Channel used to broadcast only 18 hours a day. Six hours were just colored lines on the screen. A lightbulb went off in his imagination, and he cut a deal with the channel to broadcast locally and use that otherwise unused airtime to advertise product after product. Ginsu knives were his first big hit.

Kevin went to Arnold Marks with his idea. Arnold had been selling knives at trade shows 40 weeks out of the year. "How would you like to never have to do another trade show again and sell more knives than you could in a lifetime, in no time at all?" Kevin asked him. The rest is history.

In 2009, DJ Steve Aoki played Coachella for the second time, earning $4,000, four times what he made in his previous appearance, where he earned $1,000, sitting at a picnic table doing his thing alongside other DJs. "Watching Daft Punk helped me learn more about presenting myself and my show. They did their show atop a giant glowing pyramid, playing music from *2001: A Space Odyssey*. They didn't even move during the show. The production blew me away; the production, combined with the music, showed me that music is not just visual. It's the whole experience."

The following year, a group called Justice came to Coachella and performed. They had a very aggressive punk rock sound. Marshall half-stack amps lined the stage when they played. "I loved their sound. It represented who I was and the direction I wanted to go."

In 2009, Steve put together a visual show with light boxes spelling out the letters A O K I. Friends helped him create bright-colored capes and danced on the light boxes during the performance. "I wore this crazy Jeremy Scott jacket that was reflective all over."

He decided to treat the set list like acts in a play. This was a first. He choreographed each section, sprayed champagne and super-soaked the audience. He introduced rafts for people to jump around on. The crowd quickly embraced the idea, though it was unusual and weird at the time.

"There was so much going on, I realized you couldn't see the letters on my light boxes. I worried it came off like a high school talent show."

This kind of doubt after the fact is common when one is pushing boundaries and trying new things. I often question myself after trying something new in my live speaking performances. It seems like our brains are wired to look at the negatives like "should've, would've, could've," and we become our toughest critic.

Following the event, *Rolling Stone* magazine wrote about the best acts of Coachella, and among the top stars and major acts they covered was a mention of Steve Aoki and his rafts. They shared a video on their website that went viral, along with his recognition. Suddenly, creative visual shows were part of Steve's identity.

"The turning point was paying attention to the crowd and making sure they have a life-changing experience at events." The whole concept of focusing on the audience led to better results. His attitude that anything was possible provided it excited the crowd and gave them new experiences was a game-changer for Steve. He began booking 250–300 shows per year. Where he used to play for anyone, anywhere, now he can be more selective and perform regularly for hundreds instead of dozens.

"The raft worked well for a few years, but I was ready for a new visual piece. I got this crazy idea for a slow-motion cake that would explode all over the place. I had bakeries write "AutoErotique," "Turn Up the Volume," and my label's name,

Dim Mak, on various cakes. My video artist would show the audience the cake and walk up and down the stage, looking for someone who really wanted that cake to blow up all over them. Eventually, people showed up with "Cake Me" signs. We put it up online and got the word out. People loved being "caked." Now I was bringing ten cakes to every show, tens of thousands of cakes over the next few years."

Steve is a trailblazer who understands that even the wackiest ideas have the potential to delight people and be truly memorable.

Here are a few more examples of trailblazing moments from the Asian-American community:

- Dr. Tien Liu – Play-Doh
- Kim Hyung-soon and Kim Ho – the nectarine
- Ajay V. Bhatt – USB
- James Wong Howe – deep-focus photography
- Dr. Kenneth Matsumura – the artificial liver
- Dalip Singh Saund – the first Asian elected to Congress
- Jerry Yang – Yahoo! Inc.
- Philip Ahn – the first Asian-American actor with a star on the Hollywood Walk of Fame
- Jim Lee – *X-Men* (the best-selling comic book of all time)
- Jagadish Chandra Bose – invented the radio in 1907 (years before Marconi) and made countless other scientific advances

- Ellison Onizuka – the first Asian American in space
- Patsy Mink – the first Asian-American woman elected to Congress
- Steve Chen – cofounder of YouTube
- George Ariyoshi – the first Asian-American governor (Hawaii, 1974–1986)
- Elaine Chao – the first Asian-American woman and the first Chinese American in the United States Cabinet
- Min Chueh Chang – co-inventor of the combined oral contraceptive pill
- Sammy Lee – the first Asian American to win an Olympic gold medal (Diving, 1952)
- Wataru Misaka – the first Asian American to play in the NBA
- Hikaru Nakamura – the youngest American ever to earn the titles of National Master (age 10) and International Grandmaster (age 15) in chess.
- Katherine Sui Fun Cheung – the first Asian-American licensed pilot
- Flossie Wong-Staal – cloned the AIDS virus
- An Wang – invented pulse transfer controlling device, leading to the development of magnetic core memory
- Haing Ngor – the first Asian American to win an Academy Award (Best Supporting Actor, *The Killing Fields*, 1985)

- Connie Chung – the first Asian American to be a nightly news anchor for a major network
- Ken Kashiwahara – the first Asian-American network news reporter
- Eugene Chung – the first Asian American selected in the first round of NFL draft
- Young-Oak Kim – the first Asian American to command a combat battalion
- Ed Lee – the first Asian-American man appointed mayor of a major US city (San Francisco, 2010)
- Jean Quan – the first Asian-American woman to be elected mayor of a major US city (Oakland, 2010)
- Tammy Duckworth – the first woman to have a baby while serving in Congress
- Kristi Yamaguchi – the first Asian-American woman to win a gold medal in any sport (Figure Skating, 1992)
- Young Jean Lee – the first Asian-American woman to write a play on Broadway (*Straight White Men*, 2018)

These are just the highlights of Asian-American accomplishments. If you are doubting yourself or think you can't do something, these stories will give you new faith and fire up your imagination. Remember, dreamers are the saviors of the world, and dreams are the seeds of all manmade realities.

It is essential that the products of your imagination are translated into plans. Otherwise, ideas stay in the mind and seldom become anything more than fantasies. Desire begins as a thought, an impulse. It is imprecise and fleeting. It is abstract and of no value until it has been transformed into its physical counterpart.

In other words, when you have a good idea, record it, examine it, and most importantly, act on it. Turn your creative imaginings into practical reality.

DREAM BIG TO BE BIG

In our home, we have an enormous dream board so that everyone can see the dreams of each member of our family and contribute images of things they want. It's six feet long by five feet high and hangs in a prominent area between the family room and kitchen. The board contains dozens of pictures that everyone in our household takes out of magazines or off the Internet.

I respect the value of this board so much that I had it mounted in an expensive frame like a rare piece of art.

The dream board helps stimulate our imaginations. It helps us develop clear visions of what we want and opens a wealth of educational opportunities to discuss while we break bread together. Reviewing and talking about our dreams is an instrumental tool that sharpens our focus while developing solid plans to achieve what we want. My children have experienced the power of this tool since they were young and have often seen pictures on the board become a reality in our lives. Despite everyone being active at work or in school, sports, and various activities, we all support one another.

As a parent, I teach my children that one of the most significant survival skills they can develop is their imagination. Their personal growth and the quality of their lives depends heavily on their willingness to change and their ability to imagine solutions to daily challenges.

Brad Lea embraced his creativity and resourcefulness from a young age being left alone a lot. "As one of nine kids, I had to think for myself and develop common sense early."

Raja Dhaliwal uses creativity to solve problems. "I love to draw pictures on paper and use visuals to help see the ideas through to the end."

Weight-loss expert Ilana Muhlstein's journey to success began when she embraced her imagination and started finding new ways to tackle her lifelong weight issues when others' methods didn't work for her. "I love to eat large amounts of food and feel full, so I had to look for creative ways to eat a lot without gaining weight. I started eating lots of vegetables, like several bags of broccoli with seasonings added, and the crispy, dark cheese from a pizza without the crusts."

Later, she came up with creative ideas she calls her "bunnies." "The idea is to take complex concepts and simplify them. The first bunny is 'water first, veggies most.'" This helps reinforce the idea of drinking water before meals and eating more veggies than anything else. "The second bunny is to weigh yourself every day, breaking weight loss down to small increments. Losing ten pounds is a challenge. Losing one pound or even eight ounces is a piece of cake."

Some adults believe they are not creative or that they lack imagination. Others feel that children are blessed with creativity and imagination but adults lose that edge as they get older. Do you think children are naturally more creative and imaginative than adults?

Have you ever worried about anything? Worry is nothing more than imagining fantastic scenarios about things that haven't happened yet. Your imagination works just fine.

EXPAND YOUR REFERENCE LIBRARY

Adults have a significant advantage over children when it comes to their imagination—an expanding reference library between our ears. We have more life experience. More inputs from various sources creating greater perspectives and frames of reference we can draw upon during any creative process.

A great way to be imaginative and use your ever-expanding reference library is to visualize. Look at the world through your mind's eye. Spend a few quiet moments visualizing potential solutions to a problem or imagining a successful outcome to upcoming events or challenges.

A useful tool to get the visualization process started is using a mind map. Here's how:

1. Grab a blank sheet of paper.

2. Write the central idea or topic you want to map in the center.

3. Circle it.

4. Spend one minute writing every thought and idea that comes to mind (no editing).

5. If you find another main idea in your map of thoughts, circle it and map it too (branch out or start a new map).

Each key point from your initial one-minute mind map can be expanded on the same page or brought over to a new blank page and mind mapped on its own. Within minutes, you will have successfully cleared your mind of everything you can think of about a project or challenge and have it written down for easy review. All the key points can be used to form an outline, a list of things to do, or a plan.

HIT ME WITH YOUR BEST SHOT

Your imagination can also be used to alleviate anxiety or worry. Perhaps you've laid awake at night, your mind racing about the potential outcome of a future event, creating fantastic scenarios about things that haven't happened. Sometimes the details are so vivid and dramatic that they border on the outlandish. Channel this type of unproductive worry by using your imagination as a tool to reduce stress and worrisome thoughts.

Challenge your brain to give you its most outlandish scenarios. Ask your brain, "Is that the best you can do?" Share your worries with a creative partner and try to outdo each other with outrageousness. Be silly. Create fantastic stories that go way over the top and laugh at them together. This exercise is healthy on several fronts—it's creative, it reduces stress, and it will take your mind off your worries (even while you're still thinking of them). Laughter is one of the best antidotes to worry.

STORYTELLING

Creating stories is an effective way to use your imagination and exercise your creativity because spinning yarns forces you to be more specific and expand the details, giving them greater clarity in your mind.

Once you have a clear picture of your subject, consider it in relation to your five senses: sight, sound, touch, taste, and smell. As you work through this process, your picture becomes more vivid and clearer. Practice delivering your story to other people. The more detail you provide, the higher the level of understanding will be in your mind as well as the minds of your audience.

AROUND-THE-TABLE CHALLENGE

Exercise your storytelling ability with your friends and family by picking a topic and going around the table at dinner or around the room during a social gathering. You kick it off; then pass the story to the next person, who then adds a piece; then the next, and on down the line. This is a fun game to play with children to develop their imagination, and it works for business too.

Use it as a brainstorming technique to capture ideas and solve problems. It's an excellent way to develop the ability to dream big as a team. Encourage everyone not to hold back with their input and unique perspectives, and make the goal to come up with the most outrageous ideas possible.

Be inspired by Google, who encourages their employees to work 20 percent of the time on their passion projects, most of which were born during brainstorming sessions where no idea was too crazy and nothing was off limits or controlled by management. This process gave us Gmail and Google Maps.

Every idea, no matter how far-fetched, bizarre, or out of the box it may seem, has the potential to change the world. You never know where it could lead, who might receive it, or how it might change lives and shape our future. Once an idea is released from the mind of its creator, its energy is magnified throughout time and space and becomes available to everyone. We'll talk more about the power of the brain to transmit and receive such signals along with Infinite Intelligence later in the chapters on "The Brain" and "The Sixth Sense."

The creative past is a wealth of inspiration. Engineering marvels, technology, art, and our ability to communicate in dynamic, dramatic, and detailed ways inspire awe when one realizes that everything we do starts as a mere thought fueled by a burning desire.

George Chanos's burning desire came after he had a heart attack. "That was a wake-up call. I knew I had a lot of information to share with my 16-year-old daughter and 21-year-old nephew. I decided to write my first book, *Seize Your Destiny*, to explain how to get from point A to point B, how to develop courage, be more open, and become luckier. The book started as a letter to my daughter that ultimately became a book to help young people."

George's new book, *Millennial Samurai*, is geared toward the younger generations, focusing on old core values such as character, courage, commitment, compassion, perseverance, diligence, and integrity. It also addresses topics of modern technology, artificial intelligence, advanced genomics, cloud computing,

3-D printing, stem cell research, and asteroid mining. He discusses Google's Larry Page and Eric Schmidt, who are forming a company called Planetary Resources to mine the asteroid 511 Davida, which is supposed to have $100 trillion worth of precious metals contained within its surface.

According to Chanos, "To take advantage of opportunities, you need to first be aware of them. Then, you must see the possibilities in creative ideas and new ways of thinking about the old jobs we used to do. The No. 1 job for men today is a truck driver. There are three million of them. But DaimlerChrysler is already producing driverless semi-trucks, and Tesla is making strides in the market as well. If you are a truck driver, you need to know about this. Stephen Hawking said that artificial intelligence is the greatest event in human history—greater than fire, greater than the wheel, and greater than the Internet. He's right. Millennials are looking for ways to succeed in a world where many things are changing. As a result, millennials seem to have an easier time embracing new ideas."

BUDDHIST FABLE

A farmer lived on a farm with his horse and his son. One day, the horse ran away.

"How can you work your farm without your horse?" his neighbor asked sympathetically, "Such bad luck."

The farmer replied, "Maybe it is, maybe it isn't. Who knows?"

The next day, the horse came back, bringing another horse with it.

"Such good luck!" the farmer's neighbor said.

The farmer replied, "Maybe it is, maybe it isn't. Who knows?"

The following day, the farmer's son broke his leg trying to ride the new horse.

The neighbor said, "Such bad luck!"

The farmer replied, "Maybe it is, maybe it isn't. Who knows?"

The next day, the military came to the village to draft young men to fight in a war. Because of his broken leg, the farmer's son was allowed to remain home.

You can guess what the neighbor said and how the farmer replied.

This story illustrates that we never know why or how life will unfold, so labeling events as "good" or "bad" is useless. Assigning definitions keeps us wrapped up in the ups and downs we experience, our emotions along for the ride, instead of moving forward, believing things will work out as they will. Learning to move past outcomes allows you to be more present in life and to remain flexible with what's happening in the "now."

Professional football player Lawrence Jackson views imagination as the ability to turn off our judgmental minds to explore ideas deeper, without deciding whether the thought is good or bad. Once he's uncovered an idea that fits his goals and passions and fires him up, he gets to work, setting plans in motion and fleshing out his ideas. "Most people have good ideas, but they don't write them down. They carry them around, living lives in unorganized mental offices. I'm all about decluttering my mind. I stopped driving and started taking Ubers. This gives me time to work on ideas and listen to podcasts. I don't sleep eight hours in a row. I think sleeping this long is not natural for mammals.

We're better off waking up, having bursts of energy, then going back to bed, and getting up to do it again. Just giving yourself time to think, framing things in your mind and running through them visually, creates the same electrical impulses in your mind as if it were happening for real. When I need a boost, I visualize sacking Tom Brady. It feels as good as the real thing."

Great ideas are like loose change. It's when they become a reality that they become bars of gold. Formulating brilliant new ways of doing things is easy for most of us. It's the ability to move from the idea-formulation stage to the definitive-action stage that separates the dreamers from the doers.

Musician Ray Parker Jr. said, "I'm like a monkey that sees a banana on the ground. The monkey doesn't just swing down and grab it. He thinks of ten different ways to get that banana and overcome obstacles and dangers in the process. I do that too. When problems come up, I've already thought of them."

He also turns to his imagination to further his career. He said, "I find the right people to do the stuff I don't want to do." Ray does this because he knows his strengths and appreciates the perspectives others bring to the table. He has a knack for recognizing talent and working with others for mutual benefit, letting them shine in areas where he is not skilled or interested in investing time on the learning curve.

Ray also uses music itself to spur his imagination, coming up with song lyrics first, letting them dictate what the music will be. "It depends on what I am trying to say and the emotion behind it."

Words are an essential part of communication, but what makes them memorable is the pictures they create. When we communicate in writing, the words form a bridge between the picture in our mind of what we are trying to say, and the image created in the mind of our audience as they read or listen. Hopefully, the two pictures wind up being similar.

Images are essential when it comes to remembering things. The secret is to create a fantastic picture in your mind, one that is unusual, bizarre, animated, or larger than life. Add action and emotion to it if possible, and don't be afraid to be gross and disgusting. If you were headed to the grocery store and needed to remember to buy orange juice, don't simply think, "I have to buy orange juice." Picture a giant orange cut in half and being turned into juice using your head as the juicer. Juice is everywhere, running down your face, in your hair, all over your clothes. Will you remember this? Likely.

Financial advisor Jaime Villalovos is a big believer in the power of visualization. She strives to find creative ways to express her dreams that will add fun and variety to her life, helping spark passion. Before she begins visualizing success, she formulates a plan and a detailed written statement of her intent.

When she wanted to buy a house, she figured out her plan, then regularly used all her senses to imagine what her home would look, smell, sound, and feel like. She did the same with her goal of buying a car she wanted. "My vision board is more than a to-do list. It helps me reinforce my dreams and desires, making them concrete. And it works. I won a spa day as a grand prize once, and when I got home, I looked at my vision board and realized I had a picture of the same spa I'd just gone to for free on the board. It had been there for ten years! The house I live in now? Same thing. For fifteen years, I had a picture on the board of my dream house, the same house I live in now. I have pictures of everything on my board."

Scott Williams knows his imagination is always working and gives it plenty of downtime to wander and create without distractions or rules. "There's a cartoon called *Shoe* from the nineties. One of my favorites shows a crumpled-up old bird in his treehouse office. There's a typewriter on his desk, and he's staring out the window. His nephew came up and said, 'Uncle Cosmo, I thought you were a writer. I don't hear any typing.' The old bird replies, 'Typists type. Writers stare out the window.' That bird knew that writers are always writing and that we do most of it when we're just letting our thoughts wander in a focused way. Like Jack Nicholson in *The Shining* said, 'Even if you don't hear this [typewriter], I'm still writing.' You have to stare at a blank screen a lot to get moving. It helps to have other writers involved in the outline process, working together to fill in the blanks."

Scott's daughter is a senior in high school. "She's a gifted writer, miles away from where I was at her age. 'Dad, it's hard,' she says sometimes. 'Yes, it always is,' I tell her, reminding her to look for the creativity that comes while driving, in the shower, and before deadlines, not just when she's sitting in front of her project. That's usually where the good stuff happens, where it seems effortless, fueled by nothing more than your imagination allowed to fly free."

In the next chapter, we'll explore Hill's belief that "even with the greatest imagination, you need to be skilled in organized planning."

THE BIG TAKEAWAY

Summarizing the chapter on imagination, Hill writes, "The story of practically every great fortune starts with the day when a creator of ideas and a seller of ideas got together and worked in harmony."

WISDOM FROM THE ASIAN MASTERMIND

"Passion is one great force that unleashes creativity, because if you're passionate about something, then you're more willing to take risks."

—Yo-Yo Ma, musician

"An idea that is developed and put into action is more important than an idea that exists only as an idea."

—Buddha

"It's hard to juggle being a businessperson with being a creative person. You have to organize yourself."

—Vera Wang

GROWTH EXERCISES

Before you walk into an event or a meeting today...

ask yourself, "How do I want to leave this experience? What's my purpose for being here?"

Develop intentionality.

Live your life with purpose. Start your day centered and focused. As you go about your morning routine, ask yourself what you can do this morning to create the day you want. Then, set an intention for your day. Simple is good. "Today, I will find joy all around me."

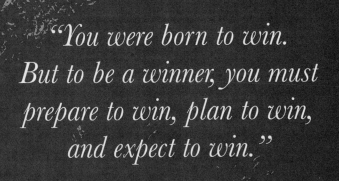

"You were born to win.
But to be a winner, you must
prepare to win, plan to win,
and expect to win."

—JOHN SHIN

ORGANIZED PLANNING

The crystallization of desire into action

D o you organize and plan for success? Hill explained that the majority of people meet with failure because of their lack of persistence in creating new plans to take the place of those that fail. Until now, we've talked about internal steps to success. But without organized plans, you can burn with passion and imagination all you like, but you most likely won't be successful.

Organized planning results in higher productivity, reduced stress, more work satisfaction, and greater life harmony and balance.

Hill emphasizes, "Your achievements can be no greater than your plans are sound."

One of my favorite expressions is "Most people don't plan to fail; they fail to plan." Waiting until the last minute, distractions, procrastination, poor planning, lack of priorities—these are all things over which you have direct control. You are your own worst enemy when you allow them to govern your time.

Fortunately, there are easy actions you can take that will increase your productivity and decrease your stress levels.

SCHEDULE IT

Many entrepreneurs and business professionals struggle with guilt and anxiety if they are not always working. I've heard countless stories from successful people who work 12 to 16 hours a day for years to build their business and achieve success. Although I am a believer in hard work and doing whatever it takes to get the job done, I also recognize the priceless value of time. Those once-in-a-lifetime moments missed are also a familiar theme and a sad reflection from otherwise successful people thinking about the price they've paid to climb the ladder.

There's inherent power in scheduling. You're opening space for things to happen. You've made a call, set a time, and made your intentions known.

Our brains perceive a scheduled item on our calendar as a priority.

"We should get together sometime" is what many people say. No commitment here.

"Let's have lunch at noon next Wednesday at Zen Garden" is concrete.

Make firm commitments to solidify your plan for success.

The best way to ensure you hit your goals and move at the pace you choose is to schedule your time. Figure out where you want to be at the end of this year and work backward from there. Break it down by the quarter, then the month, and finally by the week. Get the jump on your business tasks early in the week and early in the day. Again, this boosts confidence, builds momentum, and propels you forward.

Make sure to schedule personal time for yourself, your family, and friends. Build in breaks and buffer time for the inevitable situations that come up each week. Remember, if it's important and you want it to happen, get it on your schedule. Especially personal items. Make them non-negotiable. This commitment to yourself builds personal integrity and will help create harmony in your life.

David Fishof, the founder of Rock and Roll Fantasy Camp, has ADD but works around it. "Preparation is key. I come into the office an hour or two early to start planning and preparing for my day because I want to be the best I can be. Luck is when preparation meets opportunity," he said.

Entrepreneur Kevin Harrington prepares for his day by reading magazines and trade journals. He needs to see a visual of the next 18 months. "Laid out on my desk are pictures, schedules, Post-it Notes. Everything gets calendared. I work between 8:00 and 6:00 every day but have to be flexible. I have an active interest in 25 different ventures and deal with different time zones."

SCHEDULE TIME TO SCHEDULE YOUR TIME

Spend an hour each week creating the following week's schedule. Make this planning time a scheduled activity, and stick to it. Sunday works best for me, though any time between Friday afternoon and Sunday evening will work.

Every Sunday I spend an hour or so in the afternoon in front of my computer reviewing my upcoming week. I get organized by sending out texts and e-mails to my staff to get them moving and prepared.

Make sure to review the week that is ending so you can make a note of what you accomplished, tasks in process, and items you didn't get to this week. Make sure to acknowledge your efforts and celebrate small victories. This is super important for your self-esteem and good for your soul. Be kind to yourself.

Works in process and things you didn't get to will be the first items to go into your plan for the upcoming week. Make sure to grab your calendar and identify all the anchors—scheduled appointments and non-negotiable commitments, both business and personal. Once these are added in, you know where you need to be and how to best schedule around them.

I plan phone calls and when I'll make them. Every day, I want to talk to at least 25 people. I review the production report on Sunday and decide who I am going to call to deliver a little EPR (encouragement, praise, and recognition). I believe everyone needs some sort of CPR. People need to be resuscitated daily. So when I call them and give them some EPR, I keep them alive. Constant personal communication with clients and associates is essential to building a team.

Consider your business and personal goals and the steps you plan to take in the upcoming week to achieve them. Wrap up by adding personal and family time activities and things that make up your "we should do this" list.

When you plan for success, good things happen. Strive for harmony throughout your business and personal life.

FIRST THINGS FIRST

Brian Tracy, a personal development expert, advocates knocking out your most challenging task of the day first. He said doing so creates momentum throughout your day. Essentially, it's all downhill (in a good way) after that, making every subsequent task you do much easier and more fun.

I also take the time to let my imagination stir my burning desire as I look at my goals and refine my strategy for achieving them. In addition to task-based planning, it's important to think about results, not the activities required to produce those results. Think about value. Think long-term.

Plans need to be fully fleshed out. You should have both short-term and long-term goals connected to specific goals and tasks. And you must remain flexible and persistent, willing to try again and again if you fail.

As Hill says, "A quitter never wins, and a winner never quits."

Penney Ooi plans for success by looking at her profit and loss (P&L) statement. "Am I growing or not growing? Many people are too busy working in their business, not on their business. Every quarter, I sit with my mentorship to look at my business so I know every week of the upcoming quarter what needs to happen. Then, every six months, I have a strategic planning session to work on my business."

Planning my actions and my schedule ensures the best possible results every time. I take the time to think things through, look at all the possibilities, and examine my options. Why? Because there is nothing like having a well-thought-out plan come to fruition.

When I was younger, I tended to go off half-cocked, chomping at the bit to get things (anything) done. My engine was always revving. Today, I still have the same drive toward action, though I have found the wisdom in thinking before popping the clutch and letting her rip.

Thinking requires time and energy. Some people believe it's easier just to get moving and figure things out as you go. This is admirable from an effort standpoint, though learning from the school of hard knocks often takes longer, because you will find yourself working more as you redo things after false starts and mistakes. As the timeless expression goes, "There is never time to do it right, but there is always time to do it again."

In the simplest terms, the best way to improve results in any endeavor is to create a plan and then follow through, refining as you go.

Notice the two essential elements—creating and following through—that contribute to the power of organized planning. Most people tend to be stronger in one area over the other. Either they create elaborate plans that are never executed, or they shoot from the hip with no plan whatsoever. Look for the area (planning or execution) that you find most enjoyable, and be honest about the one you resist. Focus more energy on the least desirable element for the next few projects while you develop your strength in this area.

If it turns out you are a planner who consistently doesn't follow through, remember, "Done is better than perfect." In other words, don't get too bogged down in your planning or you will never finish anything. It's easier to edit than it is to create. Once done, you can always modify and revise.

The sweet spot of accomplishment is where thinking and action meet. Focus on this intersection. Be the rare breed of individual who thinks on their feet. And get those feet moving forward in a hurry before enthusiasm and inspiration dissipate!

BITE-SIZED PIECES

Once you identify what you want and begin visualizing the process involved, it's time to break your plan down into bite-sized pieces. The primary benefit here is you can quickly take a complex challenge that may seem overwhelming on its own and turn it into several small challenges that you can effortlessly handle without emotion and anxiety. From complex projects and lofty goals to daily routines, our brain loves to accomplish small tasks. It feels good to check things off a list, and those little victories are satisfying.

For actor Justin Chon, planning is much like identifying the reason why he makes a film. "I invest time researching and doing my due diligence. This part of planning usually shines a spotlight on the aspect of the story that gets me excited."

Preplanning helps ensure Justin finds the right partners. "Are they on board with me? Do they believe as I do in what we are doing? Will they do the work? Most of my films are low budget. Ninety percent is planning and prep; 10 percent is execution. So, organization is huge."

On the set, he can't be dogmatic and inflexible. He understands the importance of inputs and flexibility. "Sometimes things change, but keeping people on board throughout the process is essential. I rank organization ahead of managing or marketing."

Time is valuable. Justin prioritizes his time, accomplishing his top priorities first. Above all, his job and family come first. "I don't waste time or do things that take me away from my priorities. My social habits, drinking and partying, have evolved because they take away from my work and family."

PREPARATION IS 100 PERCENT CONTROLLABLE

We have total control over planning. But before you spring into action, it's important to take a few minutes and think your plan through. When you do this, two things will happen—you'll reduce stress and improve your results.

Restauranteur Katsuya Uechi is a long-term planner. "One of the most memorable parts of *Think and Grow Rich* is the part about making a blueprint and deciding how you want to be after one year, then five years. Being clear about where I am going and having a picture of what that looks like has helped guide me all these years."

Being unprepared is stressful. It's like walking a tightrope without a net. Fear takes over when we operate in the dark. We feel lost and uncertain. Having a plan, no matter how simple, will get you started. Write it down. Make a list, scribble a note—whatever it takes to unload the swirl of thoughts from your mind.

Musician Ray Parker Jr. advises young people and those who are just starting off to have a reasonable plan—something doable, realistic. "You have to believe in yourself, or else nobody will believe in you. Be respectful of other people and their time. Do the best you can do and provide quality work."

Our actions create the results we live with, and our results are all about the choices we make. Where you are today is a direct result of your past decisions. When you look at your previous results openly and honestly, you'll always see a correlation between preparation and outcome. The sooner you accept this, the better your life will be.

Some people love to analyze details and create elaborate plans, then fail to act. Or if they act, they are not fully committed. Other people jump into the deep end of the pool without thinking at all. They get in over their head and either panic or start treading water just to stay afloat.

This is when it is most important to go back to the basics and review your vision, strategy, people, and leadership.

Hill emphasizes the need for faultless plans and suggests masterminds and mentors can help you with their experience, education, and imagination, ensuring you develop well-thought-out plans that you can execute efficiently.

"People who are successful also learn to accept help from others; they don't try to do everything by themselves," says psychiatrist Crystal Lee. "They have insight into their own limitations and are comfortable going to others with strengths in their areas of growth."

The problem with some people is that they are too independent and don't know how to ask for help. They think asking for help makes them incompetent or dumb. It's actually the opposite; asking for help is a smart thing to do.

Hill agrees, saying, "No individual has sufficient experience, education, native ability, and knowledge to ensure the accumulation of a great fortune, without the cooperation of other people. Every plan you adopt, in your endeavor to accumulate wealth, should be the joint creation of yourself and every other member of your mastermind group. Most leaders begin as followers."

Hill suggests securing a team before you create your strategy and plan in order to gain from the mastermind's experience, education, innate abilities, and imagination. However, he also cautions you to pick your team and mentors with care, making sure you have the same goals in mind and that your chosen masterminds support you 100 percent.

The best mentors and leaders embrace learning, pay little attention to hierarchy, respect the feelings of their employees, and understand their customers' needs.

Hill attributes the following traits to the best leaders:

- Unwavering courage
- Self-control
- A keen sense of justice
- Definiteness of decisions
- Definiteness of plans
- The habit of doing more than paid for
- A pleasing personality
- Sympathy of understanding
- Mastery of detail
- Willingness to assume full responsibility

- Cooperation

When leadership fails, Hill says it is usually for one of the following reasons:

- The inability to organize details

- Being "too busy"

- Lack of humility

- Expecting compensation for what they know instead of what they do. As Hill says, "The world does not pay men for that which they 'know.' It pays them for what they do or induce others to do."

- Fear of competition from others on their team. Living in fear almost guarantees you will realize this fear eventually. Preparing others to take charge on your behalf allows you to be in many places and accomplish many tasks at once. Remember, if you focus on being irreplaceable, you may never be promoted.

- Lack of imagination. Without a developed imagination, you are totally dependent on others for ideas.

- Selfishness. Taking all the credit and stealing the thunder of your peers is sure to be met with resentment. A great leader attributes all the credit to her followers as she knows people will work harder for recognition and commendation than they will for money alone.

- Self-indulgence and excess. This is a sure way to lose the respect of the people around you.

- Disloyalty. Loyalty and integrity are cornerstones of every relationship. What you do and say demonstrate your true nature to others. Gossip makes people wonder what you are saying about them when they are not around.

- Emphasizing the authority of their leadership. Leadership through force is a sure sign of an insecure leader. A confident leader does not need to advertise his or her position.

- Focusing on their job titles and on the titles and job descriptions of others. As Hill notes, "The man who makes too much over his title generally has little else to emphasize."

MAKE THE MOST OF YOUR PEAK TIME

It's important to know your energy cycles. Many people are energetic in the morning when they wake up. If you are a night owl like me, your highest energy level may be in the later afternoon or evening until the wee hours of the morning.

By taking advantage of your peak energy times, you can plan your schedule to maximize the number of tasks you complete during your peak efficiency. Knocking things off your to-do list boosts confidence, builds momentum, and propels you forward. It also removes the potential for feeling guilty when you sleep in or shift your attention to other matters of importance in the afternoon.

If you haven't realized it already, planning is an essential component of success. Here is a three-step outline for achievement that spells it out plain and simple:

PREPARE TO WIN

Remember the five Ps (Proper Preparation Prevents Poor Performance).

Think about what you want to achieve. What needs to happen? What resources will you need? Make a list and get organized. The time you spend preparing to win will pay you back tenfold.

PLAN TO WIN

It's possible to be prepared and still feel lost or uneasy. A plan is the greatest natural remedy for bewilderment. A plan is a giant funnel that captures all the elements you've prepared and narrows them down to a simple set of instructions. By rounding up the pieces, you're ready to build your puzzle.

EXPECT TO WIN

Preparing and planning to win is easy for most people. The biggest challenge is expecting to win—believing you can and you will because you deserve to win.

Most people would like to have a million dollars. But do they believe they deserve it? Maybe. Maybe not. Thinking and believing are not the same. If thought is a queen and planning is a king, believing is an ace.

By believing in yourself, you expect more. When you expect more, you win more.

Solidify your belief in yourself by celebrating your goodness every day when you first wake up and right before you go to bed. Review your accomplishments and previous successes. Take a moment to believe in your potential as you examine past wins.

AVOIDING BURNOUT

Jaime Villalovos believes keeping a perfect life–family–business balance is not entirely possible. She puts the most effort toward faith, family, and business, in that order, and feels business should support your life and family. "Success is having good things happening across the board, not at the sacrifice of each other." Striving for balance, she acknowledges that sometimes a little extra effort needs to go into other categories. "I have a lot of support and delegate things when I need help. Ultimately, success means you are happy and not losing sleep at night— making a difference but not neglecting areas of your life that mean the most to you."

When her first child was 18 months old, she struggled with being a "good" mom and spending more time at home. "I shared my concerns with my mentors, who gave me insights that were helpful. Now, I spend more quality time with my kids than most nine-to-five workers. And I am happy with my choice—balanced in a way that works for me. I found it helped to cut out as many negative things from my life as I could. I had to stop watching the election news!"

Nitro Circus founder Gregg Godfrey balances his time between what I call his four Fs: faith, family, fitness, and finance. "In the beginning, I didn't balance things very well. Family has always been the most important. But I found out that pain is a good motivator. Not taking care of yourself brings you down. You can't do things and aren't motivated. That's why fitness is a big one with me. I start by keeping my body in check, my spirituality in check, and my family in check."

Despite everything he's involved in at any given time, George Chanos balances his days by trying to be more efficient with his time. "It's easier to balance and do multiple things. Balance doesn't always mean an equal division of time. One day, it's all family. The next day, it may be exclusively work. In general, your life needs to be balanced. Relationships are also important to build into the picture."

One of my favorite points George made during our interview was, "It would be better to reduce the quantity of time you spend on anything and increase the quality of time. When you are focused and mindful, you will accomplish much more. Increase your focus, increase your mindfulness, and focus on quality time." Sage words indeed.

"You need to know how to take care of yourself emotionally so you can take care of other people," says Penney Ooi.

Brad Lea believes there is no such thing as balance. "It's more about priorities. My kids motivate me to make their lives easier. I'm working on a book called *The Hard Way*. In it, I explain why setting priorities is so important and why quality time is better than a lot of time in most cases. Spending an hour or two of quality time with your kids lets you move on to other things, feeling good."

Children and family are important to Penney Ooi too. "Chinese philosophy said you cannot teach your children how to behave. You must show them. In life, you go back and forth with balance. My kids know I work hard for my family. Communication is essential. Everyone understands their roles and responsibilities and takes care of their own. At the start of the year, everyone has their own plan for the year, and we also have a family plan where we are all working toward common goals together. This helps us all feel more in balance with ourselves and each other."

THE BIG TAKEAWAY

The time you invest in planning and scheduling your efforts will pay huge dividends in your results. All planning doesn't have to look the same; it only has to work for you. Done is better than perfect.

WISDOM FROM THE ASIAN MASTERMIND

"A plan is a bridge to your dreams. Your job is to make the plan or bridge real so that your dreams will become a reality. If all you do is stand on the side of the bank and dream of the other side, your dreams will forever be just dreams."

—Robert Kiyosaki

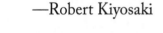

"You were born to win. But to be a winner, you must prepare to win, plan to win, and expect to win."

—John Shin

"The only difference between a rich person and a poor person is how they use their time."

—Robert Kiyosaki

"When it is obvious that the goals cannot be reached, don't adjust the goals; adjust the action steps."

—Confucius

GROWTH EXERCISES

Complete these critical steps in successful planning:

1. Write the steps to reach your goal.

2. Rank your steps by order of importance.

3. Schedule time to complete each task.

Written notes help you see the big picture, and you'll enjoy the blast of positivity when you check off items as you blaze through your list.

Take inventory of yourself.

You can only know yourself through accurate analysis. Start with these questions:

1. With whom do you love to work?

2. What businesses or activity do you find fascinating right now?

3. What can you do better or know more about than 100 other people? How can this be shared with others?

4. When do you feel the most fulfilled? What do those days look like?

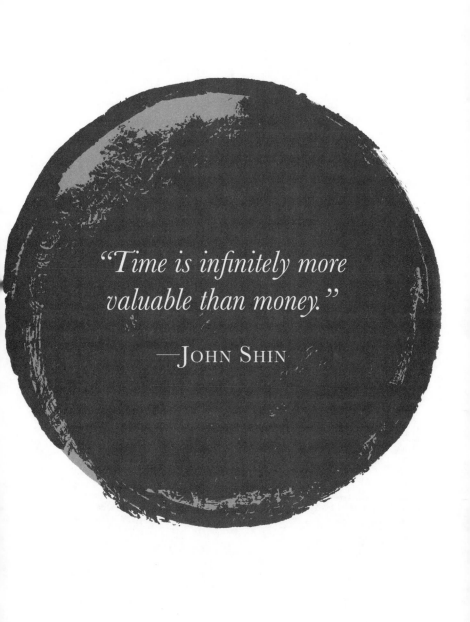

"*Time is infinitely more valuable than money.*"

—JOHN SHIN

DECISION

The mastery of procrastination

Are you familiar with the last minute? Have you waited until a deadline loomed to cram for a test, prepare for a presentation, respond to an invitation, pack for a trip, or get to the airport?

How did you feel?

Whether you felt exhilarated or stressed out, waiting until the eleventh hour is usually the result of indecision. Poor planning, disorganization, or an oversight can generally be traced back to the lack of decisive action.

According to Hill, lack of decision is near the head of the list of major causes of failure. He defines procrastination as the opposite of decision and a common enemy practically everyone must conquer.

Problems arise when indecision becomes a habit. Poor habits are usually followed by elaborate stories and excuses. This pattern generally starts when we are young and haven't formed a clear passion or direction in life regardless of our heritage or background. As the saying goes, "If you don't know where you are going, any road will take you there."

Many Asian people are raised to be more passive and not to assert themselves. Early programming from their parents and grandparents often included rules like "speak when spoken to," "don't talk back," and "don't question authority." This type of rigid upbringing compounds the problem of being indecisive and creates vulnerability to negative outside influences and manipulation from others.

Strong family heritage and rigid mindsets regarding education, career, and marriage are common among Asian families. This can morph into confidence problems later in life.

As Hill reminds his readers, "Thousands of men and women carry inferiority complexes with them all through life because some well-meaning but ignorant person destroyed their confidence through opinions or ridicule."

A tendency to be passive is a blessing and a curse. The curse is not speaking up for yourself when you clearly know what you want, letting other people make decisions for you without challenge. The blessing is the calm, peaceful warrior that exists in Asian people when they are clear and passionate about their goals. Quiet, confident, unstoppable. It's like being a superhero.

Once your burning desire and purpose begin to clearly develop, your decision-making becomes more automatic. You become less vulnerable to outside interests and manipulation because you are clear about what you want and not easily knocked off track. Clarity of purpose, mixed with a burning desire and an organized plan, makes you nearly bulletproof.

Hill says, "Analysis of several hundred people who had accumulated fortunes well beyond the multi-million-dollar mark disclosed the fact that every one of them has the habit of reaching decisions promptly and of changing these decisions slowly, if, and when they were changed."

Though it may seem easy, making decisions and getting behind them is not always simple. Numerous factors could stand in your way: poor timing; lack of money, information, or education; or other priorities. We all have busy lives, so some of your reasons may be more pressing and urgent than others. Be aware that whatever your reasons, they can easily slide into the realm of excuses. Indecision is a slippery slope.

EXCUSES, EXCUSES

If you are not pursuing your goal, acting on your plan, or making progress toward your dream, your belief in your excuse is stronger than your belief in your dream. Currently, your story about why you can't do something is more powerful, more detailed, more vivid, and more deeply entrenched in your subconscious than your goals, plans, and dreams. Go back and reread this paragraph. Let it sink in for a minute.

Jaime Villalovos made a clear decision years ago not to buy into excuses. She did it by reinforcing her belief in her dream by developing a clear vision of what she was doing. "I don't buy into excuses or let them hold me back. When I started my business, I decided up front that I was going to make it. I would plant my flag and make it happen no matter what. That firm decision made a huge difference and helped pull me through some tough times."

She learned watching others that quick decision-making led to opportunities many people couldn't be bothered to go for. "I've heard excuses from all races, nationalities, and genders. I remember talking with one woman about coming to an event, and she said, 'I can't do that. I have cookie dough in the freezer.' Another woman said, 'I can't leave. My dog will chew my furniture.' I wasn't sure how to respond to either one. It's amazing what holds people back."

The amount of energy and conviction that some people put into making and maintaining excuses is astonishing when anyone can refocus that energy into positive things. The effort is the same for thoughts of why you can versus why you can't, but there is a huge difference in the potential outcome and change in your life.

Ray Parker Jr. hit the nail on the head when we discussed procrastination and the importance of making a clear decision early in the game. "Take control of your life or else someone else is going to take control and tell you how to spend your time and your life. Success for me is waking up in the morning and doing exactly what I want to do. Make enough money to provide for your family and live in the style that makes you comfortable without stress. When my family is happy, I'm happy."

But it's not always about money for Ray. "I made some decisions in the past that required me to give up making money so I could have more relaxing times in my life. You have to balance what's important to you. If you have kids, enjoy your kids. Spend time with your wife if you are going to be married."

Ray also takes a spiritual approach to decision-making. "My process for making decisions always includes some sort of prayer, seeking guidance from a higher power to guide me. Common sense, higher power, and then what feels right. Works for me."

When making a major decision or spending a lot of money, it helps to give yourself a cooling-off period. Paying with cash can curb impulsive buying behavior. Given even a few minutes to think, it's incredible how quickly our needs can change. Thinking through purchases before making them encourages imagination, creativity, self-esteem, and character-building.

Motivational speaker Jessica Cox credits fast decision-making with her success as a speaker. "I talked once when I was a sophomore in high school to junior high students, telling them about my life, my every day. They came up afterward one at a time to say how they were inspired. Therapy is mutual. This made me realize I had something there, in speaking. Eventually, I took it to the next level and made a career out of it, never looking back."

Jessica echoes Hill, who said, "Those who reach decisions promptly and definitely know what they want and generally get it. The leaders in every walk of life decide quickly and firmly. People who failed to accumulate money, without exception, have the habit of reaching decisions, if at all, very slowly and of changing these decisions quickly and often."

Jessica loves what she does, so she hasn't questioned her choice, though some of her goals have changed along the way. "Now, I am more aware of stigmas for people with disabilities around the world who are not allowed to go to school or are hidden at home, abused time and time again. It's a horrible situation for people outside of the US with disabilities. I can use

HOW **RICH ASIANS** *THINK*

this platform to make change around the world, show the world what's possible for a woman, a woman without arms—that anything is possible."

She uses humor in her talks to break the ice and answers everyone's questions up front. "When I changed my focus toward the audience and not about me, everything changed. If I make a mistake, it's human, and they are more forgiving. Makes it a lot easier."

"I don't wear prosthetics, though I was introduced to them at a young age. I've always had exposure to the most advanced tech. I just don't like them. They were uncomfortable. It's faster and more efficient to use my legs and feet than to fumble with prosthetics. But I used them until I walked to the bus stop for my first day in eighth grade without them. I felt lighter, free, and the person God created me to be. I stepped onto the bus and promised myself that I would never wear them again. I ask people, 'What are your prosthetics?'"

In other words, what do you carry around with you that gets in the way, is too heavy to carry, and is holding you back from freedom?

Jessica doesn't let anything hold her back from life. "I might try slacklining, like a tightrope but thicker, or perhaps rock climbing with some sort of harness next."

I love people like Jessica, who inspire us all to do more.

AUXILIARY INPUTS

Most home and car audio systems have an auxiliary input. It's a way to plug in an outside source of information or additional music to enhance your experience and expand your library. When it comes to making decisions, it is essential to incorporate auxiliary inputs from your mastermind group of peers and mentors. Our ability to look at any situation is limited by our knowledge and experience and often contains blind spots. Input from outside sources helps eliminate these.

When we call upon our trusted friends and family to help in the decision-making process, we often pick up ways of looking at things we would never have seen on our own. Usually, the consensus will affirm that we are on the right track. If everyone is saying something different from what we were thinking, we may need to change course. By remaining open and honestly considering the feedback from our network, we can be decisive and move forward with informed confidence.

Chef and restaurateur Julian Serrano says, "Running a business is the way to go. If you are good at what you do, you may be running someone else's business already, so why not do it for you? It takes dedication and commitment, plus having the right abilities, to run a business. There is sacrifice and less time with your family in the beginning while you get things running."

George Chanos adds, "The more information you have, the better. We are all limited in our perspectives. Other people from different backgrounds and cultures have different perspectives. You want to seek information from as many perspectives as possible when making a decision. You have certain blind spots, and other people will see things that you don't see. Multiple perspectives are invaluable, and if they all confirm the same thing, then you are headed in the right direction. If they are all saying the opposite, it might be good to change direction."

HOW **RICH ASIANS** *THINK*

Brad Lea tends to act fast. "I just pull the trigger and act. Most people are afraid to make a move. It all boils down to making the best choices we can at the moment and moving forward. You can see the results of insignificant choices that add up over time, and you develop a pattern of making poor choices and bad decisions. But you don't have to linger there. If I make a choice and it doesn't work out, then I adjust. The key is the passion and desire that gives you stamina. Figuring out what you truly want can be difficult. Getting it is easy. Figuring it out is hard. But there is so much abundance everywhere I look, it's difficult to be negative."

Brad looks at decisions both from a short-term and long-term perspective. "Almost nothing in this life is ever done until we die. Nothing you do is a mistake unless you continue to make it over and over. You can make amends, go back to school, learn new things, say you are sorry, pray, resolve conflicts, turn over a new leaf, or set off on an adventure. All it takes is determination and a new way of looking at the chances life gives you every day."

Entrepreneur Raja Dhaliwal is a fast decision-maker too. "I see opportunities and act on them, gathering input from my team, sharing thoughts and ideas, then implementing plans quickly."

Dr. Marissa Pei believes the most powerful tool we have absolute control over is the power of choice. "We get to decide how we handle adversity, results, and obstacles in our path. A helpful perspective is to view challenges, pain, and tragedy as 'it happened for you,' not 'it happened to you.' Everyone has had some form of pain in their life. You get to choose whether you will view experiences with blame, anger, and regret; hang on to your righteous indignation; play the victim; solicit sympathy; and say that you are damaged as a result. The truth is, you're right. You have every right to do so. You've been wronged, you've been hurt, and most people will take your side. You have every right to feel that way. Everyone will agree with you. Hang on to it for the rest of your life. You are right. Or you can choose a healthier perspective and believe that everything happens to chisel you into the most glorious, beautiful, fabulous being in life. Start believing you are here to find out how beautiful you can be. Every chiseling is creating even more beauty. The more you see and experience, the fuller you become. If we don't feel pain, we do not grow. Start viewing pain as opportunity. Recognize that when you are down, you are beginning to transform again. The chick wants to expand from its shell. The caterpillar blooms from a cramped space."

Marissa doesn't regret the abuse she endured, or her divorce. "I like myself 88 percent of the time. These things didn't happen *to* me; they happened *for* me. Sure, I went through a period of the blame-shame game and, despite all the accolades, struggled to feel good about myself. I felt like a piece of shiitake, sometimes hot shiitake. It was exhausting until I finally figured out who I was."

NOTHING CHANGES

Nothing changes until you change. When you do, everything changes, including your story.

For every action, there is an equal and opposite reaction. When you choose the guaranteed return and forego opportunity, you will enjoy certain benefits and give up others. The flipside is true as well. By choosing opportunity, what you give up in guarantees and security will be offset by a wild and uncertain ride. Passion, adventure, contribution, legacy, wealth, and freedom are a few of the priceless benefits.

There is no right or wrong answer. Each route has an equal amount of costs and benefits, and only you can decide how your story ends. If you have a dream (and I believe everyone does), taking the road less traveled toward opportunity surely means fear and uncertainty. It also means an opportunity to grow as a person. It means meeting people and going places you would never have otherwise. It means exhilaration, excitement, and a far more interesting ride. Who knows what may be around the next turn? Who knows how your story will end? One thing is sure: you won't go gently into that good night.

While money is a tool that holds a finite, measurable value, time is infinite and immeasurable. Money is replaceable. Time is a one-shot deal. You can always replace money. You cannot replace time. In this regard, time is infinitely more valuable than money.

Moments and opportunities are always moving and changing. Oftentimes you get one shot at them. If you delay making a difficult decision or choice, keep in mind that the choice is only yours to make temporarily. The fact that you have the freedom to make it is one of the most amazing things about life. The not-so-good news is that eventually those choices will be made for you. Fate, the universe, or a higher power will take over. When that happens, the results may not always be what you want or expect.

Hill advises, "Keep your own counsel when you begin to put into practice the principles described here by reaching your own decisions and following them. Take no one into your confidence, except the members of your mastermind group, and be very sure in your selection of this group that you choose only those who will be in complete sympathy and harmony with your purpose."

One of the fastest ways to achieve success in any endeavor is through consistent action. This is where the rubber meets the road and unseen forces take over. We'll discuss more about this in the chapter on the sixth sense.

THE BIG TAKEAWAY

To make the best possible decisions quickly, it's important to approach them from both sides of the brain. From an analytical, left-brained perspective, think of decision-making like a game of chess. If you make this move, what will your opponent likely do? Examine your options and look at all the possible outcomes several steps ahead. Think it through. From an emotional, right-brained perspective, how does it feel? Do you trust your intuition? Do you genuinely believe you deserve the outcome you are seeking?

WISDOM FROM THE ASIAN MASTERMIND

"I do small things. I try to do good things every day. If everyone does some good, think of what a good world this will be."

—Jackie Chan

"Your choices decide your fate. Take the time to make the right ones. If you make a mistake, that's fine; learn from it and don't make it again."

—Robert Kiyosaki

"Do not let circumstances control you. You change your circumstances."

—Jackie Chan

GROWTH EXERCISES

Develop a story about your dream...

filled with benefits and personal value that outweigh any
doubts you are having. This picture in your mind must be
so vivid and incredible that you cannot live without moving toward it and making it real. Utilize a combination of
meditation, visualization, self-talk, and a vision board to
help in this process. Any tools that reinforce the images of
your success will help overcome your excuses.

Take inventory.

1. Start by writing down three things you take for granted.

2. Don't overthink; just write. Look at your list. How
   does it make you feel?

3. Next, list three things you consider to be "mistakes"
   you have made in life, things you have given up on or
   have decided are better left in the past. Examine them.
   Were they really mistakes, or did you learn something
   valuable in the process?

4. Finally, take a minute to list at least three things you
   can do tomorrow to show gratitude or go the extra
   mile for the people or things you value in your life.

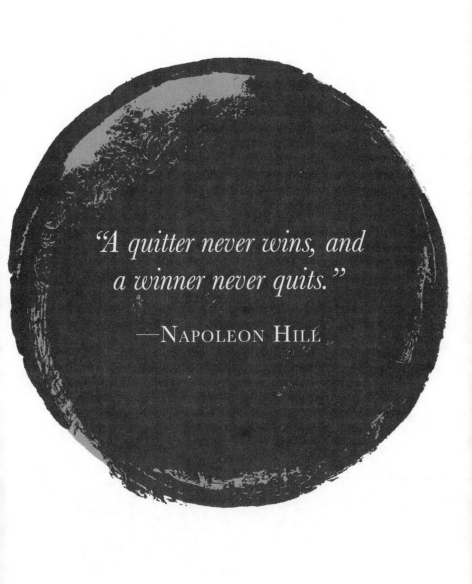

"A quitter never wins, and a winner never quits."

—NAPOLEON HILL

PERSISTENCE

The sustained effort necessary to induce faith

Have you ever been fired up with passion and burning desire, armed with a plan, only to stall out when obstacles get in the way or failure enters the picture? How do you scale that wall and stay on course?

Have you ever started out gangbusters but ran out of steam when it seemed as if reaching your goal would take a long time? Hello just about everyone who makes New Year's resolutions.

Have you ever faced your fears, kept going in the face of hurdles, and achieved victory? Have you walked through rivers of doubt and criticism to reach an achievement? Sure you have. And you have the tools to successfully battle obstacles life puts in your path. Persistence is the key to erasing fear, doubt, and negativity. It's also a requirement of achieving success.

"Most ideas need the breath of life injected into them through definite plans of immediate action," writes Hill.

Children often do not have this issue regarding planning. They try and try again, not letting the process of learning and failure stand in the way of what they want to accomplish.

You can learn a lot by watching kids. Ever seen one on an escalator when their parents aren't around? "Kid comes down, runs back up, and comes back down. Back up. Back down," notes Jaime Villalovos.

Children learn to walk and talk and eat and read, all by trial and error. As criticism, fears, and lessons about making mistakes are encountered, persistence falters. Be careful what you say to your children about their efforts and making mistakes. You want them to continue trying new things and not be afraid to make mistakes. Keep it light. Keep it simple.

"I love Jerry Seinfeld's rules for living," says writer Scott Williams. "Bust your rear end, pay attention, and fall in love. Give it all you've got; appreciate what you have and where you are at right now and fall in love. Not just romantic love. Love your parking space. Love your sandwich."

Pretty simple guidelines. Work hard—though he's not saying work long hours. Work smart and diligently when you are at work. Pay attention to your surroundings and the people around you. Take an active role in the moments that make up your day. Ask questions and be curious. I love the last one about falling in love. See how that works! Find the love in your heart for the little things. Be grateful for all that you have, and don't take things for granted.

Many people are raised to be practical and told their dreams are impossible, which makes following them easy to put off and quitting even easier when it seems like naysayers are right and the obstacles to our goals are insurmountable. My advice regarding the naysayers is to politely say, "Thank you for your opinion," and then walk away.

Everybody has an opinion. The problem is these opinions are often riddled with a lifetime of fears and doubts. It's important to the naysayer to bring other people down to an equal level to validate their decisions to remain where they are—usually, stuck in the mud.

WHATEVER'S EASIEST

It's human nature to walk the path of least resistance. Going with the flow makes good sense as it's a common strategy used throughout nature. For example, let's say you are on a raft floating on a river. You can work hard paddling upstream, going against the current and making little headway, or you can go with the flow and harness the power of the river to move you along. Going with the flow can bring slow and steady progress with almost no effort on your part. Planning helps too. Where you choose to enter the river can make all the difference.

I learned a valuable lesson from a local electrician a few years ago. In response to how we should finish a part of our project, doing it one way versus another, without a bit of hesitation he said, "Whatever's easiest." So simple it's brilliant! Use this philosophy when you are unsure how to proceed. It will allow you to get started and move forward without overthinking or working harder than necessary, things that often stop us in our tracks.

Intuition and vision are strong allies when aiming for your goals. Before you think it, you must be able to visualize it, but you also need to get across the finish line. That's where persistence comes in.

According to Hill, persistence is a state of mind, meaning it can be cultivated by anyone.

A person developing persistence will need a foundation that includes the following eight factors:

1. Definiteness of purpose

2. Desire

3. Self-reliance

4. Definiteness of plans

5. Accurate knowledge

6. Cooperation

7. Willpower

8. Habit

Notice that of the eight factors on the list, the only one that potentially includes outside sources is cooperation. All of them require your internal development. If you doubt your ability to develop any of these things, revisit the chapter on autosuggestion to increase your confidence. Then, try again.

Sometimes, looking to your past can help you with internal development. As we go through life, it can be difficult to see how far we've come or how much our background has shaped us. Evaluating where we've been can help us move forward, shedding what didn't work and embracing the rest. Your past can act as a touchstone to guide you.

When I interviewed billionaire Maurice "Maury" Gallagher, an airline entrepreneur and the current CEO and chairman of Allegiant Air, I noticed the impact his parents and early years had on him as he shared his stories with me. His parents instilled in him a strong work ethic and a persistent nature.

"My dad was one of seven children. He never went to college and became an engineer in the Navy. During World War II, he worked on several ships, some that sunk in the Atlantic, destroyed by German U-boats. He attended the Merchant Marine Academy and came out of the war as an officer. When he met my mother, a German farmer's daughter who'd grown up in Ohio, his parents didn't approve of the match because of religious differences. After her family refused to loan them money to marry, my mother married my dad anyway and stopped seeing her family. They were the type of people who showed up and took care of business, not letting anything keep them down for long. They endured hardships, family deaths, and moves made necessary by my dad's insurance salesman job. 'Talk is cheap' is something they often said that I taught my kids too."

Maury watched what his parents did, and it made an impression. "They got up, made lunches, went to work, took care of the kids, and they didn't complain."

His parents' example enabled him to forge ahead despite some false starts when he entered the working world. "I was into sports...an awkward kid who did my own thing with my parents' support. I thought I'd become an engineer like my dad, but a short time at the University of Illinois showed me that engineering wasn't what I'd thought it would be. I wasn't a math and science guy. Then, after college, I went to law school. That lasted three days. I quit, tired of school and flat broke." He spent the next few years figuring things out, working as a gopher for a road crew, helping build the I-5 freeway, going back to school to get his MBA, and working at a deli.

"I opened a pizza shop and discovered I had an entrepreneurial spirit. I'd had 19 jobs at that point," he said. "Eventually, I got a job as an accountant for a large firm and learned the language of business. Everyone should learn accounting. A few jobs later, I got a job with a leasing company that worked with the airline and railroad industry. I decided I wanted to get into the airline business."

But deciding and doing are not always the same. The industry was undergoing changes brought about by deregulation and Maury was a finance guy. Many people would have given up on the seemingly impossible dream, but Maury had learned the value of persistence from his parents. "Soon, I had two partners in an airline called West Air in Santa Rosa, California. It was a commuter airline with turboprop planes, feeding big city hubs. This first airline was a terrible business. We should have gone bankrupt a few times. I know—I was the finance guy. Somehow, we managed to keep it together for three or four years."

After a start like that, many people would have shifted focus, but not Maury. He started another airline called Pacific Express, which supported the new style of airline business called "hub and spoke," with large hubs in major cities. "We lost a bunch of money at first. The early eighties were a tough time due to inflation and interest rates, but we scraped together a few hundred thousand to get going and grew the business to what it was when we sold it for $300 million."

Many people would have kicked back at that point, called their lives a success, and retired. Instead, Maury found a new opportunity to get back into the airline business with a friend who owned a troubled airline. "I was their biggest creditor, so I made a bid and took over Allegiant Air. Then, 9/11 hit a few months later. Though I believe it's always best to start a business in tough economic times, we found ourselves in a world where airline fares shrank to less than half! We focused on leisure traffic and began flying out of Las Vegas with weekly scheduling instead of daily scheduling, and we kept everything based in Las Vegas—equipment, pilots, employees. It worked." The company that was valued at $4 million when Maury bought it grew into a billion-dollar company over the next 15 years, providing passengers with low-cost fares and no frills. "We kept things lean and efficient, looking for new ways to create opportunities."

"You must be persistent and consistent in what you do to create opportunities," says Julian Serrano, echoing Maury's philosophy. "Look for the opportunities."

Maybe you had a great opportunity and all the right ingredients, but things still didn't work out, and you find it hard to get started again. When this happens, figuring out what stalled you is the key to starting over and using a new approach.

Knowing what motivates you will also keep you on track and enable you to make choices when faced with opportunities or opposition.

"Success, to me, means the fulfillment of a goal. Working for yourself and having no boss is the American dream. Wealth is only a part of it," says Maury Gallagher, a man whose clarity and persistence helped him achieve great things despite many obstacles along the way.

Penney Ooi can easily identify times in her life that were difficult, when she faced tremendous obstacles to success. "Lots of things are difficult. It's different for everyone. Having a boss to boss you around is difficult. Not having money is difficult. Not having money to give to your kids is difficult. Seeing the disappointment of your parents is difficult. Comparing personal difficulties to business challenges is important because it teaches you what is truly difficult and puts things in perspective."

Hindsight and experience have a way of changing how we view life's challenges. As we age, we usually begin to see the bigger picture. "My parents sent me off into the unknown. I didn't think much about it when it was happening. I was too excited. It was only later that I realized what they must have been going through, what challenges they overcame to give me a chance at living a better life," Penney says.

She realized early on that her dreams were bigger than any frustration. "Ultimately, I want to have enough money to help my parents retire and then become No. 1 in my business. I make sure I am on the right track by regularly asking myself what I want to do in the next ten years. I look at how I am living my life and make sure I am making the most of my potential, that I am living 100 percent and doing something I am proud of. When I can pass along things that have worked for me to people I am coaching, I am happy. Every year we do a charity mission trip, taking the most successful partners to travel the world helping people. That motivates me like nothing else."

Still, for every story of personal triumph, we all can think of stories of failure. It can be tempting to cling to them when you go off the rails, but getting back on track is the only way to succeed. You have to act. When you stall, you must figure out why and begin again.

Maury Gallagher is a good example of this way of operating. "Because of the difficulties and regulations running a business in California, we moved to Las Vegas. Later, I got involved with ValuJet (which became AirTran in 1993), based in Atlanta. We developed a new electronic ticketing system. Before that, you had to have a paper ticket."

Maury also got into the telephone industry when the Internet boom happened and the industry was being deregulated. "I thought that because deregulation was good for the airline business, this might also work. Transition to wireless was also beginning to take hold, and things didn't work out in the end. I chalked it up to poor timing." He doesn't get that upset about adversity and challenges. "I always felt I'd find a way. Tough times reveal the people who have the chops to do the right thing."

Rock and Roll Fantasy Camp's David Fishof has always been inspired by his father, a Holocaust survivor. "My dad spent time in concentration camps, including Auschwitz and Buchenwald. He finally escaped from Sered' and made his way to Budapest, where he worked in a print shop, helping to save the lives of numerous people through the creation of false passports. He was a survivor."

Although David sometimes lacked faith in his endeavors and struggled with a tendency to let others' doubts affect him, his father's influence served him well, as he found ways around challenges, persistent to his core. "Persistence is like iron: it holds everything together."

David often thinks outside the box to achieve his goals and believes consistent follow-up is one of the most important aspects of persistence. "I once bought a ticket next to Slash at the Rock and Roll Hall of Fame dinner to talk to him about being in my camp." To get past gatekeepers, he recommends sending prospects a FedEx or UPS overnight package. "Most people open those themselves.

"Luck is all about hard work, working harder than other people are willing to do. You need to put the hours in. Some people show up at camp and feel they are great weekend musicians. I tell them they are good, but probably not as good as the pros (yet). Joe Walsh picks up his guitar five times a day and keeps his fingers moving. That's what makes him great," David says.

So, what makes us persistent sometimes, with some things, but not always, despite our desire to succeed?

Hill identifies the following signs of lack of persistence, stating, "Here, you will find the real enemies which stand between you and noteworthy achievements."

When you find yourself at a crossroads, stalled, review this list to see what area needs work.

SYMPTOMS OF LACK OF PERSISTENCE

- Failure to define exactly what you want
- Procrastination

- Lack of knowledge
- Indecision
- Blaming others
- Creating alibis and excuses
- Arrogance and self-satisfaction
- Indifference
- Believing unfavorable circumstances are unavoidable
- Lack of burning desire
- Quitting at the first sign of defeat
- Lack of organized plans
- Wishing instead of making it happen
- Neglecting to act on ideas and opportunities
- Accepting poverty instead of aiming for wealth
- Searching for shortcuts to riches
- Trying to get without giving
- Fear of criticism (see the six basic fears in "The Six Ghosts of Fear" chapter)

As you review these enemies of persistence, ask yourself if any influence your life. This might be difficult at first, but taking stock of our actions and decisions empowers us and gives us the information we need to make changes. Do not let pride stand in the way of your success.

Some people have difficulty believing they might be self-sabotaging with a poverty mentality. If you're one of them, think about Hill's words: "A poverty consciousness develops without the conscious application of habits favorable to it. The money consciousness must be created to order unless one was born with such a consciousness."

The fear of criticism and failure is often stronger than the desire for success. Hill offers the following advice for building momentum and developing persistence in the face of fears: "You may find it necessary to snap out of your mental inertia, moving slowly at first, but increasing your speed until you gain complete control over your will. Be persistent no matter how slowly you may have to move in the beginning. With persistence will come success."

Nitro Circus founder Gregg Godfrey relies on focus and passion to drive him forward. "If I'm not passionate about something, I can't focus."

He says most people fail because they quit. "It's hard. Being persistent takes effort. A lot of times people are delusional going in. Then, they give up too easily after a few setbacks. It all comes down to how many swings you're willing to take."

Sports apparel entrepreneur John Ashworth believes it is important to pick yourself up, dust yourself off, and get right back in the game when faced with setbacks. "The sun is going to come up tomorrow. The more I practice, the luckier I get," he says. Wise words.

Life is not a short sprint. It's a marathon that can span many decades. Running a successful marathon is best illustrated by the fabled race between the tortoise and the hare. Could a slow-moving reptile possibly outrun a rabbit on land? It depends. Over the long haul, both racers faced many obstacles and challenges.

When you race around at high speed, you encounter obstacles much faster, forcing you to react in an instant. This can lead to other problems: poor choices, running out of gas, mechanical failure, and devastating crashes that can delay you, set you back, or put you out of the race permanently.

Although slow and steady moves you forward at a much slower pace, you clearly see what's happening all around you. This clarity prepares you for challenges and gives you time to think about solutions. Once prepared, you execute your decisions and keep going, always moving forward slowly and steadily.

Baby steps are the best. One step to get started, then another after that, then another, moving decisively toward your goal, not waiting for life to create the conditions you need for success.

Jack Ma, the founder of Alibaba, is an expert on persistence and taking small steps that add up to big successes. As a young man, he regularly rode 70 miles on his bike to talk with, and learn English from, tourists staying at an international hotel in Hangzhou. He did this for nine years, giving tourists tours and practicing his English.

Later, when Jack was ready to attend college, he had to wait four years because Chinese entrance exams are held only once a year. But he persisted, finally earning a BA in English from Hangzhou Teacher's Institute.

After college, Jack was rejected by Harvard Business School ten times. He applied for 30 different jobs he did not get. But he remained persistent and kept moving forward, making his own breaks as he went.

Restaurateur Katsuya Uechi knew he wanted to own a restaurant from the time he first attended culinary school, but it took 20 years to make it happen. "I always knew it would happen. A friend who used to be a customer where I worked provided the money to open my first restaurant. He believed in me and invested $60,000." Katsuya paid him back $240,000 within two and a half years.

His first restaurant became very successful primarily because of the quality of the sushi. "Regular clients began coming in with many studio people. Movie stars and celebrities spread the word, and other patrons came to potentially see these people." But his success was due to more than good food. He never stopped improving, studying what customers liked. "After a while, I knew what people wanted and had their food and drinks ready for them when they sat down." Persistently pursuing his passion for presenting beautiful food and applying the input of his customers were key elements in his success.

Katsuya's story illustrates how breaks come not only from others but from ones we make for ourselves.

According to Hill, the only break anyone can afford to rely on is a self-made break. These come through the application of persistence. The starting point is definiteness of purpose.

How do you learn to open a beverage can with your foot? How do you believe you can do something that, at first, might seem impossible? "The message is, 'Here's a soda can, and I can do it,'" says motivational speaker Jessica Cox. "You can't get more definite than that." She laughs, but she's right.

One of Jessica's major strengths is that she doesn't see her situation as a challenge; rather, she views it as an opportunity.

According to Jessica, "Most people don't have a disability or need to think outside the box or come up with creative solutions. This is a disadvantage as they get older. They haven't developed this creative perspective based on a need all along."

Jessica inspires everyone who sees her. She encourages people to try something new and proves definiteness of purpose often overcomes seemingly impossible odds. The first time I saw her open a soda can with her feet, I went home and tried it, ending up with even more appreciation for Jessica. I realized that I was born with the same back and leg muscles as Jessica, but I never really used them. As a result, my back and legs began to cramp up. In business, I believe we are born with the muscles to be successful. We just have to learn to use them.

Musician Ray Parker Jr. sees no fallback either. Once he makes up his mind to do something, he doesn't let anything stop him. "Do plan A. Burn plan B. No fallback."

"A few people know from experience the soundness of persistence. They are the ones who have not accepted defeat as being anything more than temporary. They are the ones whose desires are so persistently applied that defeat is finally changed into victory. They see the punishment of defeat as an urge to greater effort," says Hill.

Highly sought-after DJ Steve Aoki started from ground zero and kept going, always believing deep down that he'd break through. "Back then, I was lucky to get $50 for a gig." He offered to work for a percentage of the door, promising to make money for clubs. "Give me your Tuesday or Thursday night," he said, knowing his partner would pack the place, drawing in crowds who'd see the flyers he distributed. "This got me in front of an audience of 40 or 50 people. I got better as I hosted more and more events like this, collecting records as I went. That helped me turn the next corner. When I started out, I was, on a scale of one to ten, a negative four! But I am a digger, good at finding great records and Spotify playlists. I learned how to DJ on the fly, before the doors were open, even when there were only a few people in the club who didn't really care anyway. It took time, but I got better as I went. I saw myself as a promoter, and pretty soon I was hosting parties on a regular basis."

Consistency was everything to Steve as he built his name and reputation. "People came to know me as the guy with a unique sound and style. I started making more money, had better turn-outs—200 here, 300 there, 500 for a downtown rave. Suddenly, I made my entire month's expenses in one week. Eventually, I paid off my credit card debt in cash; then I bought the first car I paid for myself, a Toyota Prius. My first car was actually a Ford Bronco, which was too big and obnoxious, so my mom bought me an Isuzu Rodeo. I paid for my Prius in cash that I brought to the dealership in a white paper bag! Next thing you know, I'm on my first magazine cover."

Steve is 40 now and says he's more inspired than ever, always on the lookout for things and people that inspire him to create and give back to the world in positive ways.

Breaking into creative endeavors like acting, music, or art can seem like an impossible battle. But every celebrity started out just like all of us, with only their raw talent and determination between them and success.

When Justin Chon first auditioned for roles, he stopped at nothing to get parts. His very first audition was for a T-Mobile commercial. "I put on a fake Asian accent. After, I felt as if I'd sold out with my stereotyped delivery. That's the one thing I never did again. After that, I went to an audition for a play called *Proof* at East West Players, an Asian-American theater company. I didn't have an audition scheduled, though I memorized the entire play before going in. I asked for only 30 seconds. They said no and told me that wasn't how it worked. But I waited the whole day and finally got 30 seconds with the director. She said I was too young for the role, but she loved my chutzpah. Coincidentally, there was a television show casting for a young Asian kid. The theater company suggested me for the role. I went. I was so nervous that I kept messing it up even though they were rooting for me. Ultimately, they said no, and I didn't get the part. But a few weeks later they hadn't filled the role, so I went back during an open casting call. They said, 'We've already said no to you," so I asked for 30 seconds. I'd practiced in between but still didn't get the part. A few months later, the same casting people called me in to audition for another small part in a different show. I went in and got it! It all came back to that first theater audition where I was so determined to get a shot that I wouldn't take no for an answer."

Justin's first movie role was in a horror film. "The film wasn't great, but I learned a lot about working with an ensemble and gained experience. That helped me get the part in *The Twilight Saga* movies."

At first, Justin felt his greatest adversity was being Asian. "Yeah, I got bullied. 'What's in the lunchbox? What's that smell? Why are you eating dog food? Racial slurs when I was at a drinking fountain when I was six. I didn't even know what they meant. When I was younger, I wanted to be white and live more like white people. Now, I value my Korean heritage. I draw from it. It gives me the best of both worlds, making me stronger as an adult."

At first, Justin felt he was typecast as nothing more than Asian. "Every audition, I was judged by the way I look. Casting directors had to imagine how I might fit into roles that weren't written for an Asian American. But now I see that what I thought of as my biggest obstacle was actually my greatest asset. It caused me to up my game and work on preparation. Because I didn't have as many audition opportunities, I needed to show up ready to roll as if I already got the part. That was my mindset, and it's stuck with me."

Shawn Villalovos's license plate says, "Don't Quit." He declares, "Persistence is everything! When I was younger, I read *Lincoln on Leadership*, a book about Abe Lincoln and how he overcame failure after failure—enough for a lifetime. Thirty years, decades, he failed, but he never quit, and he went on to become a world changer. I thought, *If he can do that, I can too.* Things like follow-up in business are essential. It's surprising how many people don't follow through. If people don't tell me to stop, I will continue to follow up with them. Only two people in my whole career got irritated. Most have thanked me for being there and continuing to follow up."

What about serious roadblocks? Yes, life can throw you curveballs. But you still have a choice. You control how you move forward. Embrace your excuses or come up with a new plan.

Actor Keanu Reeves, was born in Beirut, Lebanon. Of Chinese-Hawaiian heritage on his geologist father's side, Keanu translates from Hawaiian to English as "cool breeze over the mountains."

Despite being criticized as a "deadpan" actor, he's starred in a variety of roles and in 2013 directed his first feature film. A star for more than 25 years, he's still somewhat mysterious, rarely sitting for interviews and avoiding the celebrity hype and ferocious branding that many stars embrace today. He's not on social media and spends his time pursuing his passions. "I'm not looking for a red carpet to walk, and I'm not trying to have a celebrity footprint," he said in a rare interview. "I can see the appeal (of social media); it's just not to my taste."

He has overcome many misfortunes in his life before and after becoming famous. Despite each setback, he's kept pushing forward.

When he was five years old, his father abandoned his family. They kept in touch only sporadically for several years. "I spent my last vacation with him when I was 13 years old," Keanu said. "On our last day, we sat on the veranda and stared at the dark sky. He hardly said anything that evening. The next day he brought us to the airport. Then we didn't hear anything from him for ten years. No calls, no letters, nothing."

Keanu struggled with dyslexia throughout his school years. A self-described "okay student," he dropped out and never received a diploma. His dyslexia made reading scripts and memorizing lines challenging. Determined to not let this become an excuse for failure, he taught himself to manage his dyslexia and became an avid reader.

When he was 23, his best friend, River Phoenix, died of a drug overdose.

In 1999, his girlfriend, Jennifer Syme, became pregnant, but the child was stillborn in the eighth month, and it cost them their relationship. Eighteen months later, Jennifer was killed in an auto accident.

His younger sister battled leukemia for several years, entering remission in 1999. He supported her in many ways and started a charity to help other families dealing with cancer. "I have a private foundation that's been running for five or six years, and it helps aid a couple of children's hospitals and cancer research. I don't like to attach my name to it; I just let the foundation do what it does."

Known for living simply, Keanu bases his view of money and success on the freedom wealth provides—a perspective that perhaps is shaped by his losses. "It's a cliché that money doesn't buy you happiness. But it does buy you the freedom to live your life the way you want.

"Other people say, 'If you want to do what you want to do, you have to do this.' You know what? You don't. You don't."

Although he's always battled critics, many praise his acting as underrated and "natural." He takes his craft seriously, once studying Kung Fu for four months for a role, and is known for being low-key and one of the nicest people in Hollywood. He took huge pay cuts twice to get parts in films working with actors he admired. When negotiating his profit-sharing deal for the two follow-up films to his biggest hit film, *The Matrix*, Reeves opted to hand over an estimated 75 million in points to the franchise's special effects and costume design teams because he thought they deserved it. He also gave all the stuntmen Harley Davidson motorcycles.

Despite surviving several accidents, Keanu loves motorcycles so much that he started his own motorcycle company, ARCH Motorcycle. He's more than the face and money behind the company, taking an active role in design, testing, and administration. The project echoes the philosophy he said guides his life: "You're gonna die—make stuff."

He played bass in a band for several years after becoming famous for his acting, once opening for Bon Jovi.

Known for his kindness to others, his generosity, and his friendliness to everyone on set, he's found ways to turn life's misfortunes into inner strength and has thrived. "Grief changes shape, but it never ends," he said.

He seems to understand life's ephemeral, ever-changing nature, saying, "It's a particle, it's a wave," when asked how various events have shaped him.

Jaime Villalovos became sick almost overnight. "It was a shock. I came out of the shower, and my hair was falling out. I had a bald spot. The doctor discovered an autoimmune disorder and referred me to a rheumatologist, who prescribed medication I'll take for the rest of my life. He told me I couldn't have more children and advised me to get my eyes checked because my condition would ruin my eyes. He said I had lupus. No cause. No cure. I decided to pray and try anything I could to feel better. I began using affirmations. My goal was to be autoimmune disorder free. I read *Think and Grow Rich* and used the tools in it. Slowly, I started to improve, the more persistent I was with trying new things. I stopped medication and altered my diet as I continued to see and feel improvement. It was a difficult process, and I still had pain in my joints. But I kept going, believing if I continued long enough, I would beat this thing. I journaled a lot, followed my plan, applied philosophies from the book, and kept going. I never got off the horse and kept running my business and doing what I would normally do. You want to win, you don't stop."

Brad Lea says it is important to be willing to perform poorly at first. "To improve and become good at things, you need practice, repetition, and accountability. Sales is more about listening and asking the right questions, not about talking. Most people are afraid of rejection because they take it personally. In sales, it's not personal; it's part of the process. You need to deliver higher value than the money you are asking the client to pay for your product or service."

Chef and restaurateur Julian Serrano used to be afraid of failing. He shared a story about going to the park and there being many homeless people. Some of them used to be in his shoes and then they took a wrong turn and failed. The experience resulted in a new awareness for Julian, who says, "What is most important for success is consistency. The food, the staff, the atmosphere. It only takes one bad meal in a place you've gone to many times, and it might be the only thing you remember so you never come back. Consistency is essential."

Everything requires persistence. If I talk to someone and give them a lesson, they only become aware of the information. It's not until they do it over and over that they begin to develop. If you want to become good at anything or succeed, it requires persistence. Awareness plus application equals success.

Hill identifies the following steps that lead to the habit of persistence:

- A definite purpose backed by a burning desire for its fulfillment
- A definite plan expressed in continuous action
- A mind closed tightly against all negative and discouraging influences
- A friendly alliance with one or more persons who will encourage one to follow through with both plan and purpose

According to *Merriam-Webster*, the first definition of the word *action* is "a thing done." So simple. Three words that represent integrity and action. I love it!

Notice the definition of action does not include a promise to get things done. There are no assurances or grand declarations. Action is where the rubber meets the road. It's the roll-up-your-sleeves-and-get-your-hands-dirty stage. In the end, you have something done.

Actions speak louder than words and are the cornerstone of all achievement. Actions are the physical manifestation of pure truth. If you have doubts about someone or wonder whether to believe what they are saying, pay attention to what they do. Do their actions line up with their words? Are they selling BMWs yet driving a Chevy?

BE THE DIRECTOR

If I could impart a single piece of advice to you that would help you fulfill your dreams, achieve success, and change your life in an instant, it would be this: act now. Get moving on your plans and ideas. Pretend your life is a movie, filmed every day. You are the director. What does a director say when it's time to record? Action!

Take charge by creating the story of your life. It's happening every moment of every day. Be the director.

Be tenacious. Stay focused, be persistent, and never surrender, no matter what happens or how long it takes to succeed.

Be like a dog with a bone.

Tenacity works if your goal is simple or complex, immediate or long-term.

You might want to wake up earlier and spend five minutes stretching your body in the morning instead of hitting the snooze button. Or you might want to retire to Bora Bora.

To reach either goal, shift your focus from the target to the attitude and feelings you'll have once you finish. Commit to the idea of accomplishing things and focus on the pleasure you'll feel getting things done, and you will see positive results.

This small shift of focus (from the goal to the attitude) has massive potential to change your life. It's like that "magic pill" everyone is always looking for. So, listen up, and learn how to put it to work for you.

STAY FOCUSED

Our eyes focus and help us see where we are going. Wherever we point our eyes, we can potentially see whatever lies in our path—literally and figuratively.

Have you ever been looking directly at something you were looking for, yet didn't see it sitting in front of you? Have you ever searched in vain for an answer but only later realized it was staring you in the face the whole time?

Denial and fear can blind us to reality and make answers seem like golden eggs at an Easter egg hunt.

Focus, then, is more complicated than just concentrating.

Clarity (for goals, minds, and souls) requires more than focus itself. Usually, we focus our attention on where we are looking and at what we are viewing. But we can see things in our imagination or "mind's eye" too. We can see right through things or not see them at all.

Focus feels like it should require intense energy, though it is not difficult or strenuous. In fact, the more you relax and focus on the edges, on the attitude, the better your clarity will become. The easier it will be to eliminate distractions, carve out your plan, and get to it.

The ongoing effort, stress, or strain can produce results, but it's like using a hand plow instead of a tractor. It's harder and a lot less fun than learning to approach focus with a different mindset. You can set focus on fire with the right attitude.

Think of how a magnifying glass can focus the sun's energy. Although the sun is molten hot, on earth, it is not hot enough for things to burst into flames without warning. But if you take a magnifying glass and focus the sun's rays onto paper, twigs, and branches, you can start a fire. The lens focuses the sun's energy and magnifies its power to the point of ignition. You didn't have to force it. You just had to utilize the power of focus to transfer one form of energy to another.

BE PERSISTENT

According to the wisdom of Google, persistence is a "firm or obstinate continuance in a course of action in spite of difficulty or opposition."

Persistence is all about resolve and staying the course, no matter what curve balls life throws at you.

Imagine sailing in a boat through a frightening storm at sea. To reach your destination—the calm, turquoise waters of a tropical paradise—you must stay the course. If you turn back, you may never achieve your goal. In fact, you may go backward.

Being persistent doesn't mean making foolish choices that might put you in harm's way. Sometimes, it is best to turn around and regroup.

Olympic hockey player Hannah Brandt had to do this when she tried out several times for the national team and was rejected repeatedly until finally making it the last year she was eligible. "I tried out for the Olympic team in 2014 and didn't make it. The setback was a reminder to keep working hard toward the goal of getting on the team next time. But some people told me I should have made it, that it wasn't fair I hadn't." She could have taken the rejection and the words of others to heart, but instead she turned these setbacks into opportunities to grow. "I asked myself what I needed to do to make it next time. What was it going to take? What did I need to work on? I became determined to be a better, faster, stronger skater." She was passionate about what she does and willing to do whatever it took, and it paid off when she made the 2018 team.

To succeed at this level of sports, one has to be committed and persistent. "The team spent the three years leading up to Olympic year training and practicing in our own areas of the country, only coming together the Olympic year to prepare and focus on the Games. We practice three hours a day, spending an hour off the ice and another hour to two on ice," Hannah said.

Hannah's sister, Marissa, who played for Korea in the 2018 Olympics, had a different journey, though hers is also marked by dogged persistence. "The Korean coaching staff invited me to try out for the team, something I didn't think about because you have to be a Korean citizen to play for the team." After making the team, Marissa learned that the players from South Korea would be joined by the North Korean team. "Our 23-person team grew to 35. At first, we all felt a little hesitant and uncertain, but we managed to gel together quickly."

The schedule for athletes can be daunting. "We'd eat breakfast together, then have a team meeting, workout for two hours, eat lunch, have a little break, followed by two hours of ice time. After that, we'd have a motivation or goal session, then eat dinner," Marissa said.

She went back and forth between her two countries for three years to practice and prepare for the Games. "This was hard on my relationship, though my very supportive husband made it easy to decide to do it."

Marissa has the kind of persistence that lets nothing stand in her way, not even a setback like a concussion. "As a sophomore in high school, an injury made me miss a lot of school and hockey for a while. All I could think about was getting back into hockey for my teammates, to support them."

When you make a mistake or have a setback, examine it, learn from it, and then get back on the proverbial horse and ride, keeping a tenacious attitude at the forefront of all you do.

"Take care of yourself first and foremost, along with your family. Take care of business every day. You do something for 20 minutes a day, you're going to get good at it. Think long-term. Life is a struggle, and you will get knocked down. The key is getting back up again," says Maury Gallagher, Allegiant Air CEO.

You haven't failed until you give up trying. You haven't failed until you decide you have. Until your attitude changes.

NEVER SURRENDER

In the immortal words of Winston Churchill, facing death and destruction for the people of England during World War II, "We will never surrender." Given the incredible fear of the unknown during wartime, this powerful mantra united an entire country. They didn't know how they would prevail or even if they could. They knew only that they were determined to protect their ideals and people from harm. Their real power was in their belief.

Brad Lea handles rejection and the fear of it by refusing to acknowledge "no." "I keep looking. I am looking for people who are looking for me. When I was in high school, I was in wrestling and discovered I didn't like it. I recall being in a headlock under a guy's armpit. When I finally got him off me, I walked off and never looked back. I was on the basketball team briefly until I made a basket in the wrong goal and discovered I didn't like basketball either. Eventually, you will find things that resonate."

The power of "never surrender" can help you weather any storm and reach the paradise inherent in your goals.

When you adopt the mindset that you will never surrender until you've given everything you've got, you position yourself to win much of the time. This is true in competitions, in business, and in life. Winning often comes down to a fraction of a second, a final push with all you've got at the end of the race. Other times it is simply a matter of being present and in the game. As Woody Allen said, "Eighty percent of success is showing up."

Hill says, "Lack of persistence is one of the major causes of failure. Lack of persistence is a weakness common to the majority of men. It is a weakness which may be overcome by effort. The ease with which lack of persistence may be conquered will depend entirely upon the intensity of one's desire. The starting point of all achievement is desire."

Raja Dhaliwal agrees with Hill. "It's easy to be disciplined when there are tough times. It's more challenging to do it when you are successful. Reminding yourself over and over about the purpose of your life helps you remain disciplined."

If success can hinder desire and persistence, failure certainly can too, though it doesn't have to. There is always something to be gained from our mistakes. It's never a failure until you quit trying. Once you give up, you lose access to future opportunities to develop your skills. You lose valuable insights and perspectives that help you to see things in different ways. You miss the connection to the universal pipeline of support and resources.

When it comes to winning and losing, this is how I perceive what it means to fail.

Doing your best is a habit. Not showing up and quitting too soon is a habit. You have the power to choose.

Don't be a quitter. Get in the habit of playing to win. Develop the habit of being gracious and supportive of others when they win. Help them celebrate their success. In this case, everyone wins. In your heart, you will know you did your best and brought your "A game" to the table. You'll also know that there is room for improvement. A good dose of humility once in a while is essential to being a class act and a true competitor.

THE BIG TAKEAWAY

Never surrender.

WISDOM FROM THE ASIAN MASTERMIND

"Our greatest glory is not in never falling, but in rising every time we fall."

—Confucius

"You see figure skaters fall all the time. It's the way you pick yourself back up and keep going that makes you a champion."

—Michelle Kwan, Olympian and figure skater

"Throughout human history, in any great endeavor requiring the common effort of many nations and men and women everywhere, we have learned that it is only through seriousness of purpose and persistence that we ultimately carry the day. We might liken it to riding a bicycle. You stay upright and move forward so long as you keep up the momentum."

—Ban Ki-moon, South Korean diplomat

"You're only poor if you give up. The most important thing is that you did something. Most people only talk and dream of getting rich."

—Robert Kiyosaki

"When I got depressed, I watched Bruce Lee movies. I learned everything from Bruce Lee."

—Jackie Chan

"We will make it because we will never, never give up."

—Jack Ma

"You want to keep challenging yourself. And if you do well at it, great; if you fall on your face, you tried. But if you didn't try and put yourself out there, you'd never know."

—Lucy Liu

"All successes begin with self-discipline. It starts with you."

—Dwayne Johnson

"If you don't give up, you still have a chance. Giving up is the greatest failure."

—Jack Ma

"I work very hard. When people were sleeping, I was still training."

—Jackie Chan

"Success at anything will always come down to this: focus and effort. And we control both."

—Dwayne Johnson

"You can't look back; you have to keep looking forward."

—Lucy Liu

"Success isn't always about greatness; it's about consistency. Consistent hard work gains success. Greatness will come."

—Dwayne Johnson

"Without the strength to endure the crisis, one will not see the opportunity within; it is within the process of endurance that opportunity reveals itself."

—Chin-Ning Chu,
Chinese-American business consultant and
best-selling author in Asia and the Pacific Rim

"Let your actions do your talking for you."

—Dwayne Johnson

"Ideas are easy. Implementation is hard."

—Guy Kawasaki

"The road to success and greatness is always paved with consistent hard work. Outwork your competitors, be authentic, and above all else, chase your greatness."

—Dwayne Johnson

"Success to me is to laugh often and much and to know that at least one life has breathed easier because I have lived."

—Dr. Marissa Pei

GROWTH EXERCISES

Take a persistence inventory.

According to Hill, the following are the weaknesses that must be mastered by all who would accumulate riches:

- Failure to recognize and define clearly what one wants
- Procrastination
- Lack of interest in acquiring specialized knowledge
- Indecision
- Relying upon alibis
- Self-satisfaction
- Indifference
- Blaming others for one's mistakes
- Weakness of desire
- Quitting at the first sign of defeat
- Lack of an organized plan

- Not acting on ideas or grasping opportunities when presented
- Wishing instead of willing
- Compromising with poverty instead of aiming at riches
- Searching for shortcuts
- Fear

Score yourself on a scale of one to ten for each. Tackle the top two this month.

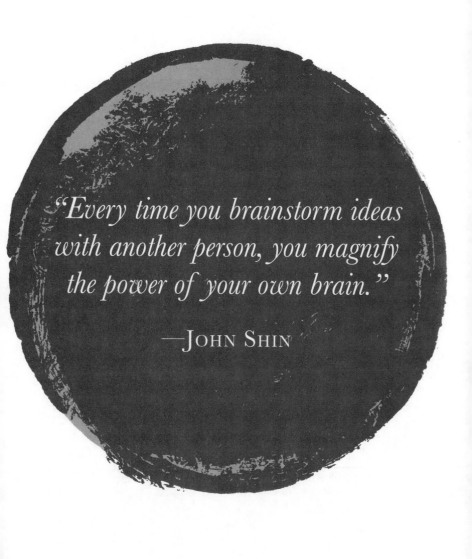

"*Every time you brainstorm ideas with another person, you magnify the power of your own brain.*"

—JOHN SHIN

POWER OF THE MASTERMIND

The driving force

S ynergy, as a term, didn't exist when Napoleon Hill wrote *Think and Grow Rich*, yet he devoted an entire chapter to the concept of synergy.

Hill believed the advantages of working with others were both economic and psychic in nature.

Let's say you are starting your own business as a financial advisor. You can attempt to learn and do everything yourself. This allows you to maintain complete control, though it might take a long time to reach your goals.

Nobody is good at everything, so attempting to do it all will likely lead to problems and frustration. You might be a financial professional yet lack bookkeeping and administrative skills. Eventually, you will run into trouble if you neglect your own accounting, especially when tax time rolls around. You could attempt to learn accounting and handle all your administrative duties, but then your client support efforts may suffer. What's the solution?

THE FAST TRACK TO SUCCESS

The fastest track to success is to leverage the power of the mastermind. Build a team that includes people who love to do things you dislike doing. Outsource everything that doesn't suit you so that you can stay focused on what you do best. Make sure everyone on your team understands the big picture and knows their roles. By taking this approach, you cover your bases and maximize your strengths and opportunities to grow your business.

The psychological advantage is that you will draw energy from your teammates because of their individual perspectives and take on things. Every time you brainstorm ideas with another person, you magnify the power of your own brain. It's as if there is a third mind created temporarily that takes both of your ideas and plugs them in together, forming hybrid thoughts that would never have been available to you individually. This is synergy, something I have experienced countless times.

Want to become better at your job or passion? Seek out the top people doing that in your area and contact them directly. Ask them to tell you the most important things they do every day that have led to their success. Brainstorm with them and take advantage of the synergy effect. Then, take their answers and apply them to your endeavors immediately. Find out what you can do to support them in their efforts and deliver value to them on a regular basis without any expectations. You have begun to build your mastermind, the group that puts you on the fast track to success.

Hill defines the mastermind as "the coordination of knowledge and effort, in the spirit of harmony, for the attainment of a definite purpose."

Merriam-Webster defines a mastermind as a person who supplies the directing or creative intelligence for a project.

"Power is organized and intelligently directed knowledge," says Hill. "Power is generated by the collective thought from a group of individuals."

The power Hill describes is the power gained from acquiring knowledge.

You may have felt this power if you've played team sports, collaborated with a team at work or in school, engaged in networking or team training, or taken part in any group activity.

Hill shares three sources of organized knowledge:

1. Infinite Intelligence

2. Accumulated experience

3. Experimentation and research

If power is achieved by accumulating all three types of knowledge, Hill points out that it would be difficult for one person to accomplish this alone. You must assemble a team of people to work with you to accelerate your learning.

Hill says, "Plans are inert and useless without sufficient power to translate them into action." This is where you'll gain the most from your chosen masterminds. You'll get more done quicker and benefit from others' experience, skills, and guidance. You'll reap economic and spiritual benefits. The whole is greater than the sum of its parts.

The opposite is also true. Disharmony and negativity can bring down a group that is not well thought out. Collective thought and energy work best if a team is in harmony, committed to achieving the same goals.

Some research suggests that women are better at forming mastermind groups that work and are more likely to enjoy working with others, reaching out to friends or colleagues for help more readily than men do.

Motivational speaker Jessica Cox brings positive energy with her into every situation. She gained much of her strength from her parents, who made a point of not pitying or coddling her. "They used to emphasize my uniqueness instead of focusing on my difference or disability." Her dad helped her develop a sense of confidence by talking about her as if she was a celebrity and someone special. "Everyone has some form of victim mentality when facing new and unfamiliar challenges. I was fortunate to have been surrounded by parents I considered my heroes and a close family that supported me in every possible way, assuring me I wasn't a victim and making me feel unique and special. They are my mastermind group.

"I didn't want to tap dance as a child. My mom encouraged me; then the dance teacher encouraged me. So I did it. But I wanted to be in the back row. Turned out there was no back row! We danced in a line. On stage, I couldn't even look at the audience. Then, we made the first few moves, and people applauded. This built my confidence. I found out when the next recital would be and set a new goal, a new challenge, to stretch myself. When you do that continuously, tremendous amounts of confidence build and build. Every time I push myself with dance, Tae Kwon Do, Girl Scouts, jumping off the high dive as a ten year old, it builds confidence."

Olympic hockey player Hannah Brandt credits the encouragement of one of her high school coaches for deciding to set the bar as high as she did. Although she'd dreamed as a child of being in the Olympics, by the time she was in high school she'd decided to play college hockey. "My coach encouraged me to dream bigger. I set my sights on the Olympics."

Her sister, Marissa, who played for the 2018 Korean hockey team, became the assistant captain and helped her teammates relax and accept the influx of North Korean players when they joined the South Korean team. "I reminded them to work together and suggested they put themselves in their shoes and focus on being a team."

Hannah says, "You have to know who you are and your role on the team. If you are a leader, you're expected to do certain things. A fourth liner may not be on the ice as much, so they'll need to support other players in other ways."

For Marissa, the people you surround yourself with are vitally important because, ultimately, they are a reflection of yourself. "The people you surround yourself with says much about you."

Hannah asks what she can learn or extract from the people around her. "Everyone has certain strengths. Knowing who to go to for certain things shortens your learning curve and helps build camaraderie." She, like many people, sees the fear of failure as a reason many people don't succeed. "But not reaching out to others for help when you need it holds a lot of people back too."

The sisters agreed that the coolest thing about the Olympics is getting to meet other athletes. They've learned that other people are needed at every stage of our journey through life, adding diversity, encouragement, and help along the way.

DJ Steve Aoki credits the people he met while earning his degrees in women's studies and sociology from University of California, Santa Barbara for changing the way he approached his studies. "Initially, I studied economics because I thought I might need it in the real world. I was bored out of my mind and didn't really get it. I got mostly Cs, maybe a B here and there, but I stuck with it to the end like a bad book. Fortunately, I needed to take other classes. For Sociology, I had the best, most inspiring teacher. She talked about cultures and struggles that people were going through. I saw an opportunity to make a difference.

"I started asking questions, looking at things differently. We as a people must speak up and go out when things aren't right. Politics are never going to be the first to change things. The people must have the presence and the power to change things. Then politics will react. Change is all about the group."

As a kid, Steve looked up to Bruce Lee. "Here was a guy the world loved, not just Asians. Why was there just one guy? It wasn't until college that I found myself in classes where the most powerful people in the room were the women. This fueled my passion and inspired me to go all in and become a double major. The chancellor of the school was talking about diminishing the ethnic studies departments, funneling money to filling in potholes or other irrelevant causes. We camped out in front of his office waiting for him to come in. Then, we created a bill of rights, keeping cultural programs going, the multicultural center open, and adding Native American studies. We wrote it with a Sharpie on the spot and got him to sign it. The experience was just as powerful as the stuff I was reading in my textbooks."

Steve's studies, classwork, and the groups he joined in school greatly influenced his music. "They were all linked. My decision to go to school was initially more of a pragmatic choice. In the end, it wasn't about using my education to go out and find a job in that field; it was about using my education to enrich my life. I absorbed the materials to make myself a better person. I never really thought of it like most entrepreneurs and startups in a suit-and-tie space. I lived in the moment and felt I was doing something meaningful that could positively affect people. My goals changed over time, but the meaning has stayed the same."

Steve said his dad has always been part of his mastermind group too. "My dad was like a superhero character to me. We had a lot of adventures together—ski trips, hot air ballooning, restaurant openings. We never sat down for weekly meetings. I had to observe and absorb things from my dad. I was happier doing my underground thing, and college grounded me even further. I made money and paid off all my dues and debts on my own without help from my dad. My father also did his own thing and didn't listen to his father either. Being independent helped me understand that I could manifest my own destiny, be in control. When my dad was dying, he let me know that he didn't have to worry about me anymore. Dad was an honest and unfiltered man and always said exactly what he thought and felt. This was a proud moment for me.

"If my dad had helped me financially, it would have been incredibly different. I probably would have had to help with some aspect of the restaurant business, not music. One of the most valuable things my dad did for me was to not help me. When he was around and saw me fall, he said, 'I am not going to pick you up. If you don't get up, you will get run over.' *Wow,* I thought. This is just the way he is, but it taught me that I needed to figure things out on my own. No self-pity. This was easier to absorb because my dad had a huge heart as well. He was just brutally honest with his advice."

Steve recalls spending time with his father in the hospital at the end of his life. His dad had hepatitis C, then diabetes, and cirrhosis of the liver. "We were alone, and I cried more than I ever had with my dad. We didn't speak. He couldn't, but it was one of the most emotionally connected moments with my dad, and I am so happy it happened so my dad could feel how much he meant to me."

He inherited his father's drive and relentless pursuit of adventure and success. "I always felt I had to prove something to my father. I got my heart from my mom. When I consider my life and the most supportive person in it, I think of my mother. I've made some radical decisions in my life that many parents might walk away from, but my mom stuck by me, never doubted me, and had such blind belief in my potential. She said, 'If this is what you really believe in, then let's take over the world together, one step at a time.' As a kid, you need your parents to reinforce your ideas. You can't always be a tough guy."

Actor Justin Chon agrees. "Being surrounded with successful, encouraging people lets me take a back seat to observe how other people operate and what they bring to the table. I believe in the power of your five best friends, being surrounded by like-minded people who have like-minded goals. It's about getting things accomplished in life, not just money. These people will be mentors and cheerleaders and guide you in your life.

"Continued study is important too," Justin says. "I take acting classes regularly. If I want to move into the big league with the pros, I have to know the basics and fundamentals, study past films, and build a strong foundation. I study people who are successful. Whatever they are doing, I should do as well. I am a big believer in habits. I listen to motivational speakers and to famous speeches like the ones Martin Luther King delivered. I pay attention to directors like Ava DuVernay, who told me, 'If your dream only includes yourself, it's not big enough.' I study confident people who clearly understand the how and why of acting. I also study systems that work like *Think and Grow Rich*, which gives me confidence. This all comes together when I say daily affirmations like 'I am' every day. What you think about you become. I break down my goals, macro to micro, into daily tasks. The more you practice, the more confident you get."

His dedication is paying off. Justin is directing now. His most recent film is *Gook*. He's directed over 40 shorts. "Practice. I did another film called *Man Up* that didn't do much but was a valuable learning experience."

It's not always easy being an Asian actor in a predominantly white Hollywood. "I went to a racist audition, and they wanted me to do a bogus Asian accent. I decided I wouldn't do it. I learned the power of 'no' that day. I don't have to do things I don't want to do. I went on to rant about it and talk about the experience. NBC asked me to write an op-ed about the experience. In the piece, I discussed the bigger problem, which is needing more Asian-American writers, producers, and directors, providing a bigger platform. The whole experience defined my purpose—to portray Asian Americans in a humanistic light."

Entrepreneur Kevin Harrington said the more successful he's become, the more mentors he's brought into his life. "I spend $150,000 a year on coaching and mentoring. That's how strongly I believe in the mastermind philosophy. Some people get to be successful and begin thinking they know everything. In my case, I'm always adding to my dream team."

Musician Ray Parker Jr. agrees. "Everyone should have a group of older and younger friends to bounce ideas off. A lot of times, everyone agrees, but there is usually one who says, 'I'm not sure.' There is a benefit from their input too. Maybe even more."

Shawn Villalovos's mastermind group has helped him succeed and has changed over time. "My major mentors came together because of similar thinking and ways of being. Faith, family, finances, and fun are part of my mastermind too. Fitness goes with fun because they usually involve something active. In the process, I build relationships with people that relate to these things, and we learn from each other. When I encounter someone who inspires me, I find a way to make them part of my life. I am confident I will find a way. Sometimes they work out, and other times the people turn out to not be what I expected. But the overall spirit is growth, so that's always there."

Shawn has learned the power in having a mastermind alliance and people surrounding you that can lift you up, helping you do things the right way. "The most impactful things were the stories I've read or heard. One guy was selling the wealthiest privately owned company in the world. By the time the deal was finished, the value of the company had increased dramatically. The buyer said, 'I'll pay more because it's worth more,' but the seller said, 'This is what we agreed to and shook on.' It wasn't about the money. He taught me that millions of dollars don't matter when it comes to integrity. Going the extra mile and character strength are essential core values of mine."

Lawrence Jackson, who played football for the University of Southern California, the Seattle Seahawks, and the Detroit Lions learned valuable success secrets from his parents. "I didn't grow up with a silver spoon in the inner city of Los Angeles. My dad was an Air Force accountant with an eye for details. Growing up, you couldn't skip a corner with a vacuum or broom. He instilled the value of excellence. My mom instilled love and nourishment and taught me how to love myself. I had asthma at a young age and was bullied, but my parents gave me a good sense of balance, so I made it through.

"Now, my mastermind circle is mostly gone. I read magazines and books about guys like Steve Jobs, Archimedes. I like to go back in time and see what I can learn from them. The blending of older thinkers into today's times fascinates me. I admire Warren Buffett and Alexander the Great, who turned paper into armor that turned a mortal wound into a flesh wound. The world holds a wealth of masterminds for those who seek their knowledge. Learning from them gives you a better picture of reality," Lawrence says.

Financial advisor Jaime Villalovos built a group of super-moms by inviting them on lunch dates. "I pick people who are strong in faith, family, fitness, and fun and get them together to talk. I cut out all negative associations with people who bring me down. Napoleon Hill talked about sitting at a conference table with his group and visualizing talking with them. I do that when I am deciding on whether or not to invite a new person into the group. My husband always gets a seat at the table. He is my partner in business and in life."

Jaime believes we are the sum of the five people closest to us. "Early on, I needed to make some changes. I became more aware of the gap, choices made along the way—similar upbringing—yet the choices were opposites along the way. Those people had to go. Stay on the horse, no excuses. This willingness to go it alone outside your comfort zone for a while is key. If you have big goals, you need to grow, a lot! Then you will be ready to connect with your mastermind group."

Gregg Godfrey's mastermind group has changed over the years. "In the beginning, it was a tight group of friends. We communicated quickly and worked fast. Now, within Nitro Circus, I work closely with my son and Colton BrockBank. As it's grown, the athletes have a lot of input. I believe the most damaging thing you can do is think you know it all.

"Getting into ESPN and big companies took a lot of convincing because there wasn't a large audience," Gregory says. "It was a struggle in the earlier days to sell what we were doing. Nitro got started because of the show *Jackass*. Johnny Knoxville was very supportive and loved what we were doing. The *Jackass* family was like ours, so we gelled. It took about six years to grow to a worldwide brand and go into different countries. I'm forever grateful to Knoxville and [Jeff] Tremaine. They were very fair and are still good friends."

The Rock and Roll Fantasy Camp, which gives people the chance to learn from and play with famous musicians, owes much of its success to the mastermind mentality. "It's more than just a music camp. Everyone gets something out of it. The rock stars love participating in the experience too. Being in a band is also about being on a team. The people who founded Oracle Software came to the camp and helped me realize there is a training and team-building aspect to what we do that goes beyond just playing music," said David Fishof, the camp's founder.

We might not all be in a position to go to a fantasy camp or rub elbows with the famous, but masterminds can come in many forms.

Restauranteur Katsuya Uechi recently hired a president to oversee the development and operation of his restaurants and recognizes the importance of hiring the right people. "In every new restaurant, the manager is the most important position. I trust them to hire the right people." He also has a head chef and works with his son, who has become the face of the business. Even though Katsuya was not initially a fan of working with partners, preferring to handle everything himself, he's now embraced them within his business.

Writer Scott Williams credits his wife as the No. 1 factor in his success. "I was succeeding at some level in things, making a living, managing an apartment building where I lived. My wife provided more permission to relax and live. This was the reminder I needed. She has always believed in me and said, 'You deserve this. You've worked hard your whole life and deserve this.' She forces me to step into a larger picture and shrink into a smaller person so I don't shadow others. I learned that the purpose of making it is to share it with others. My mom drilled it in me to live within my means. My wife helped me believe the more you make, the more you can share and help. The more you give, the more you get. The more generous in spirit, the friendlier you are, the more you get from people. That mindset comes from Catherine too. Sharing yourself and improving the lives of those around you is what it is all about."

Scott looks for people to join his mastermind group who will not shoot ideas down without providing a better idea. "In the writer's room for television, we utilize improv techniques. We don't say 'no,' we say 'yes,' and the best ideas seem to be the ones that people are the most scared to pitch. Be fearless and pitch ideas. Be prepared with many and pitch them one after another. Don't take things personally. Your mastermind should have your back either way."

Author George Chanos echoes this need for a mastermind alliance full of diversity, varied perspectives, intelligence, and integrity. "I'd look for qualities that have helped my success: character, commitment, compassion, and perseverance. Look for the same qualities you would for your partners or employees. Look for people who share the same value system. Essentially, ancient core values. Then, get them on the same page using brainstorming, encouraging them to give ideas without question or judgment. This gets them onboard. Don't eliminate anything up front. You do that later when you go through each idea and evaluate it."

George recalls a study done about luck. "A woman who considered herself unlucky and a man who thought he was lucky were both sent into a coffee shop independently. A $20 bill was placed on the floor near a businessman who was sitting there. She went in, didn't see it, ordered her coffee and left. He went in, picked it up, ordered his coffee then struck up a conversation with the businessman. You never know where opportunities will come from. Talking to a person may lead to connections that lead to connections. Don't go to the same places every day; put yourself in new situations to meet new people—that will lead to you becoming 'lucky.'"

Julian Serrano says you must like people. "The people who run my restaurants are my family and make the business. I talk with everybody in every restaurant to make sure they are all connected and happy. I feel if you make everyone feel important, they work harder for you and feel more invested. From the chefs to the waiters to the busboys, they all receive my consistent attention." In coming up with ideas for his menu, Serrano communicates and shares his ideas with the multiple chefs. Many times, he shares the idea from his head, and they make it. Sometimes Julian makes it first, and then all the chefs work it out together, adding more color, more greens, more flavor. Ultimately, he makes the final decision if it will be on the menu.

This starts from the moment he considers someone for a position in one of his restaurants. "I look first for honesty. If you are a good person, I want to hire you. I talk about a lot of different things to give myself a good feel for the person. I believe that my energy influences everyone around me. It is very important to me to bring positive energy to the business because my employees need to bring this to the customers."

When asked how he can improve and get better, Julian said, "Hire better chefs." Always thinking of the team.

He also loves to teach. "Providing opportunities, knowledge, and guidance to people who may want things but do not have the education or skills to make it happen is something I am committed to. I love being a mentor."

Mentorship is vital to Penney Ooi too. "Thinking bigger. Learning how to dream bigger. Vision. Now, I have 100 offices across the US and close to 500 franchises across the US and Canada. None of this would have been possible without networking. When I was starting off in business, my limited network made it tough at first. I had to start from square one and build."

She too had the benefit of a secure family support system that acted as her mastermind group during her formative years. "It was very important for me to show my parents I was a success. My mom borrowed the money to send me here. 'The most expensive daughter in the country,' she said. My dad always said I should get a job, learn from it, then start a business. But when things began to grow and I showed my parents all the people I was helping, it was reassuring. The best moment was when my parents knew they didn't have to worry about me anymore. I was self-sufficient."

When building new mastermind alliances, Penney says congruency is very important. "Seek out people who are compatible with you, and get together with them to build your alliance. Talk about family, life, and visions. People like you when you have something to offer. Relationships are give and take. Often, when you give first, it's easier to ask for help later."

Entrepreneur and new mom Steph Woo always ends every meeting and conversation with a question: "How can I help you?" By offering her knowledge, connections, and enthusiasm, she easily connects with like-minded people who make up her mastermind groups. At events, she strikes up conversations with speakers and leaders and those who have energy she enjoys. "I've learned not many people do that. My mentors liked my confidence." She also communicates her desire to work with them, learn from them, and help them. "They appreciate my direct approach."

Brad Lea credits his second wife for much of his success. "My first wife wasn't on board as much, and I was chasing success, out a lot, late nights. She was one of the naysayers who didn't support my efforts. My second wife is a supportive partner who is a great teammate. She stays home and takes care of the kids, one of the hardest jobs there is."

Brad also believes in expanding your network to include others outside your family and friends. "If you're starting out, reach out and put yourself in the circles you want to be in. I got a box for the Vegas Golden Knights hockey team. I look over, and there's a millionaire; over there is another. Now I know them and built a relationship with them. I want to be a millionaire, so I surrounded myself with them. Go to a country club and introduce yourself. Look them up, call them up, and say, 'Hi.' Start talking about what you do and ask if you can pick their brain for a minute. Get to talking, and next thing you know, they are your buddy. If they say 'no,' what did you lose? They weren't your buddy before anyway. Even a brief talk with experts matters in business. I am around them a lot, and it rubs off."

Sports apparel entrepreneur John Ashworth said something similar when we talked about the early days of his first company and the importance of masterminds. "When I was totally new to the clothing business, I didn't know the difference between a woven and a knit. I was honest and said, 'I don't know anything; please teach me.' Be open, be honest, and look at everyone as a teacher. Don't try to fake people out and pretend. Today I balance family and work by getting friends and family involved in the business. I want people to feel involved, secure, and have a piece of the company. When hiring people for Linksoul, I look for good, positive energy."

Dr. Marissa Pei dove even deeper into the power of the mastermind, equating your group, or lack of one, to your choices in life as they relate to fear. "Why do you think most people fail?" she asked. "Fear is certainly one reason. So is focusing on other people or on the media instead of yourself." She points out that who we surround ourselves with is largely a matter of choice and uses the term "blissipline" to describe when we use our power of choice to our advantage. "Are we calling people we should, or are we spending time with people who bring us down?"

Marissa said, "There's a saying 'Don't go to the tractor for milk.' In other words, some people keep going back to people who cannot or will not give them what they want. This saps their energy and keeps them wrapped up or stuck."

Examine your current inner circle (your mastermind group). How they have helped you succeed?

In business, my senior leaders must rank high on my list. In my personal life, I talk to my wife, Arlene, and my sister, a PhD who is knowledgeable on many subjects.

I love people. I love finding their unique qualities and character traits. I've found it only takes a bit of curiosity and encouragement to find jewels within everyone I meet. The key is to show some genuine interest.

Not sure how to show genuine interest in other people or about the world around you? Act like a child and use your natural curiosity skills. We all have an inner child. Get in touch with yours.

Offer a safe, confidential environment free of judgment when talking to others. You'd be surprised at what you can learn about people once trust and respect are established. This process is powerful because you both win. Your new acquaintance has an opportunity to reveal their authentic soul in a way they may not often do. People light up when asked about themselves and love telling an interested listener what they think. Being a good listener makes you more memorable to others. You reinforce your authentic self too when you find what resonates with you by opening yourself up to what others have to offer. By flexing your curiosity muscle, you learn more about people and life. Double win!

One of my favorite pastimes is learning—finding out about things I don't know, meeting people I've never met, and exercising my curiosity muscle daily.

EVEN THE PLAYING FIELD

Being teachable evens the playing field. When seasoned veterans in an organization are accessible to the rookies and willing to share their knowledge, everyone wins.

You might be successful and skilled, know what to say and how to say it, yet you can always learn something from people you meet. And it's not always skills and techniques. What skill rookies lack is made up for with enthusiasm. If you've been around the block a few times, a healthy dose of excitement might be a good thing to energize you. Hang out with newbies and millennials who can offer you a fresh perspective. Absorb some of their energy as if you were at the beach soaking up some sun.

When veteran performers are isolated from incoming rookies or, worse, threatened by them, a barrier exists. This separation discourages the sharing of information, ideas, and techniques that could otherwise make an organization stronger. The unspoken message is "We're too good, too important, and too busy to make time for you." As a result, the team suffers. Instead of working together, everyone forms their own island and operates in isolation, making it more difficult for everyone, including the more experienced members of the team, to succeed.

By helping rookies get stronger in less time, veterans help the workload spread more evenly across the ranks. The adage "Many hands make light work" applies to any project, team, or organization. Instead of carrying the entire load by themselves because that's how they've always done things, the old-timers benefit by focusing their energy and efforts on coaching and consulting. In the process, they become open to new perspectives that can help them expand their game.

WELCOME DISAGREEMENT

You may please some of the people some of the time, but you'll never satisfy all of them, ever. Accept this and embrace the power of this universal law. It feels good when people agree with us and accept what we do and say, not so good when they don't. Here is where I find opportunities to grow.

By welcoming disagreement or an alternative point of view, you create two opportunities to grow—education and expansion. Being open to new ideas and perspectives opens the door to your knowledge bank. Sometimes education comes when you least expect it from surprising sources. Always be ready to learn and allow your mind to grow.

Expansion happens when your mind is open, and you are willing to relax and let go a little, welcome a new point of view. By expanding your mind, you will be better able to appreciate greater diversity and alternative perspectives that exist in our world.

Welcome disagreement. By being tolerant and flexible with people, you may receive further input and develop a new take on things. Be grateful for these opportunities. Who knows— maybe it's time to let go of some old ideas and upgrade your operating system.

One of the most significant opportunities you have is leveraging the experience and success of others who have already accomplished the things you are trying to do. Instead of researching and gathering information on your own, why not copy success and become brilliant with the basics?

GREATER CONSISTENCY

At times, we can be our own worst enemy when it comes to mastering a new skill. For example, if you are new to sales and want to develop your presentation skills, you may be tempted to "wing it" instead of following a proven script given to all new salespeople in your company. It may feel as if the easier route to take is to figure things out on your own. Remember, the amount of energy it takes to create something from scratch is exponentially higher than the effort required to duplicate and improve an existing idea.

Focus your attention on the tried-and-true processes of the most successful salespeople in your company or industry. Model your business practices after theirs. Copy what they say, what they do, and how they do it. Seek out leaders and become a sponge, soaking up their wisdom. This investment of your time and attention will build your confidence faster, shave months off your learning curve, and be far less stressful than struggling on your own.

While your ego may feel doing it your own way is a more personalized way of going about it, the inconsistency of your presentation will likely yield mediocre results. Ultimately, you want to personalize your talk, but first you need to learn the script. It's proven, it works, and every top salesperson started there. Once it becomes ingrained in your mind, it will be easy and natural to add your own personal charm and make it your own.

My son is a fierce competitor. He loves to compete and is fueled by the possibilities in life. He is inspired by the achievements of others and views human triumphs as proof of what's possible. He has often said, "If they did it, so can I." He studies all the clues and instructions that already exist. Once he's educated himself, going one step further is easy because it's only one step. Instead of looking at challenges as insurmountable multi-step processes, Andrew breaks his tasks down into bite-sized pieces that are easier to accomplish. In this manner, he cuts through fear and mental static with an infectious can-do attitude.

Many people find it easier to do things by themselves because they are uncomfortable asking for help. Unfortunately, their results seldom match those who seek coaching. The go-it-alone types feel more stressed because they are always playing catch up, and they are usually the first ones to give up. Some people may feel like it's cheating to follow in the footsteps of others. To that, I say, "Learn from the best, first. Master the basics, then improve upon them." Be coachable!

If you have a hard time asking for help, remember that people love to talk about themselves and their accomplishments. Be humble. Someone who knows even a little more than you can provide the knowledge you do not have. If you still find it difficult to approach others for help, shift the focus to what your new knowledge might do for others. Aim to become an expert for people who will come behind you. By teaching others, you'll reinforce what you know and identify areas where you might need additional learning.

Once you develop your foundation by modeling what leaders do, you can personalize and improve upon their processes, making them your own. You can begin to develop new methods for doing things. In this way, you keep the horse in front of the cart. Always a good idea.

Something magical happens when you focus on others. The receiver enjoys your valuable service and the generous gift of your time. Your wisdom provides options and proven solutions based on experience. Your support helps them shoulder the load—sometimes literally. When you hop in and ride shotgun with another person, you help them make their way through unknown and unfamiliar territory.

When you serve others, everyone benefits (including you). By shifting attention away from yourself and your challenges, you gain immediate relief from stress and worry. Your mind is granted a reprieve from its primary job of self-protection.

Have you ever considered the importance of the company you keep and how the people in your life influence you? Your thoughts, decisions, and actions are affected by the opinions and input from the people closest to you. The way you feel, what you value and believe, your life in general—all are impacted by these people. My recommendation: Do some housekeeping with your relationships and make an honest assessment to see what's working and what is not.

We often confuse longevity and familiarity with depth and quality when it comes to friendships. You may be old friends with someone from high school and have decades of experience with them. This doesn't mean they are a healthy fit for you at this stage in your life if they continually hold you back or bring you down. When the chips are down, do they encourage you and help you move forward? Do their words match their actions?

Do they inspire you to be your best and provide opportunities to learn from their positive example?

This is important because the company you keep influences you as a person. It affects the way you act toward other people, friends, and family. Although it may be difficult to move in a different direction from certain people, especially family, it is possible to set some boundaries and limit the amount of time you spend with them.

THE BIG FIVE

The late Jim Rohn, a respected motivational and inspirational speaker, once said, "You are the average of the five people you spend the most time with." Take a minute to consider who these five people are in your life. You may refer to this group as your inner circle. If these five individuals are confident, successful, goal-driven people, there's a good chance you are too. It's like playing tennis with a tennis pro or practicing music with an accomplished musician. Keeping up with them is a healthy challenge for you, forcing you to up your game.

What if they are negative, cynical, and judgmental? Or they lack integrity and blame everyone around them for their situation? Although you may be a positive person at heart, with enough of this dark energy, it's only a matter of time before it begins to rub off. If one or more of the people you spend much of your time with falls into this category, it may be time to make some changes.

The company you keep also applies to your financial life. Your income and net worth are greatly influenced by your inner circle and the people you choose to help manage your financial affairs. It's easy to get caught up in struggle and strife when it comes to finances. Be careful about spending too much time with people who are always complaining about money. Misery loves company, and this is not the kind of company you want to keep.

THE BIG TAKEAWAY

The potential of your brain is magnified by harnessing the power of other great minds. When great minds are working together in concert to achieve an outcome, the whole is greater than the sum of its parts. This is known as synergy.

WISDOM FROM THE ASIAN MASTERMIND

"If you want to go somewhere, it is best to find someone who has already been there."

—Robert Kiyosaki

"Individually, we are one drop. Together, we are an ocean."

—Ryūnosuke Satoro, Japanese writer

"That was a major goal for me—to be able to reach and encourage more women, to encourage them to express themselves and be what they want to be. People get very trapped where they are."

—Vera Wang

"It doesn't matter if I failed. At least I passed the concept on to others. Even if I don't succeed, someone will succeed."

—Jack Ma

"Get a push—support from someone who believes in you. Sometimes you need a little bit of a push. I certainly do."

—Lucy Liu

"If we are a good team and know what we want to do, one of us can defeat ten of them."

—Jack Ma

"Intelligent people need a fool to lead them. When the team's all a bunch of scientists, it is best to have a peasant lead the way. His way of thinking is different. It's easier to win if you have people seeing things from different perspectives."

—Jack Ma

"Want to change the world? Upset the status quo? This takes more than run-of-the-mill relationships. You need to make people dream the same dream that you do."

—Guy Kawasaki

"I love directing. It has opened up my world so much. I love working with the crew on a different level. All of the pistons are firing—emotionally, communication, creativity, all of it."

—Lucy Liu

"The hardest thing sometimes (especially for men) is asking for help. I wish I did. You're never alone. Speak up."

—Dwayne Johnson

"There are a lot of things I can learn from Bill Gates. I can never be as rich, but one thing I can do better is to retire earlier. I think someday, and soon, I'll go back to teaching. This is something I think I can do much better than being CEO of Alibaba."

—Jack Ma
(who announced his retirement and return
to teaching as I was writing this book)

GROWTH EXERCISES

Develop your guiding principles.

Journal about the following questions:

1. How do you intend to live your life? What do you stand for?

2. What strengths and values make you different from others?

3. What are your unique attributes?

"*Love, romance, and sex are all emotions capable of driving men to heights of super achievement.*"

—NAPOLEON HILL

THE MYSTERY OF
SEX TRANSMUTATION

Redirecting your energy toward success

The word *sex* is magnetic. It immediately draws attention. Regardless of your race, gender, color, or creed, it's almost impossible to ignore. Why? According to Napoleon Hill, "Sexual desire is the most powerful of human desires. When driven by this desire, men develop keenness of imagination, courage, will-power, persistence, and creative ability unknown to them at other times."

I have updated some of Hill's 1937 statements for the 21st century to include both men and women in relation to this desire. It was a different era in 1937. The equality, expression, and understanding of the needs, wants, and desires of both sexes have come a long way.

This chapter in *Think and Grow Rich* gets a lot of attention. It's that word *sex* that draws people in, curious to know more. What's this "sex transmutation" thing all about? What does sex have to do with success?

Everyone seems to have their own take on what Hill was getting at, but I believe he was talking about refocusing energy—advising people to take their sexual energy and redirect it toward more productive pursuits. Your goals, projects, relationships, family, and whatever you are attempting to achieve will benefit.

When Hill talked about sexual energy, he noted that it comes in many forms and asked if you'd ever met someone who oozed a palpable sense of self-confidence and positive energy—the kind of person who just draws others to them. They have the rare, natural "it" factor. Hill believed anyone can develop themselves and offered a list of 21 elements that are important for achieving a magnetic personality:

- Good showmanship
- Harmony with self
- Definiteness of purpose
- Appropriateness of clothing
- Posture and carriage of the body
- Voice
- Sincerity of purpose
- Choice of language
- Poise
- A keen sense of humor
- Unselfishness
- Facial expression
- Positive thoughts
- Enthusiasm

- A sound body
- Imagination
- Tact
- Versatility
- Being a good listener
- The art of forceful (persuasive) communication
- Personal magnetism

It is worth noting that Hill specifically addressed men in this chapter. One could update his statements on sex for today to include anything that draws us away from our life's purpose and goals with addictive qualities (alcohol, drugs, and videogaming come to mind).

Ray Parker Jr. said, "I didn't do alcohol or drugs and wanted to keep a clear head. I funneled all that desire into the music instead."

According to George Chanos, "We're all involved in sales. Asking your wife to marry you. Asking your daughter to do something. Most successful people in the world are in sales. You are always selling yourself, and you absolutely can develop the talent, like anything."

Penney Ooi supported George's philosophy about sales when she said, "First, everything is sales. You must sell yourself in every area of your life. It's how you bring value to other people by seeing beyond what they can see."

Hill shared other examples of how someone's personal magnetism expresses sexual energy: the handshake, the tone of voice, posture and carriage of the body, vibrations of thought, body adornment.

Transmutation, Hill explained, is changing a lower form of energy into a higher form. By higher form, Hill was referring to more creative, imaginative, and intuitive types.

Energy equals feelings, and Hill identified three types of feelings: emotion, sensation, and intuition.

Hill felt that the sex drive in man encompasses all of these powerful, controlling emotions. Some people go to great lengths, risking everything they have, for sex. He believed this sexual energy can and should be redirected toward professional and financial success.

Tap into your emotions, Hill advised. "Love, romance, and sex are all emotions capable of driving men to heights of super achievement. Love is the emotion which serves as a safety valve and ensures balance, poise, and constructive effort. When combined, these three emotions may lift one to an altitude of a genius."

When there is trouble with our partner or in our romantic life, we can easily be knocked off balance and distracted from our constructive efforts. Fights and arguments can be draining. Until we resolve them and repair the damage, we suffer a major leak in our energy pipeline.

Allegiant Air CEO Maury Gallagher said, "Keep things in perspective. If you want to get divorced, throw all your efforts and energy into your business at the sacrifice of your family. Otherwise, understand that you need to invest time and energy into both with the benefit of an understanding and supportive spouse."

A simple yet powerful strategy for moving past hurt feelings and anger is to use the expression "just like me." It is a powerful reminder that people are all very much the same and whatever your partner did or didn't do that has you all wound up is something you've probably done at one time or another.

We all need love. We all need acceptance. Everyone makes mistakes. Whenever you disagree or get angry at a loved one, take a break, disengage, and consider what they've done. Then add "just like me" at the end. For example, they broke plans with you at the last minute. Unless you're perfect, you have likely made a similar move in your past. Just like me.

Hill said geniuses harness sex, love, and music as outlets and to open the mind to receiving inspiration. He believed the conscious operates entirely through the first faculty of the sixth sense (which we'll discuss in the chapter devoted to it), so opening ourselves to it is key to the practice of the principles.

"The human mind responds to stimulation!" Hill said. "People are influenced in their actions, not by reason so much as by feelings. The creative faculty of the mind is set into action entirely by emotions and not by cold reason."

Encourage the presence of these emotions as the dominating thoughts in one's mind and discourage the presence of all the destructive emotions.

When discussing this chapter, Dr. Marissa Pei suggested asking yourself if you are expending energy on activities that do not further your advancement toward your goals and dreams.

"Sometimes people divert their attention to the media, for example, for thrills and entertainment. They stop dreaming and get locked into one career and stick with it for the rest of their lives. Instead, take back some of that time and begin dreaming again. Spend an hour or two a week meditating, visualizing, and dreaming."

Hill said, "The mind is a creature of habit. It thrives upon the dominating thoughts fed it. Through the faculty of willpower, one may discourage the presence of any emotion and encourage the presence of any other. Control of the mind, through the power of will, is not difficult. Control comes from persistence and habit. The secret of control lies in understanding the process of transmutation. When any negative emotion presents itself in one's mind, it can be transmuted into a positive, or constructive emotion through the simple procedure of changing one's thoughts."

Hill believed no one is happy or complete without the modifying influence of the right partner.

"The man who does not recognize this important truth deprives himself of the power which has done more to help men achieve success than all other forces combined."

We discussed this in the previous chapter when we examined the power of the mastermind.

In the "Love Study," researchers wanted to show how one's thoughts affect another person. Couples were separated by steel walls and hooked up to an electroencephalogram (EEG). The results showed that when concentrating on sending an intention to each other, people with close relationships or who were experienced meditators could synchronize their brainwaves, no matter the distance between them.[18]

Next, we'll move deeper, into our subconscious mind, revealing the sometimes-hidden wealth of possibilities that lie within the part of our brain responsible for 95 percent of our thoughts.

THE BIG TAKEAWAY

Hill points out the desire for sex, love, and romance is inborn and natural. Sex and romance are forms of energies. Applying and directing our sexual urges enriches the mind, body, spirit, and bank accounts.

WISDOM FROM THE ASIAN MASTERMIND

"Mastering yourself is true power."

—Lao Tzu

"He who attends to his greater self becomes a great man, and he who attends to his smaller self becomes a small man."

—Mencius,
a Chinese philosopher, often described as
the "second Sage" after only Confucius himself

"When I let go of what I am, I become what I might be."

—Lao Tzu

"Be truthful about your emotions, and use your mind and emotions in your favor, not against yourself."

—Robert Kiyosaki

"He who conquers others is strong; he who conquers himself is mighty."

—Lao Tzu

"Defy the crowd. The crowd isn't always wise. It can also lead you down a path of silliness, sub-optimal choices, and utter destruction. Enchantment is as necessary for people to diverge from a crowd as it is to get people to join one."

—Guy Kawasaki

"He who knows others is wise. He who knows himself is enlightened."

—Lao Tzu

GROWTH EXERCISES

Journal about sex. About energy and drive. About your thoughts on the theory of sex transmutation. Google "sex transmutation exercises" and schedule a few that interest you. Open yourself to energy—yours and other people's. Try something new. Talk with your partner. Through it all, remember that sex is a powerful human drive that produces effects all its own. Harness it. Have fun with this. Take the whole month.

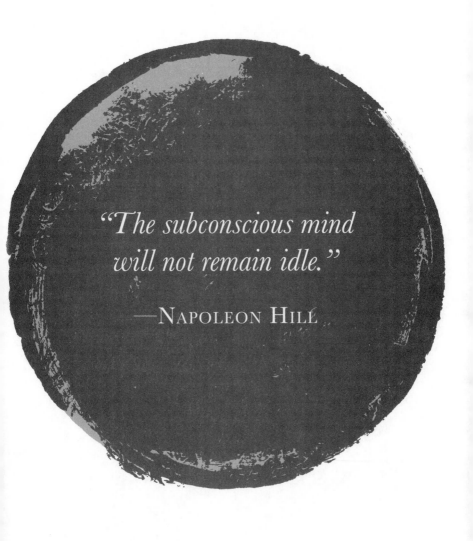

"*The subconscious mind will not remain idle.*"

—NAPOLEON HILL

THE SUBCONSCIOUS MIND

The connecting link

Have you ever overreacted to something and wondered where those emotions came from? Or immediately judged someone and wondered why? Have you ever had a dream or a great idea and not recalled it later?

These are illustrations of when your subconscious was in control and your conscious mind was at rest. Hill writes, "The subconscious mind consists of a field of consciousness in which every impulse of thought that reaches the conscious mind through any of the five senses is classified and recorded and from which thoughts may be recalled or withdrawn as letters may be taken from the filing cabinet. The subconscious acts first on the dominating desires which have been mixed with emotional feeling, such as faith. You cannot entirely control your subconscious mind, but you can voluntarily hand over to it any plan, desire, or purpose which you wish transformed into concrete form."

Because of the enormous potential of the subconscious mind, it makes sense that you would want to enhance and develop its power through yoga, meditation, self-talk, and reading. I made a point of asking my interviewees during the research phase of this book: "How do you develop your unconscious mind?"

Author and businessman George Chanos feeds his mind by reading and researching. Right now, he's preparing for a book he's writing. "I'm fascinated by the notion that we can build neural pathways in our brains with self-talk and the information we feed it. Our brain receives millions of bits of information every second. Our conscious brain can only process about 16 to 50 bits per second. The vast majority is going into our subconscious. By programming your mind, thinking positive thoughts, reinforcing yourself over time, these pathways positively flow into the subconscious. Negative pathways work the same way. So moving information down these positive pathways automatically by your self-talk and programming makes sense. Much of what we do becomes automatic over time, based on everything we've done and experienced in the past. My baby steps have turned into powerful strides. Anyone can do this by controlling their thoughts, developing their brain, making learning a lifelong thing, overcoming fears, developing courage, having commitment and resolve, then moving persistently toward their objectives."

George said, "Everything Hill talks about in *Think and Grow Rich* is still true today. Staying mentally and physically healthy and allowing yourself quiet time to think and plan are vital to the success of the tools in the book. Trying new things is good too. My wife has gotten me into yoga."

One of my daily routines is to picture in my mind the next day before I go to bed and spend 15 to 20 minutes visualizing the coming week on Sunday evening. I see things, meetings, achievements as already happening and often feel déjà vu in client meetings and when I give talks because I already did this talk; I did it in my head.

Actor Justin Chon is a big visualization guy too. Even if he misses the mark, he adjusts his vision and pictures to fit his new plan of attack. "I'm happy with where this has gotten me. If I don't hit my goals, it's okay. I no longer spend much time on negative thoughts when that happens. I just keep trying."

Visualization works exceptionally well for athletes. Richard Suinn, a sports psychologist, studied downhill skiers and found when he asked them to visualize skiing, electrical indicators from the brain were equal to the signals sent when actually skiing.

Guang Yue, an exercise physiologist, asked volunteers to imagine flexing their biceps every day for a few weeks. Afterward, the volunteers showed a 13.5 percent increase in bicep strength. Another study, at the University of Chicago, improved the basketball team's shooting by 23 percent just by visualizing making shots as part of their training. A French study showed long jumpers who envisioned their jumps improved by 45 percent.

Olympic hockey players Hannah and Marissa Brandt use mental training, imagery, and visualization to practice moves and shots in their minds to prepare for games, running through scenarios and unexpected occurrences that could come up. The day of a game, Hannah takes a half hour to close her eyes, imagine plays in the game, listen to some music, relax, and shut down her electronics. "In my mind, I might see the gold medal game going to a shootout. I visualize my shot, the moves I'll make, and the goalie's actions," Hannah said. This visualization allows her to tap into her subconscious mind, feeding it images of actions she wishes to take later, on the ice.

Marissa does this too, spending quiet time before a game, without distractions, calming her mind, consciously controlling what inputs she allows during this crucial time.

Your conscious acts like a gatekeeper, controlling what thoughts it feeds to your subconscious. Hill's principles are tools you can use to consciously influence your subconscious mind. The tools are effective and extraordinarily powerful when dealing with negative thoughts.

Raja Dhaliwal agrees. "To boost the subconscious mind, it is essential to do things repetitively for a period of time. It's also important to note that most of what we do is subconscious and to be careful what we are programming into our subconscious. You need to do things consciously to feed your subconscious mind."

If you're always worried about money and poverty or failure and pain, negative thoughts will overrun your subconscious mind. If you focus instead on abundance, your subconscious will focus its attention on positive outcomes and solutions—thus the saying "What you think about, you bring about," and Hill's core statement, "What your mind can conceive and believe, it can achieve."

"The subconscious mind may be voluntarily directed only through habit fed by faith. Be patient. Be persistent. The subconscious mind will not remain idle. If you fail to plant desires in your subconscious mind, it will feed upon the thoughts which reach it as the result of your neglect," said Hill.

Dr. Marissa Pei believes you should acknowledge the voices in your head and put them in their place when necessary. "We all have several voices like 'the critic,' 'the protector,' 'the brat,' 'fun,' and 'sad.' Have fun with them. Name them. My critic is named 'Rose,' which was my mother's name."

Marissa talks to her critic at times and lets her know that it's time to relax and shut up. "Acknowledge the selfish little brat, then move on. I allow the sad voice to express itself from time to time because it's healthy to let it out. Know that none of the voices individually can succeed on its own. It's is a combination of all of them that creates the balanced, centered self. Only the balanced, centered self can think and grow rich."

Dr. Pei echoes Hill's sentiments, for he pointed out that the subconscious mind is more susceptible to influence by impulses of thought mixed with feeling or emotion than by those originating solely in the reasoning portion of the mind. For this reason, it is important to examine your emotions, for they hold the potential to lift you up or tear you down.

In *Think and Grow Rich*, Hill breaks down positive and negative emotions this way:

THE SEVEN MAJOR POSITIVE EMOTIONS

- Desire
- Faith
- Love

- Sex
- Enthusiasm
- Romance
- Hope

THE SEVEN MAJOR NEGATIVE EMOTIONS

- Fear
- Jealousy
- Hatred
- Revenge
- Greed
- Superstition
- Anger

Positive and negative emotions cannot occupy the mind at the same time. One or the other must dominate. It is your responsibility to make sure positive emotions constitute the dominating influence of your mind.

Justin Chon recalls hanging out with one of the only other Asian kids he went to school with, Scott Nakamichi. "We were watching an HBO comedy special, and Scott said, 'That's going to be me one day.' Before I even thought about it, I said, 'That's impossible!' I went right to the negative, shocked that Scott could even have such an outrageous belief in himself. That was a big moment for me, recognizing how much power my sub-conscious had over my expectations and, therefore, my actions. Maybe you need a particular sort of naivete to believe in big, impossible dreams. You need to get past the hump of thinking your dreams are not possible."

Focusing only on positive emotions and thoughts to bring about positive changes in your life is the basis of the Law of Attraction, a principle Napoleon Hill taught years before it was popularized by Rhonda Byrne in her book and movie titled *The Secret*.

Thought equals creation. If your thoughts are attached to powerful emotions (good or bad), that speeds creation. Your life is in your hands. You can consciously choose your thoughts and change your life. There is no such thing as a hopeless situation. Every circumstance of your life can change.

Hill puts it this way: "Everything which man creates begins in the form of a thought impulse. Man can create nothing which he does not first conceive in thought."

SOME SCIENCE

Science backs up even the most New Age-sounding nuggets contained in *Think and Grow Rich*, though new research has changed what we know of the brain and how the subconscious and conscious work.

Our brains use 5 percent of their capacity for memory. The subconscious mind controls the remaining 95 percent. Our subconscious mind is always actively working, whether our conscious mind knows it or not.

Your subconscious mind is a massive memory bank that has stored and classified everything that has ever happened to you.

By the time you turn 21, you've received and saved the equivalent of 32 *Encyclopedia Britannica* books.

According to the neuro-linguistic programming (NLP) model, over two million bits of data bombard humans every second. The subconscious filters through that because the conscious mind can take care of only so many things at the same time.

The conscious mind speaks in words. The subconscious mind speaks in images, feelings, and metaphors. It responds to visualizing and communicates back with images and metaphors in dreams, hunches, and song lyrics that seem to pop into your head out of nowhere.

Our subconscious controls our breathing. We don't even think about it. It comes naturally to us. Ancient Asian medicine recognizes the importance of breath and says the breath is the link between the conscious and subconscious mind. When we bring breath into the conscious mind, we become more aware of thoughts in the subconscious. Breathing to create mindfulness is one of the founding principles of meditation and yoga.

Dr. Marissa Pei practices Balance Tai Qigong, a moving meditation that promotes inner peace, though her reasons are twofold. "Part of my goal is to change planetary consciousness toward peace, prosperity, joy, balance, creativity, and love." And Marissa knows the place to start is with oneself.

Data from epigenetics studies prove our genes do not necessarily dictate our intrinsic qualities. It isn't solely our genes that determines who we are. Our subconscious plays a huge role in our reality, responding only to its environment and the data it receives.

Studies also show that the brain prepares for action over a third of a second before we consciously decide to act. It feels as if we are making a conscious decision, but our subconscious mind has decided for us before our conscious mind can act.

It is easier to access our subconscious when we're relaxed and give it space. Many of the martial arts teach practitioners to reach a state of still communication with the subconscious as an important part of their skill-building.

Meditation works this way too, allowing you to reach the mind through autosuggestion, flooding it with quiet or calm and positive thoughts.

"Although the practice of meditation is associated with a sense of peacefulness and physical relaxation, practitioners have long claimed that meditation also provides cognitive and psychological benefits that persist throughout the day," says Sara Lazar, a faculty member in the Psychiatric Neuroimaging Research Program at Massachusetts General Hospital and an assistant professor of psychology at Harvard Medical School.

If you've never meditated, I encourage you to take up the practice. Some people find a similar effect when they walk or practice yoga. The important thing is to clear your mind so you can expand the space needed to hear and feed your subconscious. We'll talk more about meditation in this chapter's exercise section.

If you doubt your ability to create anything in your world, allowing negative thoughts to impact your subconscious, you will have a difficult time growing the faith your subconscious needs to support your success and realize your goals.

If yoga and meditation are not your thing, try daily affirmations.

The subconscious knows no time. There is no past or future. There is only now. Use affirmations with the word *now* to help align your subconscious to work with your conscious in the moment.

Actor Justin Chon is a big believer in affirmations. "What you tell yourself becomes your reality. I live it, asking my subconscious if what it is saying will bring me closer to my goal or not. Clarity of what you are trying to do is key. Books like *Think and Grow Rich* help. I love reading the wisdom of successful people with common traits. Why wouldn't you pay attention to those? They are proven to work."

Affirmations are a great way to begin a habit of uplifting self-talk by feeding your subconscious with positivity. You don't have to believe to try it and see the results for yourself (which will make believing in and implementing this into your life easier). Many people have a basis for this practice—prayer. But you do not have to be religious to do this.

Hill equated this process to prayer, saying, "If you pray for a thing, but fear as you pray that you may not receive it, or that your prayer will not be acted upon by Infinite Knowledge, your prayer will have been in vain. The subconscious mind is the intermediary which translates one's prayers into terms which Infinite Intelligence can recognize, presents the message, and brings back the answer in the form of a definite plan or idea for procuring the object of the prayer. Understand this principle, and you will know why mere words read from a book cannot, and will never, serve as an agency of communication between the mind of man and Infinite Intelligence." In other words, reading about ideas seldom translates into action.

Infinite Intelligence is the term Napoleon Hill coined to describe the source of ideas. Some might call it God, the universe, or a higher power.

Here are some simple affirmations for you to start with:

- My thoughts are under control.
- My thoughts are positive and empowering.
- Right now, I am connected with my higher self.
- I am creative and wise and open to new ideas and experiences.
- I believe I can do anything.
- Right now, I'm developing new and positive habits.
- My ability to conquer my challenges is limitless.
- My potential to succeed is infinite.
- I have the power to change my life by changing my thoughts.

Repeat your chosen positive affirmations daily to boost your self-esteem and deliver messages to your subconscious. Make sure you say or write these in the present tense. Don't wish you had a boat. Say, "I have a boat" and visualize it, feeling the emotions that come with owning one. Some people like to place a hand over their heart as they recite their affirmations. Doing this when you are looking in the mirror and getting ready for your day is a great way to kick things off.

Motivational speaker Jessica Cox talks to herself when faced with a difficult situation, using direct and straightforward affirmations. "Most of my self-talk is positive: 'You can do it. Keep going. It's easy. You've got this.' Things like that keep me super focused. I say, 'Okay, I'm going to do it,' and if it's something I want, I become almost obsessed."

Burning desire comes into play when you refuse to stop or limit yourself in any way. Football player Lawrence Jackson adds: "If you are satisfied with what you have, then you have succeeded. With life, there are no limits. Just because you have a nice car doesn't mean you are successful. Do you own it outright? The car, the house—they can be taken away. What's real is the value you create and the value you capture and what makes you happy. If you want to keep going, then keep going."

Think and Grow Rich helped Penney Ooi understand goal-setting and taught her to write her goals down. "It was like I found the key to making the Law of Attraction work for me. Having a dream and talking to yourself somehow helps the skills you need to develop and evolve along the way. Your mind is like fertile soil, and what you put into your mind is the seeds. You must be careful about what seeds you plant. When you fill your subconscious mind with positive things, it senses infinite possibilities. It's important to reinforce the positive by surrounding yourself with like-minded people and similar ideas and to feed others' minds with possibilities too. This helps us all grow."

The thoughts you think lead to the words you say. Every word that comes out of your mouth is connected to some part of you. It may be something you heard, viewed, read, or experienced somewhere along the line. You may have formed a firm belief about which you are passionate, or it might be something trivial that means little or nothing. Either way, think before you speak.

"Calmness of mind is one of the beautiful jewels of wisdom. It is the result of long and patient effort and self-control," writes James Allen in his book *As a Man Thinketh*.

"The possibilities of creative effort connected with the subconscious mind are stupendous and imponderable," said Hill.

Diving deeper into the process of controlling your thoughts, Hill devoted the next chapter to the brain, which he called "a broadcasting and receiving station for thought." This takes us from the intangible subconscious mind to the physical brain so we can understand how it controls the process of thought and harness its power for ourselves.

THE BIG TAKEAWAY

Brad Lea sums up the magic of the subconscious mind best when he says, "Anything the mind can conceive and believe, it can achieve. It all boils down to whether you believe it. The rest of the principles take over almost unconsciously once you believe."

QUOTES FROM THE ASIAN MASTERMIND

"Sight is what you see with your eyes, vision is what you see with your mind."

—Robert Kiyosaki

"Success and transformation or true impact never feel easy or safe or comfortable. That's the whole point. New is not familiar, and if you let your subconscious convince you that you made a mistake or you can't do it, nothing will happen."

—Nan Akasha, author

"My first plays were amazingly bad, but I had a teacher who thought I had promise, and he kept working with me. I finally went to a summer workshop before my senior year with people like Sam Shepard and María Irene Fornés, who encouraged me to write from my subconscious, and suddenly all this material about culture clash came out."

—David Hwang, playwright

"He who learns but does not think is lost! He who thinks but does not learn is in great danger."

—Confucius

GROWTH EXERCISES

Blow your own mind.

The next time you're typing, try to consciously recognize each key your fingers press. It's tedious and time-consuming, isn't it? Now, notice when you don't pay attention. The keys seem to press themselves much more efficiently. That's the subconscious, hard at work.

Meditate.

Try guided meditation with a purpose. Get comfortable in a quiet place where you will not be disturbed. The following is a nice meditation to try as you drift off to sleep:

Imagine a path. This is your path, so it can be through a forest, along a shore, or a hallway. Whatever you wish. At the end of this path is a gate. Picture it. Reach out and open it. Walk to a place where you feel safe and surrounded by beauty and comfort. Maybe this is on a moss-covered hill beside a river, under a weeping willow tree, or perhaps it is in the ocean, floating on your back. Go there. Be there. Breathe and relax. Notice a small box at your fingertips. You open it to find a talisman, an object you know is the key to your deepest desires. Hold it. Allow it to transport you to your dream. See it. Feel it. When you are ready to leave, replace the object in its box and leave it here to visit again whenever you need a boost.

"*Every human brain is capable of picking up vibrations of thought which are being released by other brains.*"

—NAPOLEON HILL

THE BRAIN

A broadcasting and receiving station for thought

Is there a difference between the brain and the mind?

Since Hill wrote his book, science has given us a better understanding of the brain itself. First, a few facts:

The brain is the physical part of our body, composed of neurons and supporting and nutritive structures that integrate sensory information from inside and outside the body and controls autonomic function (such as heartbeat and respiration), coordinating and directing motor responses and learning. Its complex circuitry contains approximately 86 billion nerve cells.

The brain handles approximately 70,000 thoughts per day (estimated by experts). Eighty-five percent of these thoughts are negative, according to a study by the National Science Foundation, and 95 percent are repetitive.

The brain consists of several parts that control different functions yet all work together. It is capable of change and growth, and the connections that new information makes can be seen on scans. Brain imaging studies show negative thoughts reduce cerebellum activity, affecting coordination, balance, and the speed of thought.

The prefrontal cortex determines how much attention to pay to something based on where you rank it on the scale of importance. The more you focus on negative subjects and feelings, the more synapses and neurons your brain will create, supporting your negative thoughts and multiplying them like bunnies.

The brain is slower to develop than we once thought. This can affect our choices and decisions as young people, but there are still things we can do to boost our chances of success from an early age. The good news is that our brains are elastic, capable of change and forming new connections.

Our brains alert us to potential dangers for survival purposes. Therefore, negative events and thoughts have a more significant impact on our psychological state and memories than positive ones.

Happily, our brains change as we do, and neural connections grow as we learn. Repeating the same thoughts, feelings, and behaviors increases synaptic connectivity, strengthens neural networks, and creates new neurons. The process is the same whether you think negative thoughts or positive ones.

THE ONE THING OVER WHICH YOU HAVE ABSOLUTE CONTROL

Our mind refers to our intangible understanding of things or our thought process.

Hill spends a lot of time in *Think and Grow Rich* talking about concepts like the subconscious, autosuggestion, and imagination. He lists fears and roadblocks to success that live within us and must be conquered along with positive qualities he suggests we strive to build upon, like desire and belief in oneself. He encourages readers to recognize that what we are is made up of much more than our physical bodies by showing us how our internal landscape can make or break our lives.

"You have absolute control over but one thing, and that is your thoughts. By this device, you may control your own destiny. If you fail to control your own mind, you may be sure you will control nothing else. You were given willpower for this purpose," Hill says.

The keys to developing positive habits? Mindfulness and autosuggestion.

Mind control is the result of self-discipline and habit. You either control your mind, or it controls you. There is no halfway compromise. The most practical of all methods for controlling the mind is the habit of keeping it busy with a definite purpose backed by a definite plan.

There are many things we still don't understand about the brain, but we know thoughts work because neurotransmitters pass from one neuron to another. The brain connects new information to stored knowledge and forms synapses, patterns, and connections. Positive and negative thoughts affect the growth and development of neurons and their synaptic junctions.

Every thought spurs a chemical reaction in the brain. When you think positive thoughts or you're feeling happy or optimistic, cortisol decreases, and the brain produces serotonin, creating a feeling of well-being. When serotonin levels are healthy, you feel happy, calm, less anxious, focused, and emotionally stable.

When you are calm and focused, studies have found that your brain has heightened prefrontal activity. Positivity enhances mental functions such as creative thinking, cognitive flexibility, and faster processing.

When you think negative thoughts and feel the stress that comes with them, the brain draws energy from the prefrontal cortex. Negative thoughts prevent the brain from performing at normal capacity. When stressed or scared, it's hard to absorb and process new information or think creatively.

STOP HANGING OUT IN YOUR COMFORT ZONE

Our brains like it when we're comfortable. When life is good, your brain releases feel-good chemicals, but in the long-term, comfort is terrible for your brain.

Without stimulation, networks between the brain's highways vanish. "Neglect of intense learning leads plasticity systems to waste away," writes Norman Doidge in his book *The Brain That Changes Itself.*

Michael Merzenich, author of *Soft-Wired: How the New Science of Brain Plasticity Can Change Your Life*, says, "It's the willingness to leave the comfort zone that is the key to keeping the brain new."

In other words, your brain needs newness and challenges to grow and stay healthy.

According to a study published in *Clinical Psychology Review*, optimism creates physical and mental resilience for people, even those who have experienced traumatic life circumstances.[19] Science also shows that people with optimistic and positive outlooks are more proactive when it comes to preventative health, have stronger cardiovascular health and better immune systems, earn higher incomes, and have more successful relationships and longer lifespans.

George Chanos sees the brain as a double-edged sword. "Think of your brain as a sword that requires lifelong sharpening through learning, practicing, repetition, reading, travel, attending lectures, and seeking mentors. Everything they do sharpens your sword, and you will carry that sword with you wherever they go. Think of it as a double-edged sword. The majority of information enters our minds through our subconscious, which creates a backdoor that needs to be guarded. Social media, gossip, the nightly news, negativity prey on the vulnerability of the brain if you allow them to."

DJ Steve Aoki said playing Madison Square Garden was like telling his dad he'd made it. He knew his dad equated success with popular culture in New York City. "You don't realize it until you say it out loud, but getting my father's approval, now that he's gone, is still a big deal. When I was nominated for a Grammy, the first thing that popped into my head was my dad."

I can relate to what Steve said about gaining approval from his dad. My parents used to say to my sister and me, "We didn't come here [to America] to mess this up." They made their way over to the United States to build a better life and provide greater opportunities for their children. Early in my career, I was driven by the desire to take care of them and give back for their sacrifices. My burning desire to make money was primarily about giving them a chance to see the world and experience it in ways they most likely never would have been able to without financial assistance.

"With future shows, it's much more about knowing that things will happen if they are supposed to happen, not so much about forcing the issue or needing them to happen to validate myself," Steve said. He trusts his brain and his plans to work as long as he does.

Steve plans to follow his passions. "If passion is not there, I'm not going to learn the field. Passion is essential for learning and growth. I learned through my travels and meeting great people and minds that I have so much more to learn and absorb. Music has always been the soul of what I do, though I am into many different fields involving science and tech. I believe in the neon future and merging the world together through the advancement of science and technology. Feed the brain with passion!

"The current generation should try everything like they already do. Go out and expose yourself to the world around you," Steve said. "Experience life. Be human. Be physical. Be engaged with people. Care more about the conversation you have with someone, where you have a positive takeaway that affects your life. That's a real 'like'—way better than going viral." Social media is a part of Steve's world, and he shares his reality and travels with his perceived world, maintaining a careful balance between the two.

Entrepreneur Kevin Harrington said, "Growing up, I visualized individual success as this normal thing. I saw extreme opulence in many families. That led me to create the Young Entrepreneurs Organization (YEO). I'm living the life of helping others get what they want, and in turn, I have every-thing I want."

Sometimes you just get lucky. You get an idea, and it works. Ray Parker Jr. said the genius of the *Ghostbusters* theme song was not singing the word but letting the audience shout it out—a seemly random idea we can't imagine the song without.

Sometimes paying attention involves more than listening to your brain. It means listening to other people," says Lawrence Jackson. "How do you deal with others to collaborate as a team and come together without egos getting in the way? I believe a shared purpose, where everyone can realize benefits both col-lectively and personally. The kidney doesn't get mad at the heart because it's helping keep the body running. I am there for you, you be there for me. All the individual parts of the body are beautiful organs. But isn't the human body more beautiful than the sum of those individual parts? Every role needs to be filled, not everybody is an A player or B player or C player. They all bring out the best in each other. Play upon your strengths and let each person excel at what they do best."

Hill said, "In a fashion similar to that employed by the radio broadcasting principle, every human brain is capable of pick-ing up vibrations of thought which are being released by other brains. When stimulated, or stepped up to a high rate of vibra-tion, the mind becomes more receptive to thought which reaches it through outside sources. Mind stimulation, through harmo-nious discussion of definite subjects, between people, illustrates the simplest and most practical use of the mastermind."

According to writer Scott Williams, "We all have many mas-ters that can serve us. Anything that gets you out of your own limitations, stuck in a box, nailed to the floor, and gets on the train that gets you moving is essential. An environment where people are talking positively and achieving and not withholding their own power or being stingy."

This lesson was driven home by his grandmother, who sent a check to his mom for $50. "Mom tore it up and said she didn't need to send her money. I told her she was stingy, depriving Grandmother the joy of giving. She wanted her to take the money and do something good with it. The generosity of the principles in *Think and Grow Rich* changes lives and helps others get out of their own heads so they can create more and give back to the world. If you feel bad about yourself, go out and do something for someone else. You'll feel better. Embrace books like *Think and Grow Rich* that will help you succeed. Doing nothing will keep you exactly where you are," Scott advises.

Chef and restaurateur Julian Serrano believes energy is how you feel. "In business, I've learned to push negativity aside because nothing good comes from it. Just keep moving because tomorrow will be better."

The same holds true for handling criticism from others. Penney Ooi believes approval and addiction are a big problem in the world today. "It seems as if people who are critical of others are not happy people. Ones who are happy are not critical of others; they encourage and pick them up."

DON'T BE A KNOW-IT-ALL

Have you ever met a "know-it-all," the type of person who thinks they know everything about everything? Someone who finishes your sentences for you before you can even formulate them? Having a conversation with a know-it-all is frustrating, challenging, and tiring.

The problem is their close-mindedness. Know-it-alls have their way of doing things, and regardless of what you know, they are not willing to listen to you or change their mind.

The main problem of know-it-all-ness is they miss opportunities to learn something new and a chance to develop new neural pathways in their brain. Most people will quickly tire of being around the know-it-all and will move on to a different source for answers, where a mutually beneficial dialogue is possible.

PAY ATTENTION

Research indicates that our mind and memory are essentially perfect, recording millions of bits of data every second. This doesn't mean you will be able to access information you need easily or instantly unless you organize the information on the front end. The best way to do this is to pay attention.

One of the most important aspects of remembering anything is being present in the moment when it occurs. For example, the reason most of us struggle with remembering the names of people we meet is we were not paying attention when we are introduced. We may be a little nervous during the introduction, though the main reason is we're busy thinking about what we are going to say, preparing to respond. We didn't get their name to start. Then, we begin to stress when we realize we don't know. Stress is a killer when it comes to recalling information.

How do we combat this challenge?

- Pay attention.
- Be present.
- Focus your attention on what is happening as it is happening. You stand a much higher chance of recalling the information quickly when you need it most.

In the next chapter, Hill introduces us to his final principle, the sixth sense, the "door to the temple of wisdom." The sixth sense is triggered when the other principles come together.

THE BIG TAKEAWAY

The brain is like a radio transmitter, sending out and receiving thought waves of energy. You have absolute control over but one thing, and that is your thoughts. By focusing on positive thoughts, you open the channels to receive more of the same.

WISDOM FROM THE ASIAN MASTERMIND

"The wise man does not lay up his own treasures. The more he gives to others, the more he has for his own."

—Lao Tzu

"The more you give (broadcast), the more you get (receive)."

—John Shin

"The single most powerful asset we all have is our mind. If it is trained well, it can create enormous wealth in what seems to be an instant."

—Robert Kiyosaki

"Never take for granted that people will understand your business model. You need to be in aggressive communication mode all the time."

—Eva Cheng,
world-renowned business leader

"People can get information much easier than before. That will change the way people do business, the way people live."

—Robin Li

GROWTH EXERCISES

Get up.

Set a timer on your phone to remind you to move every 20 to 60 minutes. Stretch, get your blood flowing, and give your eyes and your body a rest.

Read.

Reading increases brain connectivity; when you read, your brain translates letters and words into complex ideas and forms connections while storing knowledge. Select books based on your interests.

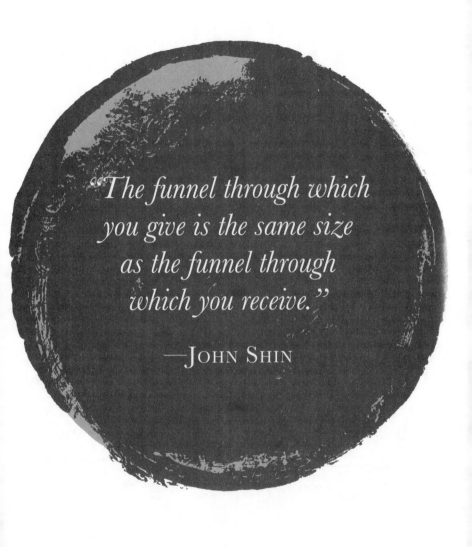

"The funnel through which you give is the same size as the funnel through which you receive."

—JOHN SHIN

THE SIXTH SENSE

The door to the temple of wisdom

What is your sixth sense? How do you utilize your intuition or sixth sense? Your instinct, your energy, your vibe, your gut? Do you sense when someone is staring at you? I catch people looking at me all the time.

Have you ever disliked someone because you "know," just by looking at them, that something is "off"?

Are you able to sense a phony when their story doesn't add up?

That's your sixth sense at work.

Napoleon Hill said, "The chapter on the sixth sense was included because the book is designed to present a complete philosophy by which individuals may unerringly guide themselves in attaining whatever they ask of life. The starting point of all achievement is desire. The finishing point is that brand of knowledge which leads to understanding—understanding of self, understanding of others, understanding of the laws of nature, recognition, and understanding of happiness. This sort of understanding comes in its fullness only through familiarity with, and use of, the principle of the sixth sense."

He identified this principle as the apex of his philosophies and said, "It can be assimilated, understood, and applied only by first mastering the other twelve principles." He also went on to say, "The sixth sense is the door to the temple of wisdom because it connects you to Infinite Intelligence."

The sixth sense lives in the subconscious mind, which Hill labels the "creative imagination." He also refers to it as "the 'receiving set' through which ideas, plans and thoughts flash into the mind. The 'flashes' are sometimes called 'hunches' or 'inspirations.'"

Allegiant Air CEO Maury Gallagher sees the sixth sense as "moments in time when the stars align. Trust yourself and take advantage of these opportunities."

Raja Dhaliwal believes our gut feelings are God's way of communicating with us. "When you have a feeling about certain things or signs appear before you, you need to pay attention. God is telling you what to do."

I have a friend who refers to these hunches or inspirations as his "spider sense" or "spidey sense"—small, almost imperceptible vibrations, as if the hairs are standing up on the back of his neck like a spider sensing when something is caught in its web.

This fine-tuning and acute sensory perception are essential to the survival of many species of living creatures. The sixth sense represents the difference between life and death at times and can act as an emergency alarm, alerting us to possible trouble.

Learning to trust your instincts and developing your sixth sense represents a huge opportunity if we learn to use it to our advantage.

Spend a moment reflecting on a time or times when you trusted your gut or followed through on a hunch. Did it work out? Did you feel a greater sense of confidence as a result?

Regardless of the outcome, trusting your instincts is a valuable tool. It builds confidence and self-esteem when you check in with yourself before making important decisions or trusting someone you don't know.

Restauranteur Katsuya Uechi trusts his instincts. "If I plan to open a new restaurant, I go there several times, and if I feel good, I move ahead. If I don't feel good, then I don't. The location of a new place is a top priority, so I look at the neighborhood and people who live in the area along with the price range, but I don't look too deep. I do what feels right."

Penney Ooi trusts her gut feelings too. "I believe somebody is sending me a message from outside. I believe the sixth sense can be developed by having enough information and experiences. I believe there is a lot of information out there we do not know."

"Wishes and prayers are only answered when they harmonize with thoughts and actions," said Hill, a reminder to plan and use the other principles too.

The sixth sense is another way to refer to intuition, which *Merriam-Webster* defines as: "1. quick and ready insight; 2. immediate apprehension or cognition."

Some people put a low value on intuition, while others believe in it fiercely.

Those who believe say the sixth sense connects us in powerful ways and anyone can develop it by choosing to live more consciously.

INTUITION VERSUS EMOTION

The sixth sense can be wrong, drawing on subconscious information that could be faulty. At times, we might react to something because of a past event we're attaching current meaning to, making it difficult to tell the difference between intuition and emotion.

The easiest way to spot intuition is that it usually comes with detached feelings, whereas emotions are affectively charged.

Emotion can feel like intuition. Strong emotions such as resentment, anger, and happiness can prevent intuition from communicating with you. Fear is very effective at blocking your intuition because this emotion sees the world as a dangerous place. It can only offer fear-based guidance.

Emotional reactions, such as fear or anxiety, happen because you are scared, afraid, or threatened. Anxiety and emotional responses come with physical symptoms like sweating, an upset stomach, panic, and difficulty breathing. Your heart might race, or you could get a heavy feeling in your chest. Anxiety and stress reactions are more instant. They demand your attention, now.

Intuition is more like the current under an ocean, gently stirring the surface of your thoughts. It is accompanied by pleasing sensations like comfortable and tranquil feelings or a calming knowledge that things have clicked into place. When you pay attention to what your body is trying to tell you, you'll easily know the difference between emotional reactions and true intuition.

Intuition doesn't come from a seeming threat or fear; instead, it is based on knowledge. It is clear and rational, and it makes sense. It has an affirming and positive quality.

Malcolm Gladwell, the author of the book *Blink*, said intuition is a "gentle inkling, a fleeting answer that happens in an instant." Intuition is a pleasant feeling, not a stressful one.

How do you engage and develop your intuition or sixth sense?

One of my favorite ways is meditation. Sit, quiet the mind, still the body, feel yourself opening, and becoming ready to receive. Search yourself for negative or positive emotions. Ask questions, and be receptive to answers. When negative thoughts come up, pretend they are clouds, and watch them float by without forming any attachment.

"Understanding of the sixth sense comes only by meditation through mind's development from within," said Hill.

Ask for guidance when you go to bed at night. Keep a notebook and pen next to your bed. Record your dreams as soon as you wake up. Dreams are your subconscious and your sixth sense working together.

In addition to meditation, you may wish to practice yoga. There is a reason it's so popular. Besides the physical benefits, yoga's Eastern philosophy is built around calming the mind and body and opening oneself to the sixth sense.

Nitro Circus founder Gregg Godfrey meditates. "I have a strong belief in a higher power. Much of what I do involves believing in myself, that I've done my homework, made the calculations. I hate to fail, so I prefer to fail fast and get on with it."

Julian Serrano enjoys going out with friends, eating and enjoying himself. He says, "I'm not too critical about what other people do, but I always sense the love a chef puts into the food."

Radio personality Dr. Marissa Pei refers to her sixth sense as her eighth sense. "Eight is a lucky number in Chinese. I believe people are forms of energy that are currently housed in their current body at this point in time. When we die, our energy continues and moves on to the next form. I am an energetic being, a pure form of energy. My eighth sense is the moment of energy connection between infinite eternal energy and me. I feel that connection as some people describe their sixth sense, intuition, or gut feeling."

Marissa believes when she is looking for an answer or walks into a room it's important to stop analyzing. "Stop thinking and start feeling what always surrounds us. Sense the energy that surrounds you and connect to it." As a result of this practice, she is a much more creative being who embraces her sensitivity. "I used to be teased about being too sensitive. Now I realize it is a gift."

As I become more in tune with my sixth sense, I have observed a powerful force at work—human nature. Although science has proven that opposites attract, I've come to a different conclusion based on the timeless idiom "Birds of a feather flock together." We're drawn to like-minded people.

Like most things, this attraction has tremendous potential, both positive and negative. The concept of "success breeds success" is as true as "misery loves company." Although each takes the same amount of energy, the difference is in the potential outcomes.

If you could spend X amount of energy on people focused on growth and success or an equal amount of energy on stagnant and complacent people, which ones would you choose? I would select the success-minded group and move one step closer to living the life of my dreams, feeling better about myself in the process. Bonus!

My grandfather used to say, "If you play with a pig, you're going to get dirty." In other words, be careful who you associate with because a part of them will rub off on you.

Have you heard of the "scotoma effect"? *Merriam-Webster* defines a scotoma as "a spot in the visual field in which vision is absent or deficient." A perfect example of this is what's behind you. We don't have eyes in the back of our heads, so without a mirror, you have a blind spot.

Less obvious are things we don't see happening right in front of us. Missed opportunities. Mistakes. Overlooked important details. Missed deadlines. We mentally slap ourselves when these things happen. But if you want to improve any area of your life, it often comes down to focus and presence. Be present in the moment and with people when you are with them. Focus on what (or who) is happening when it is happening.

When you operate from abundance, you have an open channel to Infinite Intelligence. As a result, you are blessed with many options. You see opportunity under challenging situations. Instead of focusing on winning or losing, you view challenges as learning experiences. Regardless of the outcome, you have a chance to improve your game and develop your skills and your sixth sense.

Here are three important reminders about our less tangible, intuitive nature:

1. If we spend our lives expecting apples for apples for our efforts, all we'll ever know is apples. Selfless, unconditional giving returns value to us in ways we never imagined. The less we think about WIIFM (what's in it for me?), the more positive surprises we experience.

2. Be the same person in public and in private, no matter what. It's good for your soul, and you'll be more peaceful and less stressed.

3. Internal beauty requires more effort to uncover and attracts more discerning, determined people. It forms the foundation for more profound, lasting, meaningful relationships that evolve over time.

The funnel through which you give is the same size as the funnel through which you receive. This is true across the board from money and material goods, to love, encouragement, and support. If the funnel opening is small, the flow will be restricted. If what you give is a mere trickle, what you receive will be a mirror image.

THE BIG TAKEAWAY

"With the aid of the sixth sense, you will be warned of impending dangers in time to avoid them and notified of opportunities in time to embrace them."

—Napoleon Hill

WISDOM FROM THE ASIAN MASTERMIND

"The simple act of paying attention can take you a long way."

—Keanu Reeves

"Trust your spidey sense. Be the spider."

—John Shin

"Insights from myth, dreams, and intuitions, from glimpses of an invisible reality, and from perennial human wisdom provide us with hints and guesses about the meaning of life and what we're here for. Prayer, observance, discipline, and action are the means through which we grow and find meaning."

—Jean Shinoda Bolen,
psychiatrist and author

HOW **RICH ASIANS** *THINK*

GROWTH EXERCISES

Meditate.

Yes, meditation is good for your brain too. Research shows that meditation thickens regions of the brain that control attention and interpret sensory signals. Meditation literally makes your brain bigger while silencing the mind. When the mind is silent, concentration increases, and we experience inner peace and open ourselves to the imagination, subconscious, and sixth sense.

Pay attention to your dreams.

Ask questions and become receptive to answers. Ask for guidance before you go to sleep at night. Record your dreams in a dream notebook that you keep beside your bed. Look for patterns. Dreams are your subconscious and your sixth sense working together.

Look for possibilities.

Dr. Marissa Pei recommends taking 15 minutes each day, looking at Google, breathing, and connecting to your eighth sense. "Whatever word comes into your mind or heart, look it up. The idea is to train yourself to see possibilities in life. Expand your thinking and dreaming potential, and break the habit of thinking small and limiting yourself with a narrow focus."

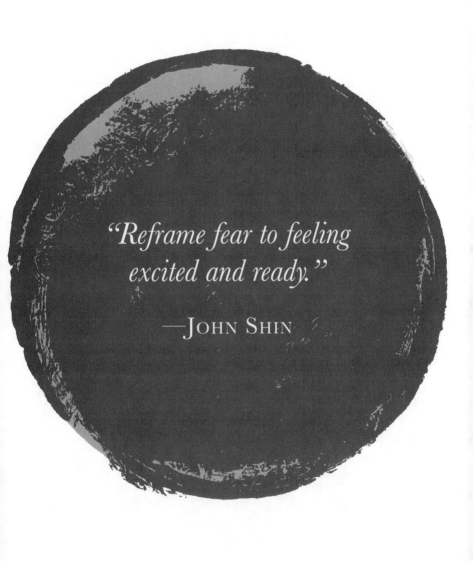

"*Reframe fear to feeling excited and ready.*"

—JOHN SHIN

THE SIX GHOSTS OF FEAR

The grand illusion

How do you overcome fear?

Your dreams must be greater, more vivid, brighter, and more magnificent than your fears.

When I was a kid, I wanted to call a girl I liked. I got her phone number, pushed past my fear of rejection and dialed it on the rotary dial phone. Her dad answered, and I hung up. After waiting a bit, I regrouped and tried again. This time she answered, and we talked for hours. I called her despite my fear of being rejected. Why did I continue to call even though my inside voice said she was going to say no to me? Overcoming this fear is how I ended up marrying my wife. When I first met Arlene, I knew I was not about to let her pass me by and lose the opportunity. So I got up, went over to her, and asked for her number. I knew I could have been rejected, but my dream and vision of being with her were clear and much bigger than my fear of rejection.

"Your dream must be bigger than your fear," Hill says.

At times, the fear of failure keeps us stuck in a place where growth cannot occur. We stick with what we know because it's safe. The primitive part of our brain wants to keep us safe. Occasionally, fear is essential to our survival, though the function of our primitive brain is largely unnecessary. Most often, avoiding risk and sticking with what we know limits opportunities and stalls our personal growth.

Penney Ooi's fear of heights is more powerful than her desire for adventure. "I could not go skydiving. I am also conscious of my health."

Personally, I fear losing my mind and having dementia or Alzheimer's. What if I cannot remember the beautiful people in my life and all the moments?

If you find yourself struggling with any of the principles we've discussed, examine what's stopping you from moving forward. Most likely, your hesitation is due to fear.

Napoleon Hill spent 20 years researching *Think and Grow Rich*, and when he was ready to publish it, he realized that most people understand the principles of success, but they don't apply them enough to make a difference in their lives.

Reviewing his research material, Hill discerned that something bigger than his principles was at work for most people—fear. These often unnamed fears hold back many people. He went back to his writing desk and added a final chapter to help people overcome their self-limiting, fear-based beliefs.

He refers to fears as "ghosts" because they exist only in your mind. These ghosts create indecision, doubt, and fear. Hill knew the influence of fear was so impactful that after completing

Think and Grow Rich, he wrote *Outwitting the Devil* to address the impact of fear and negativity and offer advice on how to overcome them.

Before you can put any portion of Hill's philosophies into successful use, your mind must be prepared to receive them. Hill says, "The preparation is not difficult. It begins with the study, analysis, and understanding of three enemies which you shall have to clear out—indecision, doubt, and fear. Indecision is the seedling of fear. Fears are nothing more than states of mind. One's state of mind is subject to control and direction."

Let's review the six ghosts of fear, the symptoms Hill identifies, to help you recognize your own fears, so that you are better equipped to blast through them.

THE SIX BASIC FEARS

- Poverty
- Criticism
- Ill Health
- Loss of Love
- Old age
- Death

FEAR OF POVERTY

Hill said the fear of poverty is the most destructive of the six basic fears. For this reason, it is also the most difficult to overcome.

He was asked why he wrote a book about money and measured riches in dollars alone, a question to which he responded, "Some will believe, and rightly so, that there are other forms of riches more desirable than money. Yes, there are riches which cannot be measured in terms of dollars, but there are millions of people who will say, 'Give me all the money I need, and I will find everything else I want.' The primary reason I wrote this book on how to get money is the fact that millions of men and women are paralyzed with fear of poverty."

When Asians come to America to start a new life, many give up previously held dreams and careers. They focus on the new hope of providing the best life they can for their children. They sacrifice so their children will have opportunities they never had.

Many children of immigrants grow up conscious of the enormous sacrifices their parents made so that they might have a better life. These children often spend their lives proving to their parents that their suffering was not in vain. They feel immense pressure to make their parents proud and can develop difficulty in going their own way, especially if their own way involves a path their parents do not approve of.

Immersion in a new culture is tough to navigate, and immigrant children often end up guiding their parents, acting as translators, advisors, and go-betweens. This can create a shift in the typical parent/child dynamic. Some children of immigrants say they feel they are obligated to care for their parents, who may not speak English or ever fully assimilate into American society.

We've all heard about immigrants who come to this country with "a dollar in their pocket." This hard life can change the way a person views money. It can either inspire them to achieve a career so they never have to worry about money again, or it can freeze them in place, afraid to break free of menial jobs or take chances that might jeopardize a steady paycheck.

Dr. Marissa Pei advises younger generations of immigrants to honor their parents and thank previous generations for going through what they did and for their belief system. "You are in a place where you can pick the best of what was and the best of what's to come, and you own the power of your ability to become anything you choose to be," she said.

While I researched this book, the United States underwent dramatic, and often terrifying, changes to immigration policies and practices. Current immigrants face new challenges and fears that are sure to affect generations to come. Now, more than ever, the hardships immigrants face have the potential to have lasting effects on their children.

To some extent, I find that most people fear poverty. Even my super-rich clients admit that the idea of losing all their wealth is daunting.

Symptoms of the fear of poverty are lack of ambition or indifference, indecision, doubt or excuse-making (usually over failures), worry, overcautiousness, and procrastination.

Hill suggests you take a personal inventory and look for these signs of an unhealthy attitude about money.

An honest assessment of where you are financially is the first step to financial health. Here are some essential steps to master your finances and conquer your fear of poverty:

- Set financial goals.

- Educate yourself on financial management.
- Strive for financial independence.
- Spend less than you earn.
- Build an emergency fund.
- Start with small investments.
- Pay attention to day-to-day money management.
- Talk about money with your family.
- Pay cash (and if you don't have the money to buy it, don't buy it).
- Be a minimalist.

Your fear of poverty will dissolve as you gain control of your money and your future.

FEAR OF CRITICISM

Viewing yourself through the eyes of others can rob you of your self-confidence, take away your initiative, destroy your imagination, and create an environment of self-imposed negativity that can wreak havoc in your life. Hill reminds us that parents often do their children irreparable harm by criticizing them.

Many Asians say that they think their parents were more critical of them growing up than other parents. As a parent, or an individual growing up with critical parents, look for the following telltale signs and symptoms of the fear of criticism:

- Self-consciousness
- Lack of poise

- Lack of firmness in decisions or ability to express opinions decisively
- Imitating others
- Boasting
- Inferiority complex
- Extravagance
- Lack of initiative
- Lack of ambition

Criticism can be helpful or harmful. It can help us grow and learn (even when it doesn't feel good at first). What we perceive can be shaken up by the opinions of others. The problem is even worse when we compare ourselves to others and come up lacking.

The solution is to remember you can disregard criticism once you've examined it for any nuggets of truth or helpful information. Instead of comparing yourself to others, work on becoming grateful for you. Tell yourself you are fabulous. Start each day by thinking of three things you are thankful for. Start a daily gratitude journal or make it a ritual as you sit down for dinner with your family to all share something you are grateful for that day. These insights will become automatic reassurances whenever you face harsh or unsolicited criticism from others.

FEAR OF ILL HEALTH

We are constantly bombarded with information about health and the latest remedies. You probably have friends or family members dealing with health issues, but are you taking care of the most precious assets you have, your mind and body? Do you prioritize exercise, rest, and healthy choices? Are you taking care of the golden goose?

Ignore your body long enough, and like a neglected automobile, eventually, it will break down. That's when worry usually sets in. Our minds are potent receivers. The negative messages we receive lead to worry, stress, and lack of self-care. All of these can trigger our fears and impact us negatively in physical ways. Symptoms of the fear of ill health include the following:

- Autosuggestion—looking for and expecting to find the symptoms of all kinds of diseases
- Frequent WebMD or Google searches for your symptoms
- Hypochondria
- Pushing your body with excessive exercise
- Talking about your health all the time
- Using alcohol or drugs to treat pains instead of eliminating the cause

Fear of ill health disappears when we take care of ourselves. Active, healthy people are confident, knowing they're proactively creating a life of sustained well-being. A positive mental attitude is also essential for maintaining good health.

I highly recommend making health and fitness a part of your weekly scheduling practice. Keep it simple, but make it happen. Stretching, exercise, walking, meditation, yoga, and time alone only takes a few minutes each day. Respect the golden goose. Be the goose.

FEAR OF LOSS OF LOVE

This fear can be the most painful of all because it touches on the other fears and attacks our self-confidence. When a relationship ends or we lose a loved one because of something we did, we tend to judge ourselves harshly. We torment ourselves with blame, negative thoughts, and behaviors like:

- jealousy
- fault-finding
- cheating
- commitment issues
- self-effacing behavior
- clinginess

Dealing with the loss of love is not easy. A person who is strong and self-confident has conviction in their values and generally will suffer less from the fear of loss of love than one who looks to others to create their happiness and self-worth.

The solution is to be more loving. If you want to be loved, be a loving person. In this regard, if one gets away, you are assured that another will be along shortly.

Practice autosuggestion and self-talk to reinforce your positive beliefs in yourself. Be grateful for your strengths and abilities. Create a list and add to it regularly to reinforce your sense of self-worth.

FEAR OF OLD AGE

Let's face it, we are all growing older each day. From the minute you are born, you are slowly dying. Not a pleasant thought, but a fact nonetheless. Surrounding our fear of old age is the general slowdown or deterioration of our health, sex drive, physical strength, stamina, mobility, mental acuity, and financial security.

All of these are facts of life, and the best antidote to all of them is to get busy living. If you've been dragging your feet about your goals and dreams, get moving while you still have the stamina and mental acuity to do so. If you hate starting over, stop quitting. Want to become rich and enjoy the options that money can afford you? Get moving on building your empire and getting your financial house in order. Do it now while you still have your health and mobility to enjoy traveling and adventures. The bottom line with the fear of old age is to know it is unavoidable. Many of the elements you may fear in old age itself can be minimized by acting now. The rest is out of your hands.

FEAR OF DEATH

As we age, our fear of ill health often becomes overshadowed by the fear of death. From time to time, we all wonder what death brings. Death will come no matter what we think about it or how much we try to avoid it. To ease these fears, strive to focus on the present and make the most of each day.

Hill reminds us that life is energy. If neither energy nor matter can be destroyed, life cannot be destroyed. Life, like other forms of energy, passes through countless processes of change, but it cannot be destroyed. Death is a transition.

The best way to get past the fear of death is to make the most of every day. If you have a burning desire for achievement and back it up with useful service to others, your focus will be on living a life of significance and will leave no room for the fear of death.

Worry and fear are enemies of happiness.

"Worry is a state of mind based on fear. It works slowly but persistently. It is insidious and subtle. It slowly digs itself in until it paralyzes one's reasoning faculties and destroys self-confidence and initiative. Worry is a form of sustained fear that is a state of mind which can be controlled." This is timeless wisdom from Napoleon Hill.

One of my favorite quotes from the original *Think and Grow Rich* is, "To worry is to pray for what you do not want." I don't know about you, but I don't make a habit of praying for things I don't want.

Make a firm decision that nothing positive comes from worry and realize its price is more than you are willing to pay. Be committed to this choice. You will find peace of mind, and calmness will follow, allowing you to focus on more positive things that will bring about joy, happiness, and success.

THE DEVIL'S WORKSHOP

Have you ever started your day feeling great, only to find your mood plummet upon reading the news or talking to a negative friend?

Hill wraps up his discussion on fears by adding a seventh he called a "basic evil." This is the susceptibility to negative influences. He warns that this fear is more deeply seated and more fatal than all of the other six fears because the ability to control the six basic fears lies with your mind and with your ability to control your thoughts. The seventh basic evil can best be controlled by your actions as well as your willpower not to allow other people's negativity permeate your spirit and bring it down.

Hill says it is important to recognize that negative influences often work on you through your subconscious mind; therefore, they are difficult to detect. "Keep your mind closed against all people who depress or discourage you in any way. Deliberately seek the company of people who influence you to think and act for yourself."

So, how should we deal with negatively from others and prevent it from stopping us before we even begin?

Some negativity seems to be a product of the duality of human nature. But you can train yourself to focus on the positive and stay removed from harmful influences as much as possible. You can choose to help others instead of being influenced by them. You can choose to lift others to a higher level of consciousness and happiness. You can become a beacon of light and create your own environment of positivity.

It's part of the human condition to experience fear and choose to remain safe within familiar surroundings. The primary role of your brain is survival, which means not taking risks and playing it safe. When it comes time to step out of your comfort zone, your brain goes into protective mode. Extravagant stories and bizarre scenarios begin to emerge. Excuses—excuses to keep you from moving forward.

Sometimes the chasm between opportunity and ideas and that critical first step can seem insurmountable. So, how do you move ahead anyway?

Think about a time when you stopped short of doing something because you felt uncomfortable or anxious. When you were faced with a yes-or-no decision and fear took over. Instead of moving ahead and being uncomfortable for a few moments, you made up an excuse.

How did you feel after? Did you feel relief?

What was your excuse? It may have been a lack of experience. Some fear or phobia. Chores, errands, demands, and responsibilities. We all have our favorites. Mine, like many other people, is that I am too busy. "I'd like to, but I can't." Sound familiar?

When you do this, after the moment has passed, do you think about the missed opportunity? Perhaps feel some pangs of regret, wishing you had another chance? Regret sticks around to haunt you. Always. No amount of explaining or wishing things were different will ever bring back a unique moment in time. There is no antidote for regret.

If you often put your dreams on hold or you've ever told yourself, "I'll get started tomorrow," it may be time to shake things up. Start thinking outside of the box and then acting. I guarantee the benefits of this behavior far outweigh the costs. In fact, the long-term cost of not acting works much like compound interest. Regret magnifies and grows exponentially over time.

Sometimes the best way to overcome one fear is to pit it against a larger and more frightening fear. This is a classic model used by advertisers for centuries. Of course, you want to do "A" because if you don't, you will experience "B." Nobody wants to experience B!

Imagine yourself older, reflecting on your life. As you reflect, you feel sad about your missed opportunities—opportunities right in front of you, pounding on your door.

Now that you are older, your perspective has changed. What once seemed frightening now seems natural. Given a chance to try again, you wouldn't hesitate. Except you can't. The moment has passed. The planets are no longer aligned. The people who made up that event have moved on. Missed opportunities involving people are the most difficult because they can never be recreated precisely like they were. It's like missing a rare performance or guest speaker who might have changed your life.

Dr. Marissa Pei told me a story that illustrates this perfectly. "There are two rocks in a rock shop. One is a beautiful, chiseled, sculpted stone everyone admires. The other, across the shop, is a dull, unpolished stone nobody gives a second glance. After years of sitting there, the unfinished rock screams out that life is unfair and complains that nobody admires it. Life says to the rock, 'Every time I came to you and offered to chisel and polish you, you screamed, 'No! Don't! I can't take the pain. So you received no changes.'" This reframing of fear is essential to mastering it, so you can handle life's ups and downs and never have to look back, regretting the times you let fear hold you back, wondering what might have been.

The pain of regret is a powerful force, thousands of times stronger than the pain of looking foolish or being a little uncomfortable in the moment. More importantly, people will overlook fumbles and mistakes because you tried. No one likes to hear a constant stream of excuses.

"At one point," said Kevin Harrington, "I was afraid of getting in front of a crowd. I just needed to get out there and do it. Practice built confidence. Coaches, Toastmasters—get out and do it before getting in front of 5,000 people. Failure is part of your life and part of every entrepreneur's life. Don't fear failure; it is part of being an entrepreneur."

When I asked Kevin if he ever feared failing or not making it, he replied, "I always believed I would be successful. Not necessarily everything I did was a success, but I learned from my attempts, failures, and I did things differently. As Winston Churchill said, 'Success is the ability to go from failure to failure without losing your enthusiasm.' You're not going to get a hit every time up to bat, certainly not a home run. One out of four, one out of five successes were good. My successes were huge, and fortunately, my failures were relatively small."

Ray Parker Jr. doesn't let fear stop him either. "I am energized and excited by music and let it move me forward. At most, I was a little unsure that I had advanced enough to keep up. I practice every day for several hours. Sometimes I play all day."

Still, like most people, Ray has fears. "What are my fears? Losing all my money and having to go back to Detroit. Believe it or not, my biggest fear is ghosts! Fear of the dark! Old hotels!" He has trouble sleeping in the house when his family is not around. He even turned his fear into one of his biggest hit songs, "Ghostbusters," about slaying ghosts.

Actor Justin Chon believes that what holds most people back is the fear of failure. "It's very crippling. Other people's judgments and what they think of you is what stops people. It's okay to fall on your face if you're learning. Practice is all part of the process. Getting over it requires action. Execute. Reflect. Repeat. It's that consistency that reduces the fear. When I know my intentions are good, I don't care what others say. Sometimes other people have good input that is valid, so I examine it and extract what is useable. When I've done my homework and my intentions are sound, I'm unstoppable!"

Pro football player Lawrence Jackson thinks about death sometimes and wonders whether he's done enough to change the world. "If I don't know when I'm going to die, why not live my life to my full potential? Courage is moving, not in the absence of fear, but despite fear. It's like walking across a piano. On the ground, you can walk across it, jump on it, play with it. Move it up ten feet, you're a little nervous. Up a thousand feet, you might be paralyzed and not want to move. What's changed?"

Perspective is everything.

Author and businessman George Chanos said, "It took 20 years to build an unassailable level of confidence. Fear paralyzes you; it prevents action. Whatever you are afraid of, you will encounter a reaction when you do it. When it's positive, you will do more. It's a process, one step at a time. One bite at a time. Some people have false confidence and portray this although they don't have the experience to back it up. Over time, confidence is earned by taking steps and building it. After 20 years, it's unassailable because it's earned."

I loved George's response when I asked him what his biggest fear was. "My daughter when she was four! She was like a locomotive and wouldn't take 'no' for an answer."

Penney Ooi thinks about the future of science and man and where they intersect. "Some people are afraid of the future. If you are afraid of the future, you are afraid of change. AI will replace a lot of jobs. In the future, robots will have all the information and data, though we will still need doctors because before the operation you need the doctor to help alleviate your fears. Communication skills will be more and more important and cannot be duplicated by machines."

Fear of the unknown is a powerful empty canvas for our imaginations to decorate. Given free reign, our fearful minds often produce dark thoughts, leading to anxiety and debilitating effects on our bodies.

A common thread linking many of my clients and prospective clients is a lack of education about money, investments, and finances. When they were kids, money was a secret between their parents, only talked about in private. This veil of secrecy about finances passed down to them.

It's time to pull back the curtain surrounding household finances and shine the spotlight on money with your children. Take away the fear of the unknown. Bring in sound education.

A potential barrier to meaningful money conversations with our children is pride. Your budget may arouse long-held feelings of societal or parental secrecy and pride in you (especially if money is tight or you've made some embarrassing mistakes you'd rather not talk about).

When it comes to cash, pride limits our ability to make essential changes in our life and the lives of our kids.

Put pride aside. Regardless of your current financial position, be open and honest with your children about your finances. There are several benefits to family-money transparency.

At first, you may feel uncomfortable, awkward, or resistant. Pay attention to your thoughts and feelings. Any time we feel discomfort or resistance, there's an underlying message. Be open to receiving it and taking advantage of the growth opportunity for yourself.

By openly discussing finances on a regular basis, you'll eliminate the unknown factor for all of you.

Your kids might be scared too. Maybe they've heard people fighting about money or using it as a weapon in a negative way. Maybe you've told them, "We can't afford this," and it scared them. Perhaps the only thing they know about finance for children is that adults don't like talking about money with kids.

So, be real. Be open and honest. Focus on facts, figures, and listening.

Conversations about a sensitive subject show your children the power of truth and integrity. They also teach them compassion. If you're struggling with a sensitive issue, it's good for your kids to know they can support you too. It shows them you're human and need help sometimes, just like they do. It's okay that some things are hard to talk about. You'll get through it together. These are powerful lessons that help us slay fears.

Teaching your children about budgets will help them feel gratitude for the things they have. Your children will learn about the rewards for a job well done when they must put forth some effort to earn money to make a purchase. A strong work ethic is worth its weight in gold and will always have value.

Finally, when you remove the curtain of mystery surrounding money and finances, you lay your cards on the table. No more mystery. No more secrets. No more fear. Your children know what's up and will better understand the decisions you must make as a parent in the future. This helps get them on board at home and provides a healthy example for them to follow.

The best way to get the most out of life and avoid the pain of regret is to act whenever possible and avoid making excuses.

CEO of Allegiant Air Maury Gallagher said, "Fear is a good thing at times. It protects you, but in business, there are times you need to go left when the world is turning right. Going out on a limb by yourself is a lonely place at times, not for everyone." The alternative doesn't appeal to him, though. "Fear is part of life. It's like the 'glass half full' analogy. A lot of people are afraid of not having enough, but there is nothing wrong with a half-full glass. If you're afraid of it and knock the water over, you've got nothing." In other words, value what you have, and never let a fear of "lack" hold you back.

When we try new things, we have an opportunity to test different ideas, hone our skills, and gain valuable experience in the process. I have always taught my children and members of my professional team to view mistakes and fumbles as learning opportunities. If you're not failing, you're not trying.

A strong tendency of all humans is to become complacent. We rise to a certain level and then remain there for extended periods. We are creatures of habit. What's comfortable and familiar is a powerful force, like a giant magnet that holds us within our comfort zone. Even when danger or deficiencies exist, many people learn to tolerate increasing levels of pain instead of changing their behavior or habits. The pain of discipline versus the pain of regret—which one do you prefer in the long run?

WORST-CASE SCENARIO GAME

A great way to get past the endless chatter in your mind is to ask better questions whenever you encounter fear or are feeling anxious. Here are a few examples:

- What's the worst thing that could happen?
- What's the worst thing people might say about me?
- If the worst thing happens, can I handle it, learn from it, and move on?

When you direct your energy to the worst possible scenario and address it head on, you remove the illusion and power it has over you. It's like drawing back the curtain of the great Oz in *The Wizard of Oz* and revealing a fearful, vulnerable man no different than us. Use the worst-case scenario game whenever you encounter fear or are feeling anxious.

Taking the first step toward change can be challenging. What if we fail? What if our new way of doing things is not as good? What if our latest creation is unsuccessful or, worse, flat out rejected? What if this and what if that? Our imaginations are almost as good at coming up with excuses as ideas.

The list of reasons why not to do something is almost insurmountable. It's our primitive brain's way of keeping us safe and secure. "Don't try new things." "Stick with the tried and true." "There is safety in numbers." All this negative self-talk serves a purpose, yet it limits us too. Our excuses and elaborate rationale keep us from spreading our wings, turning us into birds in cages.

Plato said, "The first and best victory is to conquer self. To be conquered by self is, of all things, the most shameful and vile."

"It has always been a mystery to me," said Elbert Hubbard, "why people spend so much time deliberately fooling themselves by creating alibis to cover their weaknesses. If used differently, the same time would be sufficient to cure the weakness. Then, no alibis would be needed."

Have you ever read an article, watched a video, or listened to an audio program that contained life-changing ideas? And all that was required of you to benefit from them was a willingness to change?

We've all been there. An idea or solution to a current challenge, complete with a clear set of instructions, falls right in our lap. You're in total agreement and can easily see the benefits. Yet instead of acting, you continue with your old habits and routine. Why?

Because change is unfamiliar. Change is scary and new. Our primitive brain doesn't like scary, new, and unknown things. Once we stick our neck out, we're accountable. People are watching and judging. Change also requires effort, and effort involves energy. It's easier to stick with what's familiar and follow the well-worn path of least resistance.

Change is not better or worse. Change makes you feel alive and keeps you growing and moving forward like a river. The alternative is to remain stagnant, like an isolated pond that eventually dries out, shrivels up, and dies. I don't know about you, but this sounds much scarier than dealing with something new and different.

Live each day with the wind at your back, allowing the current to help move you along. When you do this, something magical happens. Imagine riding a bicycle on the open road as opposed to riding a stationary bike. The scenery changes. What's around the next bend is yet to be seen but could be amazing. It could be awesome. It could be inspiring. It will be different. Whether it's better is all a matter of perspective.

Olympic hockey player Marissa Brandt said, "Never limit yourself by saying 'no' to opportunities. Take advantage of chances."

Raja Dhaliwal shared a story that reminded me that life is a process with plenty of room to grow and change and uncover new opportunities. "We all have potential inside of us. Like a pencil, it's all about what is within you. A pencil needs to be sharpened before it creates words. It needs to go through the sharpening process to reveal the lead. There is also an eraser on the pencil to erase our past mistakes, make changes, and rewrite our story at any time. You must go through the sharpening process to reveal the energy within so you can impact the world."

A PARTING THOUGHT FROM NAPOLEON HILL

"I would remind you that life is a checkerboard, and the player opposite you is time. If you hesitate before moving or neglect to move promptly, your man will be wiped off the board by time. You are playing against a partner who will not tolerate indecision. The master key is intangible, but it is powerful. It is the privilege of creating, in your own mind, a burning desire for a definite form of riches. There is no penalty for the use of the key, but there is a price you must pay if you do not use it. The price is failure. There is a reward of stupendous proportions if you put the key to use. It is the satisfaction that comes to all who conquer self and force life to pay whatever is asked."

THE BIG TAKEAWAY

Fear is nothing more than a state of mind. Fortunately, you have the power to control your thoughts. Feed your mind or feed your fears. The choice is yours.

WISDOM FROM THE ASIAN MASTERMIND

"Fear comes from uncertainty; we can eliminate the fear within us when we know ourselves better."

—Bruce Lee

"The fear of being different prevents most people from seeking new ways to solve their problems."

—Robert Kiyosaki

"If we can't face death, we will never overcome it. You have to look it straight in the eye. Then you can turn around and walk back out into the light."

—Maya Ying Lin, designer, architect, and artist

"Winners are not afraid of losing. But losers are. Failure is part of the process of success. People who avoid failure also avoid success."

—Robert Kiyosaki

"A lot of times people are afraid to get older. That's a shame. In other cultures, it's wonderful because you can actually see the legacy you're leaving for yourself. When you're younger, you don't really think so much about that, and you shouldn't. You're living your life and enjoying. That's great, but as you get older you want to make an impact, be an example to live by."

—Lucy Liu

GROWTH EXERCISES

Ease stress and worry. Pick a few of these to focus on for the next month:

- schedule downtime
- track how you spend your time
- schedule one thing you look forward to each day
- celebrate little wins
- concentrate on one thing at a time
- be present
- outline your priorities
- create a "stop doing" list and implement it
- say "no"
- avoid negative people
- avoid depressing events
- avoid negative media and social media
- add humor and laughter to your life and schedule it regularly
- evaluate your personal habits
- eat healthily
- exercise
- outsource what you can
- ask for help
- find a mentor or a coach
- form a mastermind group

NOTES

1. López, Gustavo et al. "Key Facts about Asian Americans, a Diverse and Growing Population." *Pew Research Center*. Last modified September 8, 2017. http://www.pewresearch.org/fact-tank/2017/09/08/key-facts-about-asian-americans/.

2. Ibid.

3. Ibid.

4. Ibid.

5. Ryan, Camille L., and Kurt Bauman. "Educational Attainment in the United States: 2015." *Census.gov*. Last modified March 2016. http://www.census.gov/content/dam/Census/library/publications/2016/demo/p20-578.pdf.

6. "14 Important Statistics about Asians." *Asian Nation: Asian American History, Demographics, & Issues*. Accessed February 10, 2019. http://www.asian-nation.org/14-statistics.shtml#sthash.hcYte6l8.dpbs.

7. Ibid.

8. Ibid.

9. "Asian-Americans Are Expanding Their Footprint in the U.S. and Making an Impact." *Nielsen*. Last modified May 19, 2016. http://

www.nielsen.com/us/en/insights/news/2016/asian-americans-are-expanding-their-footprint-and-making-an-impact.html.

10. "Statistics for U.S. Employer Firms That Were Family-Owned by Sector, Gender, Ethnicity, Race, Veteran Status, and Years in Business for the U.S., States, and Top 50 MSAs: 2015." *American FactFinder*. Last modified July 13, 2017. http://factfinder.census.gov/faces/tableservices/jsf/pages/productview.xhtml?src=bkmk.

11. "14 Important Statistics about Asians."

12. "Asian-Americans Are Expanding Their Footprint."

13. "Ryan and Bauman, "Educational Attainment."

14. "The Rise of Asian Americans." *Pew Research Center*. Last modified June 19, 2012. http://www.pewsocialtrends.org/2012/06/19/the-rise-of-asian-americans/

15. "Northwestern Mutual Survey Reveals Nearly Half of Asian Americans Define Financial Security as Pinnacle of Success." *Northwestern Mutual*. Last modified January 30, 2018. http://news.northwesternmutual.com/2018-01-30-Northwestern-Mutual-Survey-Reveals-Nearly-Half-of-Asian-Americans-Define-Financial-Security-as-Pinnacle-of-Success

16. Ibid.

17. Anik, Lalin, et al. "Feeling Good about Giving: The Benefits (and Costs) of Self-Interested Charitable Behavior." Working paper, Harvard Business School, 2009. http://www.hbs.edu/faculty/Publication%20Files/10-012_0350a55d-585b-419d-89e7-91833a612fb5.pdf.

18. Hu, Xin, et al. "EEG Correlates of Ten Positive Emotions." *Frontiers in Human Neuroscience* 11, no. 26 (2017): 1–12. http://www.ncbi.nlm.nih.gov/pmc/articles/PMC5266691/pdf/fnhum-11-00026.pdf.

19. Carver, Charles S. "Optimism." *Clinical Psychology Review* 30 (2010): 879–89. http://local.psy.miami.edu/faculty/ccarver/documents/10_CPR_Optimism.pdf.

SPECIAL THANKS

BARBARA CARRATALA BONDS

DAVID FISHOF

GERRY DZUREK & ANN WANDEEVONG

HANNA HORENSTEIN

HOLLY CHON HYANG BACHMAN

JARIYA BARTOLOME

JUMA SUEDI

KAREN FEATHERSTONE

MICHAEL HOLM

MIKEY GOMEZ

OYO & GREG BOOKOUT

RALPH & ADRIANA VILDOSOLA

VERGIL PASCUAL & LEDA DURAN

YOSHIE GUADAGNO

ABOUT THE AUTHOR

 JOHN SHIN'S family immigrated from South Korea to Los Angeles when he was a baby. Inspired by the American dream, John made his first $100 selling candy when he was six years old, and his entrepreneurial spirit was born.

John holds a BA in business administration, an MBA, and a Juris Doctorate from the University of Southern California. He is the founder and CEO of AXIANTA Financial Partners, where he leads a sales force of nearly 100,000 agents in offices across the United States. His greatest joy is helping businesses and people achieve massive success.

John serves on the boards of numerous non-profit organizations and was an executive producer of the movie *Think and Grow Rich: The Legacy*. He is an avid skier and a lifelong practitioner of Tae Kwon Do, Judo, and Hapkido. John and his wife of 25 years, Arlene, are the proud parents of four wonderful children—Matthew, Kayla, Andrew, and Jenna.

CONNECT WITH JOHN AT

www.johnshinofficial.com and www.johncshin.com.

www.soundwisdom.com